GW00983412

THE BEST AUSTRALIAN
ESSAYS
20
17

THE BEST AUSTRALIAN
ESSAYS

EDITED BY ANNA GOLDSWORTHY

Black Inc.

Published by Black Inc.,
an imprint of Schwartz Publishing Pty Ltd
Level 1, 221 Drummond Street
Carlton VIC 3053, Australia
enquiries@blackincbooks.com
www.blackincbooks.com

9781863959605 (paperback)
9781925435924 (ebook)

Cover design by Peter Long
Typesetting by Tristan Main

Printed in Australia by McPherson's Printing Group.

Contents

CONTENTS

CONTENTS

Introduction

In the *New Yorker* earlier this year, Jia Tolentino declared that 'the personal-essay boom is over', dating its 'hard endpoint' to the 2016 US presidential election, after which individual perspectives no longer seem 'a trustworthy way to get to the bottom of a subject'. In an era of fake news, she suggested, old-fashioned reportage has a renewed appeal, while the political has become so lurid that the personal struggles to compete.

Donald Trump certainly provides rich material for the essayist: so rich, in fact, that it risks being indigestible, blocking anyone's capacity to absorb anything else. As Martin McKenzie-Murray wrote in the *Saturday Paper* in March, 'incredulity has demanded rivers of ink to express itself' – a phenomenon not limited to the country that (almost) voted Trump in. Based on the submissions to this publication, it would be possible to produce a *Best Australian Trump Essays 2017*, with many choice specimens to spare.

And yet the Trump victory is not a repudiation of the personal. Nor does it spell an end to essayistic biodiversity. Instead it is a reminder to heed voices too readily dismissed. In his widely circulated essay 'In Defence of the Bad, White Working Class', Shannon Burns recommends that 'progressives *might* benefit from considering lower-class points of view, and the experiences that forge them, at least once in a while'. Engaging with other points of view and perspectives scarcely needs defending: it is one of the projects of literature. It might also provide a useful prophylactic – if not against future Trump victories, then at least against being blindsided by them.

The problem, then, may be less one of 'individual perspectives' than of the self-replicating 'individual perspective' filtered through the aperture of the Facebook feed – the technological hall of mirrors. There is no shortage of individual *perspectives* in these pages. It is possible to weary of the first person – that clamouring *me*, demanding to be heard, like the most insistent of toddlers – but perhaps there is greater humility in owning up to it than in renouncing it completely, with all the omniscience that implies. And it is not without distinguished precedent. It is almost part of the genre contract to quote Montaigne at the start of any essay collection, so here he is in his first book of essays of 1580: '*Je suis moi-même la matière de mon livre*' ('I am myself the matter of my book').

Of course, the self in itself is not enough: it is what you do with it that counts. As William Deresiewicz observed in an essay about essays for the *Atlantic*, 'what makes a personal essay an essay and not just an autobiographical narrative is precisely that it uses personal material to develop, however speculatively or intuitively, a larger conclusion.'

Is that, then, the definition of an essay? Everyone has their own theory. According to my own (evolving) criteria, an essay is not a poem (nonfiction though a poem often is); nor is it a speech, which operates according to rhythmic and textual laws of its own. Not all works of journalism, memoir or criticism are essays, though they can be if they reach beyond their subject and offer more, including the capacity to move. (Anwen Crawford represents a high-water mark here: the title of her analysis of Lady Gaga, Bob Dylan and Prince, 'Towards Joy', says it all.) That's about as far as my definition goes. The more complete definition is: *these things here*, between the covers of this book.

When a group of essays get together in a room they start talking to each other, often in surprising ways. I wondered if I had favoured subjects that interested me, or if the emergence of certain themes reflected the so-called national conversation. Birds make repeat appearances – flying heralds, perhaps, of environmental crisis – as does displacement, not least in Keane Shum's definitive 'The Tamarind Is Always Sour'. Domestic abuse and mental health are recurrent themes, reflecting a growing acceptance of these conversations, as is digital disruption. And there is quite a lot about language: not surprising, really, given that this is a subject to which writers give a great deal of thought.

There is one piece in this collection that is not penned by an Australian but takes an Australian as its subject: James Wood's appreciation of Helen Garner from the *New Yorker*. It seemed fitting to include it, not least because Garner's voice echoes through many essays here, as it does through Australian letters at large. Many times, as I read submissions, I registered the quiet skewering of *amour-propre*; the transcription of an overhead conversation; the more or less successfully deployed *reduction to tears* – Garneresque moments assimilated into a writer's own style.

Still, I doubt there is such a thing as an 'Australian essay', and nor would one wish there to be (for one thing, it would presage the un-Australian essay). As Michael Mohammed Ahmad thunders in 'Bad Writer', 'while bad writing in Western Sydney has everything in common with bad writing everywhere else, good writing in Western Sydney, and good writing everywhere else, has nothing in common with good writing anywhere else – it is good as an unhappy family is unhappy, in its own way.'

The essays in this collection are good, then, in the ways that unhappy families are unhappy, and their diversity is perhaps the most Australian thing about them. They operate at different velocities – some are sentence-savouring, others story-driven – and have different agendas. The most thrilling thing for me is the number of younger voices to be found here. Though much in these pages might lead to discouragement, the existence of these voices – stylish, vital, frequently wise – is a source of hope.

Anna Goldsworthy

Extravagant, Aggressive Birds Down Under

Tim Flannery

Towards the end of his highly enjoyable book *Where Song Began*, Tim Low informs us that 'it might be said that the world has one hemisphere weighted towards mammals and one towards birds.' The hemisphere weighted towards mammals is the northern one. And Low makes a convincing case that, in the south, birds of a most extravagant type occur. But is the southern hemisphere truly weighted towards birds? One window into the question is through bird–human interactions. We humans are used to getting our way with nature, but in the Antipodes birds occasionally gain the upper hand.

Such was the case when, in 1932, Australia decided to declare war on the emu, an enormous flightless bird whose image is emblazoned on the country's coat of arms. Sir George Pierce, Australia's defence minister, was beseeched by farmers from Australia's south-west for deliverance from the ravening creatures, which were swarming out of the desert in countless thousands, driven south by drought. Sir George agreed to help, and ' so was sparked what would become known as the Great Emu War.

Major C.P.W. Meredith of the Seventh Heavy Battery of the Royal Australian Artillery was ordered to proceed with armed troops to the environs of Campion, a small town located near the emu 'front line'. There, the army was to use Lewis guns (machine guns) to disperse the invaders. Hostilities commenced on 1 November, but the birds were at such a distance that gunfire was largely ineffective. The next day, a thousand emus were seen advancing on a dam. Meredith and his troops were in a splendid position to inflict maximum casualties, but after only fewer than twelve birds were killed the Lewis guns jammed. Frustrated by the fleetness of the birds, Meredith had the machine guns mounted on trucks, but the emus easily outran the vehicles.

A month later, a crestfallen Meredith was forced to explain to the Australian parliament that the war had been lost. He said of his foe:

> If we had a military division with the bullet-carrying capacity of these birds it would face any army in the world. They can face machine guns with the invulnerability of tanks. They are like the Zulus whom even dum-dum bullets could not stop.

The war was not over, however. Irregular troops in the form of bounty hunters were enlisted, but even they could not subdue the foe, and the conflict continued for decades.

Being defeated in war by one's avifauna is ignominious. But Australians are inured to being stung, bitten, envenomated or outright eaten alive by a hostile fauna. Incredibly, Low claims that even Australian songbirds are dangerous. The Australian magpie looks like a very large jay, and when it breeds in the spring, it turns the country into a battle ground. Magpies defend their territory by 'dive-bombing' 'invaders' from the rear, which is why you may see Australian pedestrians waving umbrellas into a clear sky, or cyclists with rearward-looking faces painted on their helmets.

Magpies, according to Low, 'can distinguish kindly adults from scheming boys'. Postmen are particularly detested: Australia is perhaps the only country on earth where they fear songbirds as much as dogs. And those whom magpies particularly loathe will be identified and targeted, even if they haven't been seen for years. Low tells of a 'terrorized school in Brisbane' where 'throngs of screaming parents at the gates were trying to get their terrified children to run quickly across the open area to the main building where the school medical officer was waiting with the first aid kit.' Over two weeks, more than a hundred children had their faces cut by magpies. But the damage can be much worse. Magpies will sometimes land in front of a person they despise, and then leap at their face. Each year, one or two people are stabbed in the eyes.

Surveys indicate that 85 per cent of Australians have been harassed by magpies, so it seems remarkable that a magpie that blinded a boy in the Queensland town of Toowoomba was relocated rather than killed. In 1856, the naturalist George Bennett said of these remarkable creatures, 'It is a bird of much importance in its own estimation, struts about quite fearless of danger, and evinces, on many occasions, great bravery.' It says something of the national character of Australians that they can forgive such a creature almost anything.

Australia and New Guinea are joined at times of low sea level and share many species in common. Consequently, Low uses 'Australia' as shorthand for Australia–New Guinea throughout his book. The flightless cassowary inhabits the rainforests of New Guinea and north Queensland. The size of a man, it has a gaudy purple, yellow and red head that bears a high crest and a frighteningly malicious eye. On its foot is a four-inch-long dagger-like claw, which Low suspects is used to 'kill many more people in New Guinea than tigers do in most countries in Asia'.

I worked for twenty years in New Guinea, and am certain that Low is correct. It's the male cassowaries that incubate the eggs and care for the chicks, and they will attack out of the blue if you go anywhere near their young. There being so very few accounts of cassowary attacks (because most happen among remote tribes living in dense jungle), it is worthwhile recounting one instance here. Professor Joe Mangi is a friend and archaeologist who told me of an attack that occurred in the 1980s in Papua New Guinea's Southern Highlands. The victim had found a cassowary nest and was taking the eggs (which are bright green and up to five and a half inches long) when he heard a booming noise. He barely had time to grab his machete and leap to meet the attacking bird. They met midair, the man severing the cassowary's leg, the bird disembowelling the man with its claw.

Joe dispatched the wounded cassowary and gathered the man's intestines, which were stretched over yards of forest floor. Uncertain about medical treatment, he emptied the entire contents of his medical kit onto the guts before gathering them up and stuffing them back into the abdominal cavity. When the villagers arrived, they daubed their faces with white clay and began mourning: they considered the victim a dead man. With the nearest airstrip a full day's walk away, Joe urged that a stretcher be made. But the victim sat up and said, 'You take my first wife. You the second. And you get the pigs.' Joe's reassurances that the man would survive if he could be got to a hospital were as cries in the wilderness.

Carrying the stretcher over the broken limestone country was hard going, so Joe sent two boys ahead to request fresh carriers. They never arrived, and when Joe got to the village he found it in mourning for the victim. The village chief was so enraged at the youths, who had told him that the victim had died, that he struck them on the head with a piece of timber. Now the cassowary had claimed three victims.

When the stretcher carrying the first victim approached the airstrip an aircraft was heard, but Joe's feet were so torn that he was crippled, so he sent a muscular villager ahead to ask the pilot to wait for the casualties. The young Australian pilot was naturally alarmed at the sight of a Papuan charging towards his plane, his grass pubic covering waving wildly in the breeze. He leapt into the cockpit and began preparations for take-off when he noticed that the Papuan, who spoke no English, had grasped the propeller. Joe arrived in time to explain things, and the victim made a full recovery.

Low offers a curious aside about emus and cassowaries. They are some of the few birds that possess penises. Only 3 per cent of all bird species are so endowed, the other 97 per cent getting by with a 'cloacal kiss' to transfer sperm. Possession of a penis is an ancestral condition inherited from the dinosaurs, and just why most birds have lost their penis is a curious question. Low puts it down to hygiene, saying that 'birds face more disease risks than mammals since they use the same opening for defecation and sex'. But what to make of the Argentine lake duck, whose sixteen-inch phallus is longer than its body? Low offers the rather feeble observation that ducks are cleaner than most birds because their bottoms are immersed in water. But if there is no disease risk, then why do some female ducks possess multiple false vaginas?

Another curious question concerns why Australia's birds are so aggressive, and often so large. The continent's mammals are mostly marsupials, and Low claims that they are rather poor competitors for the birds, so birds have come to dominate some ecological niches, including fruit-eating in tropical forests – a niche exploited by cassowaries. But there is more to the story than that. Strange as it may seem, neither the cassowary nor the magpie can claim to be Australia's most aggressive bird. That title must go to a rather drab grey member of the honeyeater family known as the noisy miner.

Accused in a scientific paper of 'despotic aggressiveness', the species has been recorded driving off fifty-seven rival types of bird. Indeed, the noisy miner's aggression has led to it becoming 'one of the most important mechanisms through which habitat fragmentation and degradation threaten populations of eastern Australian woodland birds'. 'They will turn on almost anything,' Low says: 'koalas, cows, bats, pigs, snakes, lizards, people', as well as other birds. And worse, they recruit allies in their bullying, including the aptly named butcherbird – a sharp-beaked, shrike-like predator that the noisy miners leave alone – provided they refrain from taking their eggs and young.

Noisy miners will even recruit humans as allies. Some years ago, a great fracas emanating from a mob of noisy miners outside my house in Sydney induced me to leave my work and investigate. As I stepped outside, the birds fell into silent expectation. Looking down, I saw a python. I got the distinct feeling that the noisy miners expected me to deal with it. But I like pythons, so I left it and returned inside. The howl of disappointed rage emerging simultaneously from dozens of beaks had to be heard to be believed. To get any peace, I was forced to move the snake.

Many Australian birds are highly intelligent, a factor that contributes in no small measure to their success. Parrots and songbirds – groups that thrive in Australia – have large brains relative to their body size. According to research, they can outdo apes in some tasks, exhibiting 'cultural transmission of tool design, theory of mind, and Piagetian object permanence to a high level'. Like many humans, they are also playful. The apogee of avian intelligence arguably occurs on New Caledonia – an island adjacent to Australia – where a native crow (a songbird) makes a variety of tools, including hooks.

Low notes that 'complicated calls and intelligence seem to go together'. There may be a link here with our own species. Charles Darwin wrote that birds

> have nearly the same taste for the beautiful as we have. This is shewn by our enjoyment of the singing of birds, and by our women, both civilized and savage, decking their heads with borrowed plumes ...

Indeed, it may be that songbirds taught us humans how to sing by 'influencing the evolution of human acoustic perception'.

The highly social nature of many Australian birds is also notable. In some species it's not only the parents who feed the chicks, but distantly related or even unrelated birds. According to Low, white-winged choughs – a large black bird with a sinister-looking red eye – even practise a form of slavery. They abduct fledglings from the nests of other choughs and induce them to feed their own chicks. But in this 'dishonest society' the abductees sometimes only fake helping.

For those feeling safe from large, intelligent and aggressive birds in their mammal-dominated northern hemisphere homes, Low has some alarming news. Australian birds have taken over the world. The remarkable fact has been revealed through genetic studies, and when first announced it was flatly disbelieved, for it flew in the face of all that we thought we knew about the way evolution works. Prior to the discovery, it was thought that species from the larger, northern continents were competitively superior, which means that faunal exchange should be one-way – from north to south. Darwin put the idea as succinctly as anyone:

> I suspect that this preponderant migration from the north to the south is due to the greater extent of land in the north, and to the northern forms having existed in their homes in greater numbers, and having consequently been advanced through natural selection and competition to a higher stage of perfection, or domineering power, than the southern forms.

The first significant questioning of the idea came from Charles Sibley, an ornithologist working at Yale in the early 1970s, who discovered that if he boiled double-stranded bird DNA, when the mixture cooled the strands would recombine. He found that if he mixed the DNA of two species, the strength of the rebonding was an index of evolutionary relatedness. His work revealed that 'Australia's robins, flycatchers, warblers and babblers were not what their names suggested'. Instead, they were part of an ancient Australian group that over time had come to resemble birds from elsewhere. They were, Sibley concluded, part of an ancient songbird radiation as diverse and unique as Australia's marsupials.

Since Sibley's day, genetic studies have become immensely more sophisticated, and some have revealed entirely unexpected relationships. Several detailed genetic studies, including a comprehensive mapping of retroposons (repetitive DNA fragments that insert randomly into the genome), for example, agree that songbirds, parrots and falcons are one another's closest relatives, and that this group probably originated close to the time of the dinosaur extinction in what was then the Australian section of the supercontinent Gondwana. It seems astonishing that falcons and robins could be more closely related to each other than are falcons and hawks. But the avian body plan is highly restricted by the requirements of flight, and because there are so few options for becoming a flying predator, convergent evolution is widespread among birds.

Occasionally, anatomists and behaviourists discover clues to relationships by re-examining the earliest members of a bird family tree in light of genetic studies. New Zealand's kea, for example, is a member of the most basal branch of the parrot family tree. It is a predator with a vicious beak, and can kill and eat sheep, making a relationship between parrots and falcons seem a little less improbable.

Songbirds are by far the largest and most successful group of birds in the world. Their 5000 species, divided between forty orders, make up 47 per cent of all bird species. Eighteen of Britain's twenty most abundant species are songbirds, as is the most abundant wild bird on earth, Africa's red-billed quelea, of which 1.5 billion are thought to exist. The great majority of songbirds fall into just one order, the perching birds or Passeriformes, which take their name from the Latin term for the sparrow. All of the little birds that forage among leaves are perching birds, as are crows and magpies, and one thing that sets them apart from all other birds is the possession of a hind toe operated by an independent set of tendons.

In 2002 a genetic study revealed that New Zealand's wrens sit at the base of the songbird family tree. They are mostly extinct, and the survivors don't sing at all, instead vocalising with high, thin squeaks. Other studies show that the second branch of the songbird family tree includes Australia's lyrebirds and scrub birds, while the third includes Australia's treecreepers and bowerbirds. None of these branches has many species, and all are exclusively Australasian. This abundance of early types, along with the discovery in Australia of the oldest songbird fossils in the world, provides convincing evidence that Darwin's dictum, at least when it comes to the songbirds, is wrong. One of the most successful groups of vertebrates ever to have evolved – the songbirds – originated in Australia and has since spread around the globe.

Low has some fascinating ideas about why and how the songbirds evolved. The group that first spread successfully outside Australia seems to have discovered a new ecological niche that developed, paradoxically, courtesy of Australia's infertile soils. Australia is low, flat and geologically comatose, so its soils have not been rejuvenated by volcanoes, the uplift and erosion of mountains, or glaciers for tens of millions of years. As a result, its ancient soils are largely leached of nutrients, so plants growing in them tend to hoard what nutrients they can get. Nectar, being sugary, requires minimal nutrients in order to be produced, and Australia's eucalypts and their relatives are some of the greatest nectar producers on earth. Moreover, their flowers are simple in structure and animals require no special adaptations to harvest the rich liquid, making it attractive to a wide range of species. Visitors to Australia will easily see the consequences: flowering gum trees pulsate with the screams of lorikeets and the raucous cries of half a dozen species of honeyeaters. Relatively small species like noisy miners have triumphed in this melee only by becoming highly social, aggressive and intelligent.

Beginning around thirty million years ago, Australia's aggressive, social songbirds found their way across the stepping-stone island arc lying to Australia's north. When they reached mainland Asia, an entire new world opened to them. The fossil record of Europe, which is particularly complete, tells the story of what happened next. Prior to the arrival of songbirds, Europe was host to myriad primitive birds such as mousebirds (a few of which survive today in Africa). As soon as the songbirds arrived, they vanished permanently. The initial songbird invasion was no one-off event. Just as Africa has been the point of origin of one hominid type after another – from *Homo erectus* to modern humans – so Australia has acted as a fountainhead for songbird lineages that have gone on to spread around the globe. One example of a more recent invasion concerns the orioles, a group of songbirds that, until a few million years ago, were most probably restricted to New Guinea.

The oriole family is a small element in New Guinea's avifauna. But it does include the world's only poisonous bird, the hooded pitohui. So toxic are its feathers and skin that merely handling a stuffed museum specimen that is decades old can induce nausea. It was only after one branch of this family reached foreign shores and gave rise to all the Old World orioles that orioles became an avian success. Fans of the Baltimore Orioles should know, incidentally, that the bird is a member of an entirely different family, the Icteriidae, which is restricted to the New World.

Where Song Began provides a novel interpretation of Australia's avifauna that will enrich the understanding of anyone interested in birds. As a professional biologist familiar with much of its matter, I found myself again and again astonished. Indeed, it seems to prove that what Mark Twain said of Australia's history – that 'it does not read like history, but like the most beautiful lies' – applies equally well to Australian nature.

Lessons from Camels

Robert Skinner

For reasons that are still unclear to me, I agreed to go on a ten-day camel trek with my parents. When they invited me my initial reaction was *I've got a whole LIFE going on here, I can't just take off.* I had a pile of junk mail to read and some pretty firm dinner plans. A few weeks later I was at a party where I didn't think much of the people. Or, more accurately, I didn't think the people thought much of me. So I wandered outside, thought, *Phooey to you, city living,* and texted my parents. 'I'm in.'

A week before departure they called me from Adelaide, huddled together and shouting into the speakerphone.

'When you get here, we need you to pick up thirty kilograms of potatoes. We're in charge of the potatoes.'

'Don't stress him out,' said my mum. 'You just bring yourself.'

'Yeah, yeah, but just – and the potatoes.'

My dad explained where we'd be going: from Orroroo, in the Flinders Ranges, east towards Yunta, north to Koonamore, and then south-west along Pipeline Road.

'It's a triangle, Bob. We're doing a triangle.'

I asked how far we'd be riding, all up. There was a moment's silence.

'We're not riding, mate. They're wagon camels.'

We would be walking, said my dad. Next to the camels, and for twenty-five kilometres a day. He paused.

'You have been training, haven't you?'

I said yes, in the sense that I'd managed to keep my legs in pretty much mint unused condition. I started to panic.

'I thought I was supposed to be practising sitting down.'

*

My dad's cousin Robyn had married a bushman called Don, and together they raced camels and went on wagon expeditions. This was the first time they were bringing other people along. There would be between nine and fourteen people on the trek. Being in such close quarters with strangers for ten days was not my dad's idea of a good time. He would have preferred to be at home with a book or tinkering in his shed. But his own dad had a reputation for disappearing out the back door every time someone showed up at the front door, and *my* dad was forever trying not to be that guy.

The night before we left Adelaide he did that thing nervous parents do, where they start fussing over their kids instead. He looked at me gruffly and said, 'Now listen, Bob. What are you going to do out there for entertainment?'

'I dunno. I brought a few books.'

'You understand that these are country folk we'll be travelling with. They like different things to us.'

'Well, what about you? What are you going to do?'

'I'm going to look at the fire,' he said. 'Don't worry about me.'

*

My parents and I drove north from our house in Adelaide to meet up with the crew in Orroroo. On the way we picked up a thirty-one-year-old cameleer called Brian. He had a huge camel-coloured beard, and a smile that took over his whole face. 'G'day, folks,' he said as he climbed in.

We drove for four hours through small towns and low ranges, alongside dry creek beds and stubbly wheatfields. We peppered Brian with questions about camels. ('Is it true that they spit?' 'Can Jewish people eat them?' 'Why don't you ride horses instead?') He had two camels of his own, Firestorm and Vicky, and every time he talked about them he got a faraway look in his eyes.

In the late afternoon we drove down a dirt driveway and pulled up outside a big shearing shed. The head of our expedition, old bushman Don, came up to the car. From where I was sitting I could only make out his waistline. His jeans were covered in dirt and were about six sizes too big. They were held up by a rope, a belt and a pair of braces.

He leaned in through the window and said, 'Now, the important thing about this trip is not to panic.'

The first thing we were supposed to not panic about was the state of one of the wagons. It had been refurbished by Greg, a local naturalist and council worker who would be joining us on the trek. 'You can tell he worked on the highways,' said Don, pointing at the wagon. 'It's all held together by street signs.' That wasn't the problem so much as its rickety, lopsided canopy. The wagon looked as though it wanted to veer off into the bushes and lie down.

I walked over to the holding pen to see if maybe I had a magic touch with camels. This is the persistent dream of dilettantes: that we will, at some point, uncover a superpower that will make sense of lives filled with false starts, failures and endless dabbling.

I stood up on the railing and said 'Hello, ladies!' to what I would later learn was mostly a bunch of bullocks. The camels looked at me with long-lashed eyes. The biggest camel, Weet-Bix, came over and nuzzled my hand. I stroked his fleshy lips and hummed a Middle Eastern tune I knew; he bit me affectionately on the arm. Things were looking good!

*

On the morning of departure I asked Brian if he wanted some help wrangling the camels. 'I've got kind of a special rapport with them,' I said, and explained about the deep looks, the nibbling and so forth.

'They've been *biting* you? Mate, you can't let them *do* that!'

So I went and helped my dad instead. He had designed and built a solar-powered electrical system and was ready to install it.

I wanted to be useful, so I kept suggesting we bolt things to hard-to-reach poles that only I could climb up to.

Our procession was two wagons long. The main one had a canvas roof and was fitted out with bench seats from an old Kingswood. The smaller wagon was still looking pretty rickety, but they'd braced it as best they could.

We spent the rest of the morning loading the main wagon with our worldly possessions, and then (it sounds crazy when you see it written down) attached the wagon to four camels. Those outback camel trains look so stately and peaceful in the photographs! But when our camels felt the weight of the wagon they bolted, and took the wagon bouncing through bushes and rabbit holes. One of the camels started bucking wildly, throwing his head around and generally not taking very good care of our things. Brian was pumping the handbrake and hanging on.

'Pull 'em up, Brian!'

'I'm fucking trying!'

In the ruckus, another four camels broke loose and charged off in the direction of Brian and the wagon. They were tied together but going at high speed. Brian had, by now, managed to stop the wagon/get tangled in a fence line, but the four-pack of rogue camels headed straight for him.

Don yelled out to me, 'Get between them and the wagon, Bob! Head 'em off!'

Leadership is a hard-to-pin-down quality. But if, after two days of knowing someone, they tell you to jump in front of a pack of charging camels and you find yourself willingly obliging, then they've probably got it.

The camels were looking like a pretty dumb idea, but we were on to a good thing with Don.

We managed to round up the camels and get the wagons back on track. Don took his hat off and wiped the sweat from his face. 'That's normal,' he said. 'They always start off like that. Let's push on.'

One of the reasons we go bush is to trade our old, boring problems (scrounging for rent money, beating the traffic) for new and refreshing ones. On our daily treks we had to pull down stock fences, navigate creek crossings and get cooking fires started in the rain. *This is living!* I thought to myself. My dad didn't quite share my enthusiasm. He was up to his neck in living already. What he really wanted was a nice sit-down.

Getting the camels mustered every morning was a real snafu. There was one problem camel called Blister who'd been raised as a pet and suffered all the same problems as a trust-fund kid. Don was trying to break him in as a wagon camel and get some herd mentality back into him. One morning Blister was really making him sweat. Don was yelling, 'Fucking *hoosh down*, you bird-brained bastard!' and the camel – stubborn, outraged – was bellowing back. Meanwhile, Brian and his friend Chantelle (a dreadlocked camel racer) were trying to corral the two lead camels, who'd gotten tangled up somehow.

My dad saw me writing in my diary and came over. He stood next to me for a while. Just the two of us.

'If *I* was writing a book,' he said, 'I'd call it *Why We Invented the Internal Combustion Engine*.'

*

Brian or Nat usually drove the main wagon. Nat was a bosomy powerhouse who raised a family, kept a menagerie of pets and broke in camels for a living. She wore the same singlet, shorts and thongs the whole trip. Even on frosty nights. One evening she reached into her bra looking for a cigarette, and I saw her pull out a lighter, a tobacco pouch, a packet of tissues, a hunting knife, $20 (*in change*) and a bundle of keys before she looked up and said, 'Oh, here it is. It's in my fucking mouth.' On the fourth day she got kicked full in the face by a camel and just started kicking it back.

The smaller wagon was driven by the camp cook, who drank white wine and soda with one hand and swished the reins around with the other. She shouted so relentlessly at her camels (Chrystal and Sapphire) that they could no longer tell what was a command and what was general chitchat. So they ignored her completely and just ambled along cheerfully at their own pace. If you really wanted the camels to do something, you had to put on a high-pitched voice or a foreign accent to get their attention.

Don was in charge of getting us out of trouble ('If Plan A doesn't work there's always Plan B, and if that doesn't work, well, there's plenty of letters in the alphabet') and Robyn made us welcome wherever we landed. She was tireless and enthusiastic, looked out for everyone, and had none of the high-school bluster and faux toughness of other people we met along the way.

The walkers usually went up ahead, or drifted along between the two wagons. We passed through mallee country and sheep stations, along ancient valleys and across plateaus covered in saltbush. If you got far enough ahead there was a strange buzzing stillness. When it was overcast you didn't even hear bird calls. Just the gentle clanking of the approaching wagons, and the muffled shouts, like a distant football game, of people urging the camels up a hill or over boggy ground.

We'd stop once for morning tea, once for lunch, and whenever something went wrong. It never felt like we were covering any great distances, but the nubs of old mountains would appear in the morning and disappear behind us by the end of the day. Greg, a birdwatcher, would come up to us in camp and say, 'Twenty-seven kilometres today, as the crow flies.'

When I got fed up with walking, or with being awake, I would climb into the back of the main wagon, curl up between rifles and saddlebags, and go to sleep. The wagon rocked back and forth and I dreamed endlessly about women. Of soft voices and deep looks. I dreamed of the brownest eyes I've ever seen, of blonde-haired guitar players kissing me behind stage curtains, of great poets reading in small, smoke-filled rooms and looking up coyly between stanzas. I dreamed of warm bodies tangling up in soft sheets, of curved shoulders and plunging necklines. The relentless masculinity of the bush was starting to wear me down.

In the afternoons we'd pull up an hour or two before sunset and let the camels out to feed. They'd trundle off and start pulling apart the native vegetation, and we would start a fire and get cooking. The camels didn't need to drink for the entire trip, though I can't say the same for their handlers. They started drinking port from a goon sack at lunch, and were pretty much trolleyed by the time dinner was served. Sometimes around the camp fire we heard bush stories: about desert crossings, about a guy who had to shoot the bull camel he was riding in the head because he couldn't get it to slow down. But mostly we got the Nat and Chantelle show. They had shouting matches about semen swallowing. (I remember this particularly well because it was the same high-volume argument, almost verbatim, three nights in a row: Chantelle was for, Nat was against. It was Chantelle who kept bringing it up.)

My mum loved it. She thought they were hilarious. But it was all too much for my dad. (I think it was being twerked on that finally broke him.) It will come as a surprise to anyone who's been to a dinner party with my dad that he actually has quite delicate sensibilities. One morning he said to me, 'That Chantelle's got a mouth like a *sewer.*' Which was a bit rich coming from the guy who got up at my brother's twenty-first birthday dinner and – reminiscing on the night of conception – said, 'Yep, we should have settled for hand jobs *that* night.' But I got his point, which was that he really wanted to be alone for a while and there was nowhere to sit.

It was a gruelling regime for my parents. They were hardly sleeping at night and were walking all day. When the wagons stopped for lunch, the cameleers would climb down to stretch their legs, and my parents would look around desperately for somewhere to rest. My dad didn't want to sit on the ground because he honestly thought he wouldn't be able to get back up. I started climbing onto the wagon at lunchtime and pulling down camp stools.

On the fifth day I was walking with my dad and he said that he wanted to go home early. I was shocked. I don't think I've ever seen my dad give up.

'What does Mum think?'

He grunted. 'She won't even talk about it.'

He was looking pretty beaten. He'd walked thirty kilometres that day, and was chilled to the bone. (For days after the trip he would walk around our house shivering and trying to get warm. 'It's *cold*,' he kept saying, when it wasn't.) He'd developed cracked lips, a patchy white beard and various other ailments that had afflicted the early white explorers. My mum wasn't looking crash-hot either. Her face was red and puffy because, for complicated reasons, she didn't believe in sunscreen.

There's a peculiar anguish to seeing your own parents suffer. If it's your children suffering, you know or hope that it's because they're still building their characters, that the world will accommodate them somehow. But if it's your parents, you know that things are probably only going to get harder for them. The world for them is a cruise liner steaming towards the horizon, leaving them bobbing alone in the vast, lonely ocean with only each other.

My dad said, 'Jesus Christ, Bob, do you have to say this shit out loud? It's pretty bleak.'

We trudged through flat, heavily grazed country that had the feeling of a ghost town. Rain had washed out some tracks ahead, so when we reached the ruins of the Waukaringa pub we turned around and started back the way we'd come.

The camels never trudged. They held their heads up high like queens at a ball, for days. A horse pulls in a straight line. But the camels were always looking around as they walked, with a prospective optimism that eluded us now that we were heading back the way we'd come.

I tried to entertain my dad with half-baked theories about possessions. I had visited a camping store on the day before the trip and everything in there had felt so *essential*. I got so excited by the gadgetry that I would have blown all my money in one go, if I'd had any. And what you realise, once you actually leave the city, is that it's all crap. That's why they never have those stores out in the country. I can't think of one thing in those shops that we could have used out there. What we needed was a pair of pliers and some wire. Throughout the journey we fixed everything with that combination. The broken steering column, the billy can, the bracket on the solar-powered system. I remember being impressed by the quality of Don's camp oven. It was a thing that would last a lifetime. I'm through with flim-flam, I said. What is it about city living? All I want to do when I'm there is *buy* stuff. What I want is just a few beautiful, useful things.

My dad asked, 'Is that why you bought that camel skin?'

Well, OK. So you can get fooled in reverse, too. At the camp fire one night I was talking to the manager of the local meatworks, and got a great price on a camel skin. Twenty-five bucks! Say what you want about my decision-making, but don't tell me that's not a bargain. When I arranged to buy it I honestly thought, *This will become one of my most useful possessions.*

I've been back home for two months now and I'm lumbered with this camel skin. I also find myself in the ridiculous situation of trying to find an apartment big enough to keep it in. Too many people have gone to too much trouble for me to throw it away. Robyn drove it from the Flinders Ranges to Adelaide. My parents – who did finish the trek, and walked the whole way – salted it themselves and sent it to a tannery. But I have it rolled up in the corner of my room. Just as I have the vision of my dad and mum on the last day of the trip, utterly miserable, but walking side by side and leaning into each other on the road to Orroroo.

Endlings

Harriet Riley

In 1996 a correspondence published in *Nature* coined the term 'endling' to refer to an animal that is the last of its species. It's a fantastical word, like something out of a fairytale. An endling lives deep in a dark forest beneath distant mountains, and can only be seen at midnight once every hundred years.

In a way, this isn't so far from the truth. Every now and then there's a sighting of an animal, like the Australian night parrot, long thought extinct. But just as often we know exactly when and where the last member of a species died.

Whether it's Martha the passenger pigeon or Lonesome George the Pinta Island tortoise, every endling is a lesson in how humans should – or rather, shouldn't – interact with the natural world. But the word 'endling' itself tells us something important, too, about how we relate to species on the brink of extinction. We do not see them as real.

Or, perhaps more accurately, we do not see extinction as real.

I first noticed this while consoling a heartbroken ornithologist. It was winter in Sydney and my friend, Katie – who has a PhD in parrots – had just split up with her fiancé, Gus. As rain streaked down the windows of her kitchen, I told her to focus on her other great love. Birds. Gus had never been the only thing in her life, after all, and it was important to do what makes you happy after a breakup.

A few days later Katie was in New Zealand, keeping busy with kea and kiwi deep in the valleys of Fiordland National Park.

The plan worked, or it would have, had she not encountered an endling.

One night in a bar after a long day's tramping, the locals told her about the kakapo. The kakapo is a greenish, ground-dwelling parrot that looks like an overfed corgi. It's the world's only flightless parrot, as well as the heaviest, and because it's nocturnal it has whiskers to help it to see in the dark. To attract a mate, the male kakapo selects a location in front of a large stone or tree on the side of a mountain, and digs a basin about the size of a paddling pool. He then sits in the centre of the amphitheatre and 'booms' – a deep, low call that can be heard by females for miles around.

But European settlement decimated the kakapo. Dogs, rats, cats and weasels – even the settlers themselves – all found the bird delicious and drove it to extinction. This wasn't unusual; most of New Zealand's endemic birdlife had fared the same, and Katie knew it. Nevertheless, the story of Fiordland's last kakapo got to her.

The locals explained that by 1970 all the females had died. Just one lone male remained, and he continued to perform his booming ritual night after night in a nearby valley. Kakapo live for a hundred years and their calls – which are lower than 100 hertz – can carry for five kilometres. Each night the kakapo boomed, and the locals heard him, like the bassline of a song being played in the next room.

Finally, in 1985, he fell silent.

Just like that, Katie fell in love again. The next morning she set off into the mountains with a notebook and Wanderstöcke to find the lost kakapo.

I went along with the kakapo ride. Every few days, Katie would text me a picture from somewhere they'd filmed *Lord of the Rings*. This, she'd point out, was definitely kakapo country. Of course it was, it was Middle Earth. All sorts of impossible species existed there.

Perhaps that's why we associate extinction with fantasy: nothing but the epic scale of myth can capture the immensity of losing an entire species. I say an entire species. We actually lose about 383 a day. Because this is the Holocene Extinction Event, the sixth great extinction since life evolved on earth. The first two were the Ordovician–Silurian Extinction and the Late Devonian Extinction, but it's the Permian Extinction, known to scientists as the Great Dying, that really takes the cake.

When volcanism and bolide impacts heated the atmosphere 252 million years ago, in much the same way that human activity is heating it today, huge quantities of methane and carbon were released from the land and sea. Runaway climate change took hold and destroyed a full 96 per cent of life on earth. It was ten million years, longer than any other extinction event, before the planet recovered its former biodiversity. Then came the Triassic–Jurassic Extinction, and the Cretaceous–Tertiary Extinction, when a meteorite obliterated the last of the dinosaurs.

But it's the Great Dying that the Holocene resembles most, with the same changing atmosphere, and the same seismic scale. According to the Living Planet Index, more than half of all living creatures have died out in the last forty years. Reading this report didn't give me a conscious sense of dread like most environmental papers do. Instead I felt a deep, primal pain – a disturbance in the force.

That's how I realised, as Katie was grieving her relationship, that I was in mourning too. I'm a climate scientist, but for the past nine months I hadn't read a thing about climate change. Friends would email me links to articles and I would delete them, telling myself that I was too busy, or that I knew that study already.

But the truth was I was avoiding it, because all the news was bad. I'd worked on the issue for years – going to UN summits, prepping lab reports, writing articles – I'd dedicated myself to it night and day for a decade. And every new article felt like a fellow doctor telling me about a cancer patient – how they were getting worse, how they'd been in remission but it had come back. How it had metastasised, how they had found a new drug but it wouldn't be on the market for another ten years, how it was growing and changing and shifting and spreading and how we had to prepare for the worst.

So I stopped reading. I started working on other issues. I slunk away from the bedside because nobody wants to watch their patient die. The Living Planet Index was the first climate paper I'd read all year and, sure enough, it led to an eye-scratching, skin-tearing, dirt-in-hair-rubbing outpouring of grief.

I'm not the only one. We call it a climate depression (yes, that's a weather joke) – and it's the main reason for the unusually high burnout rates among environmentalists and sustainability experts. But new research from around the world shows that it's not just professionals who succumb. Kari Norgaard, a sociology professor from the University of Oregon, ran a study in which she asked people whose towns had been impacted by climate change to describe how it made them feel. They spoke of fear, frustration, anger, hopelessness and guilt. One of the most telling responses came from a participant living by a river: 'It's like, you want to be a proud person and if you draw your identity from the river and when the river is degraded, that reflects on you.' Climate change destroys your sense of self-worth.

Another survey, this one by Yale and George Mason University, found that 'most Americans (74 per cent) ... "rarely" or "never" discuss global warming with family and friends, a number that has grown substantially since 2008 (60 per cent)'. In other words, the closer we come to destruction, the less we want to talk about it. It's counterintuitive, but these negative feelings make us less, not more, likely to fight the problem.

So this is climate change – something that, before depriving us of our lives, first deprives us of our self-worth, and our agency. Thankfully, psychologists know all about this. They've studied it everywhere from smokers to drinkers to people in bad relationships. It turns out that when someone thinks they can't solve a problem, their brain tells them to ignore it.

This insight led to one of the most successful climate interventions ever made. A team of researchers asked a group of climate deniers to install energy-efficient light bulbs, explaining that it would save them money. Several months later the researchers returned and told the participants their light bulbs also saved energy, and had significantly reduced the carbon footprint of each household. They then asked the participants about their views on climate change, and this time, they all believed. The fact that they had already made a difference meant that making a bigger one didn't seem impossible anymore. They could let themselves believe in the end of the world, because they'd been given a way to help stop it.

Katie, meanwhile, was still in denial. Every day she found signs of the kakapo – tracks, droppings, the severed stems of tussock grass. It wasn't a completely crazy idea, she told me. The takahe, another flightless bird, had been rediscovered in this very same part of Fiordland, and thanks to conservation efforts there were now 300 of them. Why shouldn't the kakapo be there too, nestled beneath a stand of pampas grass?

It's easy to empathise with an endling when you're single. I've thought a lot about how that parrot must have felt, on the night that it died, curled up in the cool loam, drifting off to sleep. He must have been confused at still being alone, but he would have assumed, as we all do deep in our primitive hindbrains, that his mate would arrive tomorrow.

And that's the problem with the weird romance of extinction. The strange thrill that something might be the last of its kind wakes up an ecstatic hope that it's not: that maybe, just maybe, there is a thylacine, or a passenger pigeon, or a fat, bewhiskered ground parrot out there beyond the mountains, if we could just go out and find it.

There might as well be unicorns.

We can't bring extinct species back from the dead any more than we can escape the consequences of climate change. And one day one of us will be the last human being on earth.

I was brooding over this solitary image when Katie arrived at the cafe to meet me. She was back from New Zealand, no parrot, no Gus. But she was happy; 'I wouldn't marry him now if he was the last man on earth.' I laughed out loud. 'Now we know what happened to the kakapo.'

To feel grief is to admit that we loved. And sometimes it's easier to pretend the lost thing didn't matter than to confront the fact that it's gone. That's why we call endlings such a fanciful name, because pretending that they never existed means that there's nothing to grieve. But any psychologist will tell you that you have to grieve to move on.

We sat in the sun with the galahs and the lorikeets like a float left over from Mardi Gras. A magpie sidled up and gave my carrot cake a long, entitled glare. It was hard to feel depressed around birds like these, and hard to give up the fight.

Then Katie told me about the Kakapo Recovery Programme.

In 1989 Stewart Island's last sixty-one kakapo were moved to three predator-free islets nearby. A government team took charge of the birds and, since then, their population has risen to 123. The project aims to one day reintroduce the kakapo to Fiordland and has begun restoring two islands in the park for the purpose.

This, we agreed, was the better way to love – to work for the living, not hunt for the dead. After all, humans aren't endlings yet, and we can always find new people and new species to care for. Katie got out her phone to show me her photos. It turns out the Kakapo Recovery Programme has some very handsome park rangers.

Hello, Stranger

Sonya Hartnett

This place doesn't look the way I've expected it to. It's much flatter: in every direction, you can see for miles. It's as flat as a pan, and as dry. The paddocks are yellow and mostly empty, although there is the occasional herd of cows and some sheep. The open ground that hems the road is greener and more densely treed than I'd imagined, with massive silver-trunked eucalypts that have stood here a hundred years and more. The dirt they grow in is rocky, coloured ochre. The sky is huge, brilliantly blue, and uncrossed by birds. It is bakingly hot, and, at midday, shadowless. I don't see any roadkill on the rubbly verge. The train line snakes alongside the farm fences, a scalding, greasy, burgundy vein. The pale grass growing beside it stands as high as the paddock posts.

Things would have been different when you were here, of course. It was winter then. The paddocks would have been green, the leaf mulch cold, the tarmac black and mirrored by rain. But the sky would have been just as wide above you, and the landscape as unsheltering. The few houses and scrappy businesses on the outskirts of town do not look like they would welcome a stray at any time. For all that it is broiling now, it was doubtlessly bitter then. Summer or winter, this is hard country for a homeless dog.

*

You are Dog the Third. First among you was Zak, a whippet in a time when no-one knew what whippets were except very old men who, at the sight of him, were taken tearfully back to the rabbit-hunting days of their boyhoods. A pizza delivery kid once asked me if Zak was a baby kangaroo. Then there was Shilo, the Black Prince of Hounds, my husky wolf, my beating heart. No-one ever mistook him for anything he was not. Both of them came to me as puppies, Zak like a tiny grey jewel fit for an empress, Shilo so endearing that I couldn't believe the breeder was willing to let me take him. I was with them for almost every day of their long lives. What they learned, we learned together. I knew where they had come from, I'd seen what they had seen. Their worlds were my world, our lives meshed together. They were my friends and familiars, and they still are, though they are both gone now.

You, however: no-one knows exactly how old you are. No-one except you knows where you've been and what you have seen. You are mine, and I am yours – but part of you is unknown to me. Part of you is the stranger who eats from my hand, plays in my yard, sleeps in my bedroom. You aren't completely mine, not truly, not fully, not absolutely – not the way Zak and Shilo were. For you, there was once somebody else, and an entire other life. And that somebody loved you in that life, I'm sure of this for several reasons: yet you were found outside a country town at the end of winter, and how you came to be there is a mystery known only, of the two of us, to you.

So we have come here, to Cobram, to search for you.

*

What I know of your history, I know as scraps. There's a frustrating lack of detail to the story, missing people, undefined lengths of time. The ranger who found you is no longer working for the shire, so there's no-one to ask what you did when the dog catcher's van pulled up beside you that afternoon, or even if there actually was a van, and if it was in fact afternoon. For all I know you walked into a front yard, or were found curled up in a hay shed, or followed someone home from the hotel. I look at you and try to ask, How did it go? I think it had a great impact, the time you spent as a stray. It's an experience that has burnt into

SONYA HARTNETT

your bones. I imagine you traipsing an outback road, nose down to a scent, ears up at the sight of birds. You hate bad weather, you would have fretted about the damp and cold. The slightest prick of a burr is traumatic for you, and rain horrifies you to your core: your travels must have been so uneasy. How did you know when to sleep, or which path to take when the road forked? You aren't particularly forthright, so I suspect you journeyed loosely, buffeted along like a leaf. You didn't find much to eat, because you were thin when the ranger picked you up, and becoming unwell. Yet you survived those rough, long, drifting days, possibly for weeks. And to do that, there has to be a thread of steel in you.

*

In the absence of facts, I imagine it like this. A bony black and white dog walks the broken edge of a road. All around are towering gums and flat paddocks, clusters of sleek cows. The ranger pulls up in a white van, stones popping away from the tyres. The dog isn't timid, and comes willingly when the ranger slaps her thigh, its head lowered, tail wagging. It's a handsome dog, the size of a sturdy whippet, black patches over amber eyes, the coat a mottle of spots. Outsized ears, like a puppy's. Pointer-cross-spaniel perhaps. Bird dog, certainly. The coat is peculiar, wispy, like the silk of a corncob – it's so unusual that everyone who sees it will remark upon it. A friendly mutt who leans against the ranger, who'd climb all over her if given the chance, across her shoulders, into her arms. Soft-natured and good-looking, a nice dog all round. There's no collar, and the animal hasn't been neutered. At an educated guess, about a year old. The ranger opens the door of the van and the dog jumps right in.

*

The relief you would have felt, I can imagine. You're not a pack leader, nor a lone wolf. You are a mild and accepting sort of fellow. Rambling, scavenging, hungry, roofless, you had doubtlessly assumed that this was how life was always destined to be.

*

Cobram is 250 kilometres north of Melbourne, on the Victorian bank of the Murray River. It is part of the Shire of Moira, a vast municipality that extends far along the river and deep into surrounding farmland. It's a comfortably sized country town, with long streets and wide roads. The people are friendly, and nod hello; the traffic, on a sunny Saturday morning, is slow. Cobram has won the Tidy Towns award in the past, and today its grassy median strips are spotlessly clean. I watch you closely as we walk, but you show no sign of recognising anything or anyone we pass. In bringing you here, it has been my greatest fear: that somebody will shout a name that I don't know but you do. As it is, the only person who takes any notice of us is a shire worker who advises we should keep clear of the Rottweiler chained up in a nearby ute. I look around, and the Rottie is glaring gleamingly at us. Your tail is wagging, as always.

At the veterinarian's I ask the girl behind the counter where I might find the dog pound. She tells me it's eight or ten kilometres out of town, and winces. 'It's opposite the tip, which is a bit horrible,' she says. We drive east on the pretty Goulburn Valley Highway, past orchards advertising peaches, plums, oranges and olives, past a very smashed-up car.

A road sign points to the municipal tip, but not to the pound. At the tip sit many more smashed cars, lined up in a snaggle-toothed row. From some of their bumpers flutter ragged strips of yellow-and-black police tape.

The dog pound is a largish area overlooking a field of apricots, or possibly they are nectarines. To the side, a single gum tree casts a blot of shade. There is no-one in attendance, and no sign stating any information at all. There is a high cyclone-wire fence, and then another fence: I can get close, but not onto the actual property. Beside the gum tree there's a row of eight wire cages, rectangular and tall, tin-roofed and dirt-floored. I don't know if you stayed in one of these, but they do look long unused. At the end of the cage row stands a spacious Brunswick-green shed, reasonably new. The sun bores down unhindered onto its metal roof. Inside the shed a dog is barking, lonesome and dismayed. I can't get past the fences to see him, and I'm guiltily glad. Beyond us, at the tip, two men in high-visibility vests are hauling dusty tyres. Here, as everywhere, the sensation is of heat, dirt, insect song, arid stone. It's not a place where anyone spends one minute more than they have to. Returning to town, I tell myself that inside every car we pass is that barking dog's owner on their way to collect the poor thing.

State regulations stipulate that a stray must spend a minimum of eight days in the pound before being offered for rehoming, or being euthanased. I guess the ranger watched you while you were in her care, deciding which would be your fate should your owner fail to claim you. Because there's no doubt that you had been owned: you love people, you love to be fussed over, you can never resist a lap. I've never seen you flinch at a raised voice or a lifted hand. You've always preferred to travel in the front seat of a car. Someone not only kept you, but indulged and cared about you. And yet you walked the road so long that you started to fade away, and then you spent at least eight days in the pound, and nobody came.

*

If Zak or Shilo had become lost, I would have searched for them forever. I would have walked the world. I would have looked twice at every dog I ever saw. I would have wanted to die. But life can be different in the country – harsher, less sentimental. And people are different everywhere, the things they will do and not do.

I think about what might have happened – I have thought about it a lot. A gundog like you, I think you were a man's dog. Youthful and adventurous, did you escape a poorly fenced property, possibly not for the first time, and did your owner lose patience with you, and feel unwilling or unable to pay the pound fees even if you were found? Or maybe you were distracted flushing rabbits out of the scrub one evening, and accidentally lost sight of your owner, and he of you? Or did he lose you deliberately, because you were distracted too readily? Were you lost and given up for dead, or were you let go, to live or die as you would?

Neither of those scenarios ties neatly with the man who let you on his lap, who drove with you in the front seat of his car.

*

There are photos of you from this time, presumably taken by the ranger. You sit on wet concrete, eyeing the camera warily. I know you well, and I recognise the expression on your face. Uncomfortable, unsure. You do not like a surface that is wet. There is a rope around your neck, and it's crossing close to your face. You do not like that kind of carelessness, it might turn out badly for you. The whole situation would have made you unhappy, but I see you enduring without complaint. Good dog.

Everyone who meets you sees your good heart. The first time I brought you to meet him, my vet said, 'You've got a good one here.' The ranger saw it too. She took the photos and, because the shire was trying to improve outcomes for its strays, and because you were 'one of the best dogs she had met', the ranger contacted a city-based rescue group with which the shire had recently begun to work.

*

We're staying in a motel ten minutes out of Cobram. I couldn't find a place in town that would take a dog. It's fine, though, the motel is charming, full of young fruit pickers who smile when they see you, click their fingers to encourage you to come to them. The lady who runs the place says she's never been busier than since she started accepting pets. She says that dogs have been among the best guests she's had. She has a bold Jack Russell–cross–Shih tzu which her husband calls a 'jack shit'.

I tell my hostess I'm writing about rescue dogs, but that usually I write novels for children. Immediately she phones a friend who owns a bookshop in New South Wales, eager to know if he's heard of me. Her face falls as she listens. No, she tells me, and her husband, and the fruit pickers who sit around listening, her bookseller friend has never heard of me. And she considers me with a tinge of suspicion and dislike. I babble and smile and walk away, face burning. You fly loyally after me, your low and humiliated companion.

All the time you were on the road and in the pound, I was looking for you. Not for you specifically, but for the dog who spoke to me. One who would be different from Zak and Shilo, because I had no wish to replicate or compare. Most importantly,

I wanted a rescue dog, because you only get to share this life with a certain number of dogs, and one of them at least should be lifted from the pool of need.

You can send yourself crazy looking at needful dogs. Pound dogs, pet shop dogs, backyard breeder dogs, puppy farm dogs. The most poignant are the ones who are unwanted because of baby, because of job, because of travel, because of getting married, because of allergic partner, because of divorce, because grown too big, because too old, because need too much exercise, because just not right anymore. Dogs who are said to be nice dogs, happy dogs, great with kids, adore walks, car, cats, beach, playful, loving, family member, no trouble, suddenly cast aside. Dogs in the hands of people who don't think an animal matters. Dogs who smile for the camera without realising their time is ticking. Dogs who haven't understood that the person they want doesn't want them in return. Dogs who have had sad lives, and for whom this advertisement on the internet is just another step on that lonely downhill trudge. You can give yourself a nervous breakdown.

It's easier to look at rescue sites. At least you know the animal is, for the time being, in safe hands.

*

When the Victorian Dog Rescue Group accepted responsibility for you, they sent you to the Cobram vet for needles and a health check. I have the report the group received.

There is wear on your teeth which isn't typical in a young dog – my own vet would wonder if your time being homeless could be to blame, the weeks spent chewing what you could find. A few days after your first visit, the ranger – this decent woman, this passing guardian angel of yours – brought you back to the vet clinic, because you seemed poorly. You were tested for parvo and found negative, so you were given a course of antibiotics.

There's no mention anywhere, because presumably it wasn't known then, that you cough occasionally and terribly, as if the dust of a stony road coats your nose and throat.

*

The group gives names to the dogs they take on, and they called you Coleridge, I don't know why. The moniker caught my eye, as it would. It's a ludicrously fancy name for someone of your hobo background and mongrel blood, but you are undeniably distinguished-looking, so the name does suit you. I'd intended to call my third dog Wyatt, but what with your other life and then the road, the pound, the foster care, the country, the city, you'd already endured enough change. So you are Coleridge Wyatt, as there is Zakary Star and Shilo Hagrid. You are Cole, Colly, Colly Dolly, Colly Flower. Once, I told a tiny dog-shy girl that your name was Little Flower, and immediately her fear left her, and she reached out to pat you. Little flower.

*

It was quite the process, getting you. At times it made me doubt myself, as if I had no experience with any animal at all. As if I'd never tamed the wolf lord, nor found a path through a whippet's eccentric mind. But at some point amid the waiting and the phone calls and the inspections of the backyard you became mine, enduring the labyrinthine application process made you mine, returning to look at your photograph – that droll tolerance at the pound – made you mine.

The first night you stayed, you slept beneath the dining table. When I bathed the dirt out of you, you fought like a steer. You couldn't catch a ball, you were intimidated by the cat, you couldn't swim, you were frightened by noisy play. We were strangers, but we belonged to each other now, and I told you I would always care for you. There'd be times when I'd have to leave you, but I would always come back for you. One day, driving along swooping streets with you in the back seat, I glanced in the rear-vision mirror and saw you galloping along the road after the car. Some luggage had toppled across the seat and, to escape it, you'd jumped out the window without a sound. I pulled over and you ran to me, desperate but joyful, absolutely forgiving. My heart smarted with grief for you. Had you once chased a car until you couldn't see it, and stood in the dust cloud trying to work out what was going on? Why would anyone stop wanting you, Cole? There's not an ounce of unkindness in you. You ask for almost nothing. You try at all times to be a good dog. I've puzzled over it so often and so futilely, how a person could simply not bother to care.

*

We leave Cobram after three days. No-one has tried to claim you, and nothing we've seen has seemed familiar to you, but nonetheless it's a relief to turn the car towards home. Two and a half hours down the Hume, through horse country – Black Caviar country, no less – the fire danger rating signs becoming less lurid the further south we go. You sleep soundly, waking to gaze out the window sometimes. Home to the bitumen, power poles, car horns, rubbish left by kids in the street: this inner-city suburb is very different from the landscape you came from, but I hope you like it here. I hope you're glad to be with me, as I am glad to be with you. We didn't find anything in Cobram, but we also found quite a lot. I think I know you better, yet you retain much mystery. It's good, I feel happy. Home, you trot straight out to the chicken coop, because chasing the pigeons which congregate at the feeder is the bird dog's favourite sport.

*

Something happened yesterday. We were walking our usual track along Merri Creek. In the near distance an old man appeared between the trees. He was wearing a broad-brimmed canvas hat and walking in a slow but steady way. The moment you saw him, your tail whirled. You ran – you really bolted – to press yourself against his legs. The old man bent to greet you, and I saw you realise he wasn't somebody you recognised. The incident was nothing, yet there was something remarkable about it. I said, 'He thought he knew you.' The man said, 'Yes, I think he did.' And he was a dear old man, with a sweet gentle face, so dapper in his hat and tidy clothes, and it occurred to me then, something I have not considered before. Maybe he died. Maybe your owner, who loved you, couldn't search for you because he died.

*

Well, who knows: someone might, but I never will, and maybe you don't know either. I would say it doesn't matter – sure, it doesn't matter to me – but it matters to you, I think, and always will. The past has left its shadowy mark on you. Cole, it happens to us all.

But you are here. This bed is yours, this bowl, this collar. You have a microchip, a registration tag, a phone number on a disc. I shift house a lot, house after house after house – we've been together only two and a half years, but already we've shared three different houses. Probably our roaming will continue, but know this, Cole: where I am, you can be. Bird dog, lost dog, found dog, good dog, you are free to stay.

Commonplace

John Clarke

A little while back I took some photographs of shorebirds, many of which are migratory and fly to the Arctic in our autumn to breed. Some of the godwits I photographed had orange leg tags and when I zoomed in I could read the letters and numbers, so I reported these on a website that tracks migratory birds and which tells me these birds were tagged one year ago, in exactly the same place. This means that during 2016 they flew from here, over the South Pacific and southern Asia to China, where for millions of years they have fed on the mudflats in the Yellow Sea between the mainland and the Korean peninsula. Then they fly further north to either Siberia or Alaska. And after the breeding season they fly all the way back. Recently a small transmitter was put in a godwit that flew from Alaska to New Zealand in one go without stopping to eat or rest.

As a result more research is being done about how the birds sleep. We used to think that each godwit would take a turn at the front, go like the clappers for a while and then slip back into the peloton for bit of a rest while fresher godwits moved forward and took over. Not the case apparently. Microsleeps is the current wisdom. The birds have a capacity to close down part of their brain while flying. Exactly how they do this, and here's an ornithological term, is anyone's guess. Godwit numbers are down this year and the curlew sandpiper and eastern curlew numbers are so far down both are now classified as critically endangered.

The reason is that the birds can no longer feed on the mudflats in the Yellow Sea on the flight north. The mudflats aren't there anymore. Despite international agreements on the crucial importance of the feeding grounds of migratory birds, the area has been reclaimed for housing.

For some reason I've been to a few florists lately. Last week I went into one about an hour out of town and was having a look around when a man came over and asked what I'd like. I said I wasn't quite sure and he said that was fine and he pointed and said he'd be over there if I wanted any help. I thanked him and in fairly short order I moved away from the arrangements and settled on some fresh flowers. I caught his eye.

'Worked it out?' he asked, coming over.

'Yes, I believe I have,' I said indicating my choice, 'I think I'll just have a swag of these.'

'Lilies,' he said. 'Yes, beautiful. Good choice.' And he collected a generous handful and we went over to the counter where he began to wrap them.

'You've been out of the florist game for a while, haven't you?' he said.

'Yes, I have,' I conceded.

'Thought so,' he said, and continued wrapping. 'We've pretty much given up the term "swag" these days.'

'Really?' I asked. 'What expression do we use these days?'

'Oh,' he drawled, in what A.A. Milne would call a wondering kind of way. '"Bunch", mostly, these days.'

'Is that right?' I said. '"Bunch" of flowers.'

'Yes. A lot of people call them bunches now.'

'Goodness,' I said and I paid him and left.

I'll be going back there. He's good.

A friend's house was burgled the other day. A couple of replaceable modern devices were taken and a small amount of cash but the main contribution to her sense of shock and violation was that there was stuff everywhere, books pulled out of bookcases, accounts and professional records tipped out of folders, the filing cabinet upended and the contents tossed about and clothes hauled out of wardrobes and cupboards and thrown all over the floor. All the king's horses and all the king's men were quickly on hand and eventually order was restored.

When she was explaining the drama to her neighbours one of them reported that his brother's house had been completely cleaned out while he was away over the summer. Everything worth anything was stolen in broad daylight. The police investigation revealed that entry was effected by jemmying the back door open and the rest of the crime was committed as follows: a large van was backed up to the front of the house at about 9.30 in the morning and for the next hour or so, several men carried things out of the house and put them in the van while another man mowed the lawn.

In 1972 I was driving a delivery van for Barkers, which was a titanic London retail institution in Kensington until encountering an iceberg one night in dense fog about a decade ago. Some of the people to whom we delivered were very grand and a bit Miss Havisham, but a great many of them were kind and interesting. Lady Fremantle, for example, was about eighty-five and she had a maid who was hot on her heels, so when I arrived with the week's groceries I'd carry them through into the kitchen. We'd often have a chat and on a cold day we'd sit at the table and have a hot chocolate. If they needed anything shifted, lifted or removed, they'd ask me but 'only if it would be no trouble' and if anything needed to be posted, I'd drop it in the mail.

Lady F was from a naval family and hanging in a slightly askew frame on the wall was the first order Nelson had written with his left hand after he'd lost his right arm. There was also a couple called Lord and Lady Graves, who were in films and were stars on the London musical stage and to whom I was delivering one day when I was invited in. 'Come in,' said Peter Graves. 'I'm Peter Graves. You're a New Zealander, aren't you?' I said I was and he said, 'Yes, please come in. We're very sad today. It's is the anniversary of the death of our dear friend Inia Te Wiata. We're just going to have a quick drink. It would be great if you could join us.'

A bottle of whisky was produced and Peter spoke about the great baritone and we had a quick drink. They then both told some excellent stories and we had a couple more quick drinks before speaking of a great many things and there was some very enjoyable singing at some point and I think we had some salmon as a few more quick drinks were put away. I then left and continued my delivery round, of which I have no clear recollection.

During the 1980s I worked on a television series on which one of the senior writers was James Mitchell, who'd written *Callan* and *When the Boat Comes In* and whose experience in writing series television was considerable. After the first script meeting Jim came over and said, 'We've worked together before, haven't we?'

'No, I don't think so,' I said.

'Yes we have,' he said. 'I've seen you before.'

'I used to deliver your groceries, Jim,' I said. 'You live in Bedford Gardens.' James was a working-class Tory and was inclined not to speak to people who delivered things, but he was always very nice to me after that first script meeting.

One of the advantages of the Barkers job was that if I wanted to go somewhere in London, to the National Gallery or the Tate or the V and A, I could drive up to the front door and, provided I left one of the back doors of the van open to indicate I'd just ducked in to deliver something, I could park there as long as I liked.

Long before winning the Nobel Prize, Seamus Heaney was aware of the danger of allowing oneself to be elevated by others. He told the story of Antaeus, a great warrior in ancient Greece, enormously strong and born out of the earth itself. Antaeus would challenge his opponents to a wrestling match in which he would neutralise them, wrap his arms around them and crush them to death. Antaeus was eventually defeated by Hercules. Hercules was a famous warrior too, but he was also very smart and he'd been studying Antaeus. He had worked out that when an opponent threw Antaeus down on the ground, it made Antaeus stronger because he drew his strength from the earth. So when Hercules and Antaeus fought to the death, Hercules defeated Antaeus by lifting him off the ground and holding him up.

Something else we get from ancient Greece is the story of Narcissus, although perhaps our understanding of it has drifted slightly from its mooring. In a nutshell, Narcissus is out hunting one day when Echo sees him and falls in love with him. She follows him and talks to him. She has never seen anything as beautiful as he is and she declares her love for him. When Narcissus rejects her, Echo is broken-hearted and disappears, leaving only her voice.

Then Nemesis, the goddess of revenge, punishes Narcissus by leading him to a pool in which he sees an image so beautiful he becomes enchanted and visits the pool each day to gaze at it. Ultimately he realises that the image cannot love him and cannot even exist independently of his act of looking at it. As with Echo, Narcissus's love is obsessive and unrequited, and he kills himself.

Oscar Wilde, who was a Greek scholar, recognised that characterising Narcissus's obsession as 'self-love' misses the fact that what he is enthralled by is a reflection. It is not himself as he knows himself to be. The image is reversed. He is beguiled by a perspective of himself he hasn't seen before.

In order to highlight this otherness, Wilde included an addendum to the story in which, after Narcissus dies, the pool weeps and becomes salty with its tears. The forest creatures gather around and sympathise. They understand that the pool would mourn for so beautiful a young man as Narcissus.

'No, no,' says the pool, and it explains that it mourns because when Narcissus bent over and looked into it, it could see itself reflected in his eyes.

Wilde's two sons were brought up under the name Holland after the surname Wilde, previously illuminated by one of the greatest gifts in the history of the theatre, had become associated with what was called 'gross indecency'. Both Cyril and Vyvyan Holland served as officers in the First World War. Cyril was killed by a sniper but Vyvyan survived and after the war he worked sometimes as a lawyer and sometimes as a writer and translator. In 1947 his second wife, Thelma, who was from Melbourne and who later became the Queen's beautician, was invited to Australia and New Zealand to give a series of lectures on fashion in nineteenth-century Australia. Between 1948 and 1952 Vyvyan and Thelma Holland lived in Melbourne.

Among Vyvyan's published works is *Drink and Be Merry*, which, although it is essentially a book about wine, contains a story about the remarkable skill level of the painters Braque and Derain. The two young men shared a rather long studio and each operated at one end of the room. They developed the habit of throwing things to each other and once they'd reached Olympic standard at hurling and catching any article regardless of shape, they worked out how to throw a carafe full of water underarm the length of the room, spinning it backwards so that the water stayed in it. At the other end of the room the recipient would judge the rotation exactly and would catch the carafe by the neck as it arrived.

At the time it was common to be offered all sorts of wine in a restaurant, but it was difficult to get the waiter to bring water. One evening Derain dressed for dinner and entered the Café de Paris at the fashionable hour and ordered a meal and a carafe of water. A few minutes later, after Derain's water had arrived, Braque entered and sat at a table about the distance from Derain's as existed between their easels in the studio. Braque ordered his meal and then stood up and said, 'This is monstrous. I've been sitting here for twenty minutes and I've asked for a glass of water and what do I get? Nothing!'

Those assembled were further astonished when Derain stood up and said, 'You want a carafe of water, sir? Voilà,' and he spun the full carafe over the heads of diners to Braque, who caught it perfectly, slowly poured himself a glass of water and flung the carafe back over the heads to Derain.

'Thank you, sir,' Braque said, and both painters sat down as if nothing had happened.

Another admirable piece of spontaneous public theatre was established by the Australian cartoonist Paul Rigby in the late 1950s, through the formation of the Limp Falling Association. Members of the association would gather, often in venues where refreshments were available, and would go limp and fall to the ground. This would happen in the middle of a room or along a wall or at a dinner table, and in a couple of more orchestral instances, in a group of twenty down a full staircase. At a time when Australia has lost touch with its identity, it is regrettable that not only has this tradition been lost but that there is not a federal Minister of Limp Falling, charged with revitalising an important symbol of folkloric independence. It cannot be that the activity is too absurd. There are many federal ministers engaged in idiocy of a far greater magnitude than going limp and falling to the ground. In fact it might help if some of them made enquiries and joined the association.

A Makarrata Declaration:
A Declaration of Our Country

Stan Grant

Salman Rushdie – the great Indian writer – once said of the importance of stories: 'Those that do not have the power over the story that dominates their lives, the power to re-tell it, re-think it, deconstruct it, joke about it, and change it as times change, truly are powerless because they cannot think new thoughts.'

As our world spins around us, consumed as we are by political upheaval, economic uncertainty, terrorism and war, I have wondered about this thing: story and its importance. What is this great story of us? What captures this thing of life? This transcendence; this beauty and terror; this hope and despair; this fleeting performance measured in minutes before the curtain falls and we fade into the black and others mount the stage.

> *In a world*
> *full of*
> *temporary things*
> *you are*
> *a perpetual*
> *feeling*

The Indian poet Sanober Khan speaks of our need to find solace in nostalgia; to create the everlasting from fleeting moments. She says 'the magic fades too fast, and nothing remains ... nothing lasts.'

I contemplate that now as I think of us: people from all points tossed together here on this island to become a people, a country: a nation. Nothing remains ... nothing lasts. Yet despite this impermanence, we struggle as human beings to make sense of ourselves and our place on this earth. When all passes, all too soon, what is left is the fact of our humanity and how we embraced it; the time we had and how it was spent. Each age asks much of us: we have been tested by war, and horror unimaginable except that our imaginations are what gave rise to it; we have endured disaster, collapse, tyranny, poverty, and above it all we endure. As Sanober Khan tells us, we 'create the everlasting from fleeting moments'.

The greatest story of us? For me it isn't written or spoken; for me it is a painting on a ceiling in a world far from my own. My epiphany came in the Sistine Chapel. There, in a throng of tourists crammed into the Vatican, I gazed at our eternal struggle. Michelangelo laboured four years to produce this, his depiction of Genesis.

Here is the outstretched hand of Adam, reaching for the hand of God. They extend but they do not touch. Between them is all of us: all we want to be; all we fail to be; all our ambiguity. Between them is the very spark of life – not in the fact of existence but the act of striving.

It is twenty years since I gazed on Michelangelo's masterpiece, and I have never ceased pondering that distance – what is it that separates us, even as we reach for each other? To me it has always seemed that we live in that small, empty space, reaching for that connection, between the certainty of ourselves and the possibilities of togetherness.

How do we fill that space? We fill it with history, identity, hate, myth, longing, love, resentment, memory. We reach for each other and yet we don't touch. The philosopher Hegel would see it as the struggle for our freedom – that space the essence of our being and non-being.

I glimpse that in Michelangelo's Adam and God – an outstretched hand and a space of endless possibility.

World history, writes Hegel, is the 'interpretation of spirit in time'. The Polish Nobel Prize–winning poet Czesław Miłosz wondered about this journey of time and people, this quest of the spirit. In his poem 'The Spirit of History', from *A Treatise of Poetry*, he writes:

Amid thunder, the golden house of is
Collapses, and the process of becoming ascends.

Certainty – being – gone; and ahead, possibility and change: inevitable, unrelenting change. As Miłosz writes:

You without beginning, you always between …

The Australian novelist Eleanor Dark captures that impermanence in her great trilogy *The Timeless Land*. She explores the birth pains of modern Australia, and the upheaval for the First Peoples. She begins by imagining the moment of the coming of the whites. The boy Bennilong (sic) has come to the shore with his father. Only six years old, he was expected to act as a man.

He was conscious of the world, and conscious of himself as a part of it, fitting into it, belonging to it, drawing strength and joy and existence from it, like a bee in the frothing yellow opulence of the wattle.

Dark imagines a blue cloudless sky, the sea a 'silver line', the surf breaking on the rocks. Bennilong was tired but his father did not notice; he kept his eyes peeled for the 'boat with wings'. He had been looking year after year after that strange morning when a 'magic boat had flown into their harbour'. It had 'folded its wings like a seagull' and come to rest. From the boat came 'mysterious beings with faces pale as bones'. Bennilong had been told this story in corroboree: how these strangers came and left as suddenly.

It was long ago and the memory of the 'magic boat' had faded, but Bennilong's father remembered, and so they came to stand on the rock and watch and wait for the white faces' eventual return. So vivid is Dark's recreation that I feel as though I am the young boy himself, standing with his father, his head filled with old stories and imagining, dreaming and becoming.

Bennilong stared at it. The unending water. He looked up at his father's lean figure, still motionless, still watching for the boat with wings, and there was born in him a conviction which all through his boyhood was to tease him now and then – that the water was not really unending after all; that somewhere, far, far away there lay another land; that some day he, Bennilong, not in a bark canoe but in a boat with wings, would go in search of it.

A generation later, another Australian writer, Thomas Keneally, in his book *The Chant of Jimmie Blacksmith*, imagines a scene long after the whites have come. For Keneally's Jimmie Blacksmith, the golden house of *is* indeed has collapsed, and Blacksmith emerges as a new type of being, a creation possible only here.

The bone-pale face of the white stranger has darkened, and the curly hair of Dark's Bennilong has straightened. This is the Australian synthesis: Blacksmith born of black and white – from ancient and new – Australian in a way that no other can be.

Half breed Jimmie had resulted from a visit some white man had made to Brentwood blacks' camp in 1878. The missionaries – who had never been told the higher things of Wibbera – had made it clear that if you had pale children it was because you'd been rolled by white men. They'd not been told that it was Emu-Wren, the tribal totem, who'd quickened the womb.

Keneally's Blacksmith was based on a historical figure, Jimmy Governor. The real Jimmy was a mixed-race Wiradjuri man who, like his fictional equivalent, married a white woman and searched for a place in this new country, on the eve of Federation. Governor found instead derision and rejection, his wife endured humiliation, and Jimmy – aided by his brother and an uncle – responded with a violent rampage that ended with nine people dead and sparked the biggest manhunt in Australian history.

Keneally sees his Jimmie as the man between: finding a place in neither the white nor the black world. He is a potent symbol of a country in transition: what has been and what is to come. In one scene Keneally depicts two office clerks debating Federation as Jimmie looks on, awaiting an instructional pamphlet on what wood to use for fencing. The clerks fall into a discussion about the American Civil War.

'Wouldn't happen here. Could yer imagine Australians shooting Australians?

'... And you seem to forget, my friend, that there's no such thing as an Australian ...'

They eventually notice Jimmie.

'Jacko?' he called. 'He's an honest poor bastard but he's nearly extinct.'

'And, surprisingly, that is the work of those you so fancifully call Australians.'

Keneally grapples with this emerging nation: a people – as Hegel would have said – in a process of 'becoming'. His Jimmie Blacksmith is as much a part of this transformation as the two arguing clerks. Rejected, he massacres the Australians who would tell him he was not one of them. However this nation was founded, whatever the injustice and brutality of British settlement, Jimmie is tied inexorably to its fate even as he is mocked, excluded and doomed, and even as he so violently rejects it.

In film and art and song and literature we have sought to make sense of what it is to be this thing called an Australian. I recall the film *Picnic at Hanging Rock*. I saw it on a very rare visit to the cinema as a young teenager. The memory has never left me, and I have returned to it time and again. It is a haunting meditation on place, with the vanishing girls seemingly swallowed by the land itself. Remember the voice over of the doomed girl, Miranda: 'What we see and what we seem are but a dream ... a dream within a dream.'

The use of that word *dream*, spoken by the whitest of white girls, symbolically connects us to the *dreaming*, in that place – the rock – that stood for an eternity just waiting for them. Their disappearance would become part of the dreaming story itself. *Picnic at Hanging Rock* has always struck me as a film about the thesis of Britishness set against the antithesis of terra nullius – an empty land for the taking. Those who emerge from the disappearance of the girls are forever changed: the synthesis of a new people in a new place. The girls lost have become a part of this place, initiated: a mystery now part of an even greater mystery of this old land.

One scene has always captivated me. As the girls arrive for their picnic, an obviously British family are having their own gathering. They are overly and stuffily dressed, sweltering yet making no concession to the heat, their basket of food laid out before them. As they eat, ants swarm over the meal, and there is a plague of flies. Here was the incongruity of imposed Britishness on a harsh, hot, foreboding place: Europeans trying to tame an untameable country. As the search for the missing girls continues day after day, the family return for their ritual picnic. In this way, the film's director, Peter Weir, grapples with the themes of alienation and belonging. The Indigenous presence is felt more than seen: the land itself represented as blackness.

Eleanor Dark, Tom Keneally and Peter Weir: they have tried to tell the story of us – of our place. They set us in an ancient continuum ruptured by a cataclysmic clash of culture and civilisation. Out of destruction we are born anew: uncertain perhaps of our place, but with no other place to call our own. Whiteness must struggle with its blackness: it is in the land itself, it is in the memory of the people displaced, and it is there in blood – hidden blackness, or blackness denied.

For the First Peoples, it is a fashioning or refashioning of belonging when the very essence of belonging itself has been ruptured and the certainty of heritage blurred. Jimmy Governor (Jimmie Blacksmith) is part white, married white and yet is rejected for being black. What it is to be Indigenous has become a puzzle not easily explained, nor simple to comprehend.

The young Indigenous writer Ellen van Neerven, in her book of short stories, *Heat and Light* – a dazzling collection that crunches genre and gender, where plants speak as people and the past and future collide – grapples with ambiguity and the fluidity of identity and belonging. Van Neerven is of Aboriginal and Dutch heritage, and many of these stories are tales of ambiguity.

'So much is in what we make of things,' she writes. 'The stories we construct about our place in our families are essential to our lives.' In this story of a girl looking for herself in the image of a grandmother she never knew, Van Neerven writes: 'If I didn't know my grandmother, then how could I know myself.'

The French historian Michel de Certeau says we live with a history of absence. We use stories to fill the void. What we call history he saw as a collection of artefacts we assemble to try to make sense of ourselves. Here is the crux of recognition, constructed out of a past reimagined, history written and history denied. As a nation, we struggle to reconcile ourselves to our past and our place. Always there is story.

The story of Australia speaks to us from the dry shores of Lake Mungo. Forty thousand years ago, the waters were full, sustaining a thriving community. Here a man was laid to rest with full ceremony, his body smeared in ochre. In all of humanity this was rare, among the earliest examples of such ritual. The mourners sang a song in language now lost. As modern Australia celebrated its birth at Federation in 1901, the historical inspiration for Jimmie Blacksmith, the real Jimmy Governor, sat in a Darlinghurst jail cell, alternating between singing songs in his traditional Wiradjuri language and reading the Bible – the synthesis of the old and new worlds that collided here so violently, given form in a man soon for the gallows. It is a synthesis Keneally saw as contradiction, and yet the essence of being Australian. Joan Lindsay wrote the book of the missing girls of Hanging Rock, and director Peter Weir fixed it in our imaginations: the land itself a potent character in an ethereal tale of place and being.

These are Australian stories, ancient and modern, and all efforts at recognition – a need to be seen. It is a fleeting project, an attempt to capture a people – a people always changing – in a time and place. A drawing on a cave wall preserved for antiquity to tell future people: 'This was us.' It is so human, and it is essential.

While story grapples with timelessness, with ambivalence and ambiguity, we live in a land of laws, and the law demands certainty. If the First Peoples are to have justice, it must truly be acknowledged at law. It must reside in our nation's founding document. But I would argue that we seek something more, that we write a declaration of our nation – a Makarrata Declaration of Country – that speaks beyond race or history. In the United States this is captured in the Declaration of Independence, a poetic document that resonates beyond the American Constitution: 'We hold these truths to be self-evident, that all men are created equal, that they are endowed by their creator with certain unalienable rights, that among these are life, liberty and the pursuit of happiness ...'

Never before in human history had that noble sentiment been so explicitly set down. The Declaration of Independence pledged a government as the right of the people. The people were then considered to be white: equality did not extend to those in bondage. Yet far into the nation's future – beyond the imaginings of the American founding fathers – a black man would occupy the White House. The new American nation pledged 'to each other our lives'. Through Civil War, assassination, disgrace and protest, it seeks to hold to that pledge.

The very idea of *nation* sits uneasily in a world of fractured, contending loyalties, a world of blood feuds. How can it hold us all? Globalisation is testing the limits of sovereignty – of identity. I return to the words of French philosopher Ernest Renan. Writing in 1882, he pondered that which made a nation. 'A nation is a soul,' he wrote, 'a spiritual principle.' For Renan, we draw from the past to live in the future: 'the nation, like the individual, is the outcome of a long past of efforts, sacrifices, and devotions.' Yet he counselled against clinging to memory, to grievance or division: 'Forgetting, I would even say historical error, is an essential factor in the creation of a nation.'

In Australia we are presented with a challenge to our nation, one that stems from history itself; its unfinished business. The idea of Indigenous recognition seeks restoration in an exercise of reconciliation. But recognition walks a national faultline: history, race. These things that can divide, yet cannot be ignored. Recognition itself challenges us to make good on the past, yet live free of its chains – to remember in order to forget. Renan told us a nation demands it of us: 'Man is a slave neither of his race, his language, his religion, the course of his rivers, nor the direction of his mountain ranges. A great aggregation of men, in sane mind and warm heart, created a moral conscience that calls itself a nation.'

Recognition is the struggle for our moral conscience. It is also a test of how we are governed. Can our constitution satisfy the demands of what Canadian philosopher James Tully calls our 'strange multiplicity'? Tully says we find ourselves locked in intractable conflicts of nationalism and federalism, linguistic and ethnic minorities, feminism and multiculturalism and the demands of indigenous rights. He writes: 'The question is whether a constitution can give recognition to the legitimate demands of the members of diverse cultures that renders every-one their due ...'

Our constitution – our founding document – must reflect what came before: it must acknowledge the place of the First Peoples. Others have described it as our nation's rule book. It is a rule book that still carries the illegitimacy and stain of race, so it surely needs amendment. This land's First Peoples have felt the sting of exclusion and discrimination. It is the challenge of a nation to rise above its past. Can our constitution meet the aspirations of those locked out at the nation's birth? Will the First Peoples be given full voice to shape our destinies and complete our union with our fellow Australians?

These things need not be incompatible. The First Peoples do not have special rights, but inherent rights. It diminishes no-one to acknowledge and protect that unique status, in keeping with the spirit and limits of our constitutional democracy. In this way we ensure allegiance. In this way we narrow our differences and strengthen our bonds. Without meaningful, substantial recognition of the status of the First Peoples, a Declaration of Country will ring hollow. But with it we are free.

A nation is not just a set of laws. Above all, it is a story: a never-ending story of us. It is the story of a land steeped in time, await-ing people from many other lands, who in time will call themselves Australians. It begins with the first footsteps taken tens of millennia ago, and continues in the newest-born child of this land. It will live on in those still to come. A Makarrata Declaration, a Declaration of our Country, must speak to us all. It should speak to our sense of place: our home. It should be the work of poets. It should stand alone, apart from the Constitution. Its words should be carved in monuments to fall from the lips of children not yet born.

The bones of my ancestors are buried in this land. They are the bones of black and white. They are dust, the very land itself. When the political debates of our age are past, there will always be our country. Our challenge – all of us – is to live here and call it home. The work is undone to make a nation, this thing of the soul.

A Makarrata Declaration must tell the story of Eleanor Dark's Bennilong and the story of Peter Weir's missing white girls. It must tell the story of a man called Wongamar, my Wiradjuri forebear, and the story of an Irishman, John Grant, whose name I carry, a man who came here clasped in irons with no hope of return. This would be his home. A Makarrata Declaration should speak to who we have been and allow for who we may become.

A preamble could read:

> *The first people touched this land as our continent was being formed.*
> *They came in boats when humanity had yet to cross an open sea.*
> *Here they formed a civilisation that continues to this day.*
> *Their birthright has never been ceded.*
> *Those people live still in their descendants.*
> *We enter into their heritage and respect their traditions.*
> *We honour too those who have come from other lands and carry with them their cultures and faiths.*
> *Though our bonds may strain, we seek to live together in harmony.*
> *Though we may disagree, we find no enemy among us.*
> *We cherish the foundations of our nation, and our rule of law and democracy.*
> *We abide by the will of the majority but defend the rights of the minority.*
> *We are all equal in dignity.*
> *Opportunity is for all.*
> *Worth should be measured not in privilege.*
> *By our efforts we prosper.*
> *In a land of plenty, we care for those without.*
> *From the first footsteps to the most recent arrival, this land is our home.*
> *Here, together, we form a new people bound not by the chains of history but committed to a future forged together.*

When I think of a Makarrata Declaration, a Declaration of our Country, I think of the Scottish poet Rabbie Burns, who said: 'If I could write all the songs I would not care who wrote the laws.' A Makarrata Declaration should be the song of our country.

Uluru Statement from the Heart

We, gathered at the 2017 National Constitutional Convention, coming from all points of the southern sky, make this statement from the heart:

Our Aboriginal and Torres Strait Islander tribes were the first sovereign Nations of the Australian continent and its adjacent islands, and possessed it under our own laws and customs. This our ancestors did, according to the reckoning of our culture, from the Creation, according to the common law from 'time immemorial', and according to science more than 60,000 years ago.

This sovereignty is *a spiritual notion: the ancestral tie between the land, or 'mother nature', and the Aboriginal and Torres Strait Islander peoples who were born therefrom, remain attached thereto, and must one day return thither to be united with our ancestors. This link is the basis of the ownership of the soil, or better, of sovereignty.* It has never been ceded or extinguished, and coexists with the sovereignty of the Crown.

How could it be otherwise? That peoples possessed a land for sixty millennia and this sacred link disappears from world history in merely the last two hundred years?

With substantive constitutional change and structural reform, we believe this ancient sovereignty can shine through as a fuller expression of Australia's nationhood.

Proportionally, we are the most incarcerated people on the planet. We are not an innately criminal people. Our children are aliened from their families at unprecedented rates. This cannot be because we have no love for them. And our youth languish in detention in obscene numbers. They should be our hope for the future. These dimensions of our crisis tell plainly the structural nature of our problem. This is *the torment of our powerlessness.*

We seek constitutional reforms to empower our people and take *a rightful place* in our own country. When we have power over our destiny our children will flourish. They will walk in two worlds and their culture will be a gift to their country.

We call for the establishment of a First Nations Voice enshrined in the Constitution.

Makarrata is the culmination of our agenda: *the coming together after a struggle.* It captures our aspirations for a fair and truthful relationship with the people of Australia and a better future for our children based on justice and self-determination.

We seek a Makarrata Commission to supervise a process of agreement-making between governments and First Nations and truth-telling about our history.

In 1967 we were counted, in 2017 we seek to be heard. We leave base camp and start our trek across this vast country. We invite you to walk with us in a movement of the Australian people for a better future.

The Tamarind Is Always Sour

Keane Shum

If you crouch and hug your knees to your chest, and feel the skin
of a man's arm peeling against your own, and the sweat collecting on your nose drips onto the back of another man hunched
over in front of you; if slices of light sift through the wooden slats
a foot above your head, and your stomach feels like it is grinding
stones, your throat clenches against swallowing each waft of
urine and vomit, and the sting from a gash torn through your
thigh by a rubber gear belt swung at you like a mace burns like
the entire limb is being ripped off, like the chilli powder a filthy
hand ground into your eyes; if you and the hundreds in the hold
with you have been like this for twenty days, the gentle but mad-
deningly offbeat rocking of the sea pierced only by the occasional screams of women above deck, and you don't know when
it will end, and even when it ends you don't know how every day
after that will end, if you will be in bed with your wife or in jail,
as confined to a cell as you were to the village your grandparents
built a thousand miles from here, where you had a house but no
quarter, land but no country, time but no future; if you do not
exist on paper, anywhere, if no-one will take you in, and you are
drifting, always, then you know what that means. You know the
tamarind is always sour.

*

When I travel for work, it is neither a president nor a queen but the Secretary-General of the United Nations who requests free passage for the bearer of my passport, officially called a laissez-passer, French for 'let pass'. Its sky-blue cover is embossed not with the seal or flag of any one nation but with an outline of the world, all the inhabited continents as seen from the North Pole, swaddled in olive branches. I have presented it to dozens of immigration checkpoints nearly every month for four years now, but I still feel charmed every time I do. I possess no other document that gives as true and full a picture of my identity, shaped as it has been across several of the continents emblazoned on my laissez-passer.

My grandparents fled interregnum China nearly a century ago to colonial Hong Kong and Indonesia, where my parents grew up before studying and then settling in Australia in the 1960s. I was born an Australian citizen and a British subject in 1983, left for Taiwan when my parents' careers took them there in 1986 and never went back. I ended up growing up mostly in both British and Chinese Hong Kong before going to university and law school in the United States.

After working for some time as a New York corporate lawyer in Hong Kong, I found a job in Thailand with the South-East Asia office of the United Nations High Commissioner for Refugees. A week after I arrived in Bangkok, I came to the office to find my new work passport sitting half open on my desk, the visa pages trying to flutter out like the thrill I was trying to contain in front of my grizzled UN colleagues. When no-one was watching, I took a photo of my laissez-passer and messaged it to my closest friends and family.

It was 2013, not long after Barack Obama's second inauguration. I had stood for six subzero hours on the National Mall in Washington, D.C., during his first inauguration, waiting for the new dawn, for a multicultural child of immigrants to become the most powerful person in the world, a man whose childhood in Indonesia included tying string to dragonfly tails and eating *soto bakso* from a street stall, just as my mother's did. And when Americans re-elected Obama in an actual Electoral College landslide, confirming that it had been no fluke the first time, that this was not an aberration but the full forward march of history; and again later that year, when the immigration officer at Suvarnabhumi Airport stamped my laissez-passer and admitted me into the Kingdom of Thailand as an official of these United Nations, I could not help but feel like I was being certified on a cutting-edge assembly line, like I was a prototype for our new globalist age, friend of all nations, citizen of the world.

*

My job is to follow the movements of refugees across South-East Asia so that we know where and how they might seek asylum, and what kind of needs they will have when they do. For the last few years, by far the largest group of refugees moving across South-East Asia has been the Rohingya, an ethnic minority from Myanmar. The Rohingya are Muslims who have lived for generations in the western Myanmar state of Rakhine, but are considered by virtually all other Myanmarese – most of whom are Buddhists – to be interlopers from neighbouring Bangladesh.

By law, the more than one million Rohingya in Myanmar are almost all excluded from Myanmar citizenship, making them the largest stateless group in the world. They are cut off from livelihoods, medical care and schools. Systematic discrimination, punctuated by occasional eruptions of violent conflict, has pushed hundreds of thousands of Rohingya to seek refuge across a vast expanse stretching from Saudi Arabia and Pakistan to Bangladesh and Malaysia. There are anywhere from two to three million Rohingya in the world, and the large majority of them do not exist on paper.

When I first started talking to Rohingya refugees in 2014, most of them were fleeing Myanmar by boat because they were generally prohibited by local authorities from crossing by road into even the next town. Every month, thousands of Rohingya were committing US$2000 a head to a multinational network of Myanmarese, Bangladeshi, Thai and Malaysian people smugglers whom they entrusted to bring them across the Bay of Bengal and the Andaman Sea to Malaysia. My team and I interviewed hundreds of Rohingya who made this journey, and their testimonies were remarkably consistent and consistently terrifying. The only more inhumane crossing I have ever heard or read about is the Middle Passage, the part of the slave journey across the Atlantic that killed millions of Africans between the sixteenth and nineteenth centuries.

To be clear, the Rohingya were not enslaved on ships – most at least started the journey voluntarily – but the conditions were so brutally coercive that they were arguably all victims of human trafficking. Seven or eight hundred and sometimes over a thousand Rohingya and poor Bangladeshis hoping to find work in Malaysia would be packed into the hold of a fifteen- to thirty-metre-long fishing trawler, modified to fit the maximum number of human beings that could possibly crouch shoulder to shoulder on multiple levels below deck, none high enough to stand in. The 12 per cent who were women or girls were usually kept above deck, near the crew quarters.

Each passenger was given one cup of water and one scoop of rice per day. The toilet was a couple of wooden planks resting on iron bars welded to the side of the boat – the outside – and you could only use it once or twice a day in turn, following everyone else in your row. If you tried to go out of turn, or asked for more food or water, the crew would pistol-whip you or belt you with a plastic pipe. The business model was to get as many passengers to Malaysia alive as possible, but crews were not shy about shooting or beating people dead to maintain order. The murdered would be thrown overboard, along with the handful on each ship who perished from starvation or sickness. Based on our interviews, we think about twelve of every thousand passengers died at sea, almost all from abuse or deprivation. There could be over 1800 Rohingya and Bangladeshi bodies on the floor of the Bay of Bengal and the Andaman Sea.

Crossing by sea from Myanmar to Malaysia should only take one week, but most Rohingya I spoke to were in the hands of their smugglers for months. Boats would drift for weeks while waiting to fill to capacity or, at the destination, for a moment to disembark without being detected by authorities. This usually took place off the coast of southern Thailand, where it was easier for smugglers to land than on the Malaysian coast, which is heavily patrolled.

In Thailand, smugglers hauled their human cargo by truck to jungle encampments near the Malaysian border. There they would sequester the Rohingya and Bangladeshis in wooden cages until their families could pay off their debts. To extract payment, the smugglers called the family members of their captives as they beat them, forcing their screams into the phone. Only after payment was received were the prisoners released to Malaysia.

One sixteen-year-old Rohingya girl travelling on her own told us she was repeatedly raped in the jungle for fifteen days. Hundreds of bodies have been found haphazardly buried near these camps along the Thai–Malaysian border. Survivors have told me there may be hundreds more, killed while trying to escape or simply left for dead because they were too ill to transport when smugglers moved camp to evade authorities. I have met dozens of Rohingya in various states of paralysis, a symptom of the beri-beri they developed from being so severely malnourished.

One long weekend in 2014, I went sailing with my brother in the waters just up the coast from where these mass graves would eventually be discovered. It is paradise. From Phuket to the north and Langkawi to the south, the towering karst outcroppings that dot this seascape and the snow white sands that line them are unreal in their beauty, unmatched by any natural scenery in the region, maybe the world. Tourists from Europe and Russia and China and Australia live out their fantasies here in plush beach resorts, watching the sky turn brilliant shades of magenta and indigo as the sun sets over the same seas where refugees and migrants have languished near death for months.

*

Walking through a village in Maungdaw, a mainly Rohingya district in the westernmost point of Myanmar up against the border with Bangladesh, is akin to navigating a maze. The walkways between homes are like hiking trails: unpaved, narrow clearings with irregular dips and rises. Some are covered overhead by arches of brush, making it dark even during the day, and the woven bamboo fences express a kind of bounce and flow, as if the whole village bends in the wind. The taste of the sea is never far.

It is not hard to imagine Kamal (names have been changed to protect those involved), a twelve-year-old Rohingya boy, walking through his village one autumn night, suddenly being encircled by a group of young men. Some have guns. They grab his hair and make him walk towards a riverbank, where dozens of people are being herded onto a large canoe of sorts. There are a few other children like him, alone and confused. After several hours out to sea, they sail up to a fishing trawler. Everyone boards, and Kamal is forced underneath deck, into the hold. He does not know where he is going.

Six weeks later, in November 2014, I spoke to Kamal and his friend Ismail in a featureless mosque in Ampang, a modest suburb of Kuala Lumpur home to a sizeable Rohingya community. The two boys told similar stories of being abducted in Maungdaw, loaded onto a boat against their will and shipped to Malaysia via the jungle camps in Thailand, which is where they met. Their parents only found out where they were when smugglers – or, more properly in this case, kidnappers – called them from Thailand, demanding and eventually securing $2000 ransoms to release Kamal and Ismail to relatives in Malaysia.

Kamal was sullen and withdrawn when I spoke to him, and my colleague who was helping interpret could not hear him well over the evening call to prayer. We did not press him for details, and we did not need to. He was obviously vulnerable, and Ismail in any case happily recounted their journey for the both of them. There was adrenaline in Ismail's voice, almost excitement about what had happened to them, as if it had been an adventure. He had re-established contact with his parents, and their plan was for him to work in Malaysia for a number of years until Ismail could afford to join a brother in Saudi Arabia. Ismail was also twelve.

Kamal and Ismail's circumstances were not common, but they were also not unique. In late 2014, my colleagues and I began to notice a few worrying trends in our interviews with Rohingya who had just arrived in Malaysia. One was the abductions of children like Kamal and Ismail. Ten thousand Rohingya and Bangladeshis were being loaded onto boats every month. Smugglers in Bangladesh and Myanmar, paid per passenger they loaded, had apparently promised to deliver full boats to their counterparts in Thailand, who leased each boat against the income they expected from maximum capacity. The profit margins were so robust that the smugglers seemed to grow over-confident, leasing more boats than could be filled. To artificially bring demand in line with supply, they started abducting children and stuffing them into the unfilled boats. It was riskless kidnapping: you could get caught for holding someone for ransom in your own country, but not if you shipped the victim overseas and could still bank on the ransom being paid.

Another worrying development was the increasing number of women and girls on these boats. At first they only carried men, but by early 2015, about 18 per cent of passengers were female, often teenage brides sent off to marry Rohingya men in Malaysia. With so many young Rohingya men having left Myanmar, finding a husband locally had become difficult and incurred a more expensive dowry. Marrying a man making a relatively good income in Malaysia, and willing to pay for his bride's journey, became an attractive option. For brides under eighteen, it was also, unambiguously, a form of human trafficking.

Hasina was one of them; she was fifteen when I met her. In January 2015, Hasina's *nikah*, or wedding, took place at the home of the groom's parents in Maungdaw. Hasina had come to stay with them two days earlier, and on the wedding day her own parents arrived, along with a *mullah* who would officiate the ceremony. As the afternoon heat gave way to a cool winter evening, a full moon rose above the north Rakhine sky.

Shortly after the *Isha* night prayer, they gathered and sat down on a mat, and the groom's voice sprung from the speakers of a mobile phone; he lived in Penang, Malaysia. Months before, he had called his parents looking for a wife, and they had approached Hasina's parents, who were struggling to marry off their daughter because they could not afford a dowry. Not only were the groom's parents not asking for a dowry, but their son was also willing to pay for Hasina to join him in Malaysia. Hasina's parents agreed.

During the *nikah*, over the phone, the mullah asked both Hasina and the groom if they agreed to marry each other, which they did. Food was served: they had chicken, Hasina remembers. The next day, she saw her husband for the first time when a cousin lent a smart phone that allowed them to video chat with one another. They talked for two hours, about what they had eaten and their health, and he told her about the arrangements he was making for her boat journey.

As she recalls the conversation to me and my colleague, Hasina smiles shyly and chuckles, saying she has not thought about any of this since getting on the boat. 'It's like a lesson I'm learning from you,' she says, surprised to be asked about her wedding.

After leaving their homes in Myanmar, Hasina and two other girls, also hoping to join husbands in Malaysia they had never met, were cloistered in the same pre-departure hideout on the Bangladesh side of the Naf River, the natural boundary between Myanmar and Bangladesh. It was the home of a *dalal*, or smuggler, named Jahangir, whom Hasina later heard, and news reports seem to verify, was shot dead by Bangladeshi police in May 2015. 'He was a good man,' said Hasina, echoing the grudging respect, even gratitude, often shown to people smugglers all over the world, from these *dalals* in the Bay of Bengal to the snakeheads of southern China and the coyotes along the Rio Grande.

The three girls were taken together to a green and white wooden fishing trawler not more than fifteen metres long, with distinctive dragon insignias painted on either side of the bow. They waited sixteen days for smugglers to fill the ship's three decks with the target load of 500 passengers, which could potentially bring in as much as one million dollars in income before ship and crew costs.

Hasina's own costs, to be paid by her husband, amounted to $1400, plus a $120 upfront 'boat fare' to board. The ship sailed for six days, then hardly moved for weeks once it reached Thai waters. Hasina was allowed to speak to her husband over the phone on several occasions, but mainly so that he could be threatened by the captain into delivering payment. The captain, a portly polyglot with short hair fronted by a fringe, was called the Kachin – after the ethnic minority still engaged in armed conflict in northern Myanmar. On his orders, the crew routinely beat passengers with rubber gear belts.

Sometime in late March or early April 2015, Hasina and 200 others on the main deck were transferred to an empty red and white boat for four days, then again to a red and green boat already carrying around one hundred passengers. Word spread that these were people with no means and no sponsor to pay, and that this boat was a kind of floating market of bad debt, where new smugglers could assume the passengers' payment obligations at a lower price, in the hopes that they would eventually be able to extract the funds. Fearing this would only reduce their chances of disembarkation, Hasina and others pleaded to the Kachin to keep them. 'Don't worry, I'm not selling you,' he said. 'We'll take you back.' It turned out to be true; they had been moved between boats because of a shortage of rations, and while waiting for new rations to arrive, the Kachin had paid the crews of the other boats to temporarily feed his passengers. Five days later, they were all returned to the original ship.

Hasina thinks she spent another month at sea. She would know more clearly had she not lost consciousness several times, so deeply once that the crew was planning to throw her overboard until other women convinced them she would live. They went days without food, and still, 'I vomited a lot,' said Hasina. 'Sometimes ten times in a day.'

This was the other worrying trend my colleagues and I noticed in late 2014 and early 2015: smugglers were diverting from their usual practice of disembarking and holding people ransom in jungle camps in Thailand. Instead, Thailand was being bypassed altogether, and demands for ransoms were being made on board, meaning boats full of malnourished refugees and migrants were just drifting in the Andaman Sea for months. Upon payment, smugglers were disembarking groups of sixty to eighty Rohingya and Bangladeshis directly to Malaysia, either to the resort island of Langkawi or to the mainland.

Around the same time, according to a Reuters report, Thai authorities had opened an investigation into a Rohingya smuggler named Anwar, based on a complaint filed by a Rohingya roti seller whose nephew was being held by Anwar's subordinates, even though the roti seller had already paid the ransom. Reuters reported that the nephew was killed in retaliation, and that Anwar was arrested on 28 April 2015, three days before authorities in Songkhla, in southern Thailand, discovered the first batch of bodies hastily buried near jungle camps.

The triad-style hierarchy of the smuggling networks makes it difficult to know for certain, but many Rohingya my team and I spoke to believed that their boats were under Anwar's control, and that his arrest was what led smugglers to convene an on-water meeting in early May among their various crews in the vicinity of the Thai–Malaysian maritime border. The Kachin was one of the attendees. There were rumours that the Thai navy was out in force looking for smugglers' boats, so the smugglers conspired to cut their losses and abandon ship en masse, leaving thousands of Rohingya and Bangladeshis stranded.

Survivors from different boats told us nearly identical stories of how they were abandoned. Crews returned from the on-water meeting and distributed extra servings of food and water, hinting that everyone would disembark in Malaysia soon. Then, in the evening of 9 May, the 578 passengers aboard Hasina's ship watched in the twilight as a speedboat approached. Four men emerged and boarded their ship, stripping it of instruments and equipment as the entire crew made their way to the speedboat. When passengers began to protest, warning shots were fired. The Kachin, as he stepped onto the speedboat himself, told the Rohingya men on board to sail due west, then offered some consolation. 'I didn't destroy the engine,' he said.

Around the same time, the captain of a larger smuggling vessel nearby, carrying as many as 1000 Rohingya and Bangladeshis, also abandoned ship. He also fled on a trailing speedboat, after telling his passengers to sail at 220 degrees in order to reach Malaysia the next morning. But there is nowhere in the Andaman Sea where a heading of 220 degrees will point a ship to Malaysia. The captain was almost certainly directing them towards Indonesia.

Wherever this ship was headed, it ran out of fuel the next day. Passing fishing boats gave some fuel and directed the Rohingya and Bangladeshis to Indonesia. The following morning, 11 May 2015, two Indonesian navy vessels arrived with water, dry instant noodles and biscuits, and returned later in the day to tow the ship towards Malaysia. 'We gave them fuel and asked them to proceed,' an Indonesian navy spokesperson told Agence France-Presse. 'We are not forcing them to go to Malaysia nor Australia. That is not our business. Our business is they don't enter Indonesia because Indonesia is not the destination.'

The ship drifted for nearly two days until being approached near Penang on the afternoon of 13 May by two Malaysian navy vessels, which also provided food and water. Overnight, the Malaysians towed the ship back into Indonesian territory. When the Malaysians untied from the ship, multiple passengers remember the Malaysians giving instructions to stay put while they went to retrieve other boats in the area. *Then we'll bring you all to Malaysia*, the passengers said they were told.

The next day, Malaysia's Deputy Home Minister, Wan Junaidi, acknowledged to the Associated Press that Malaysia had turned back both this ship and Hasina's. 'We have to send the right message,' he said. 'They are not welcome here.'

*

I speak regularly to Moy, another teenage bride who spent a month at sea trying to make it to Indonesia to join her husband. The groom's family was originally from the same town as Moy but had fled the conflict and poverty at home to strike out across the sea for the Javanese hill station of Bandung, 150 kilometres south-east of Jakarta. Moy was sixteen when their parents arranged the marriage and barely seventeen when she boarded the ship that took her away from a civil war and also her mother. They exchanged letters for years after Moy arrived in Bandung, writing to each other until Moy's mother died, having never again seen her only daughter.

When nationalist Indonesians began suspecting Moy's community of embracing a radical ideology, there was a fear that any links to home, including correspondence, would be used as evidence of subversion. So Moy burned all her mother's letters. She has never told me about this herself, but I know because her eldest daughter remembers watching, and shared this memory with me because that is what mothers do with their children. Moy is my grandmother. She arrived in Indonesia by boat from China in March 1947, and she, too, knows something about not being welcome there.

Often when I meet Rohingya refugees, they will shake my hand with one arm and with the other present scraps of torn papers with faded Burmese script documenting their residence in Myanmar, and their parents', and grandparents'. It comes almost from muscle memory, an automatic reaction to meeting officials of any kind, as if to say, *Look, I exist, I belong.* And it makes me think of the tattered administrative forms with faded Dutch and Indonesian type that my family still keeps in plastic sleeves, decades after we all became Australian citizens.

There is my grandmother Moy's visa from the Dutch consulate in the south-eastern Chinese port of Amoy, now Xiamen, allowing her admission to the Dutch Indies, now Indonesia, dated 24 February 1947. Also in a plastic sleeve is a form signed by my mother on 10 July 1967, changing her name from the Chinese name she was given at birth to an Indonesian name no-one has ever called her by, pursuant to Cabinet Presidium Decision 127/U/Kep/12/1966, which stated 'That replacing the names of Indonesians of foreign descent with names which conform to indigenous Indonesian names will assist in assimilation'.

Without context, this regulation and all our family forms appear benign. The photos of my mother attached to them show her in smart dress and well-coiffed hair, making the kind of scarcely perceptible smile permissible in official photos; a little wider and they could be from my high school yearbook. The transition from Chinese to Indonesian citizenship and nomenclature could seem like the natural assimilation of an immigrant community.

But here is the context: from the beginning of Dutch rule in Indonesia, Chinese who had immigrated there since the sixteenth century were eliminated from the body politic, most violently in 1740, when Dutch authorities ordered a bloodletting in Jakarta that killed as many as 10,000 Chinese. After Indonesian independence in 1949, the Dutch policy of categorising ethnic Chinese as 'foreign orientals' was effectively continued through legislation that barred them from doing business in rural areas. To continue their trades, Chinese Indonesians were confined to urban ghettos like the one in Bandung where my mother grew up. In some cases, they were violently expelled from rural areas, as when thousands of Chinese Indonesians were killed in 1965 and 1966 for being suspected Communists. My mother remembers hiding with her siblings in the bathroom one afternoon as mobs descended on their home. When my mother finally emerged, the family car was missing. It had been rolled down a hill and torched.

The smoke combusting from that car, curling from my grand-mother's letters, still signals to me today, in the fires that have consumed Rohingya villages as recently as late 2016, but also in 2012, when an orgy of intercommunal violence in Rakhine State disintegrated whole villages and led to a surge of Rohingya taking to the seas. 'There were no fire brigades, no rescuers,' one Rohingya man once told me. 'Villages were just burnt to ash.'

No-one came to put out the flames of my mother's family car, either. Instead, in 1967, Indonesian president Suharto signed the Basic Policy for the Solution of the Chinese Problem. Public displays of Chinese literature and culture were prohibited. The importation of anything bearing Chinese characters became contraband, which is when my grandmother burned all the letters from her dead mother. And when Cabinet Presidium Decision 127 suggesting Chinese Indonesians should adopt Indonesian names did not prove persuasive enough, Suharto dispensed with any pretence. 'Indonesian citizens of foreign descent who still use Chinese names', read his Presidential Decision No. 240 of 1967, 'are urged to replace them with Indonesian names'.

By the end of that year, my mother had left Bandung for North Sydney Girls High School, cramming enough Shakespeare in one year to earn admission to the University of Sydney. She went on a student visa; her family never sought asylum per se, but if they ever had, and if I were the one assessing their claims, as I have for hundreds of asylum seekers, I would have had no qualms recognising them as refugees, defined under the 1951 Convention Relating to the Status of Refugees as individuals with a well-founded fear of persecution on account of, among other things, their race and nationality. The tattered forms we keep in plastic sleeves are not benign records of integration into Indonesian society; they were the bureaucratic tools of discrimination. When I showed the documents to my mother recently, including one registering her when she was six years old – in the photo, she has a bow in her hair – for no obvious purpose, she asked, indignantly and rhetorically, 'Why did we always have to sign all these forms?'

Those are nearly the exact words Rohingya say to me, also indignantly, also rhetorically, every time the Myanmar government makes them apply for new documents or turn in old ones, or register their identities or participate in verification exercises. Intentionally or not, the terminology of exclusion has been recycled: where Chinese Indonesians used to be required to carry around a Proof of Citizenship card to get a passport or register their marriages, Rohingya are now being required to apply for a Nationality Verification card to travel to the next town or fish or go to school. Even if the Myanmar government one day genuinely seeks to recognise them, the Rohingya have lost all trust in processes, which only ever end badly for them. They sit on plastic stools in a dirt courtyard in Maungdaw and ask me, 'Why should we have to apply for citizenship?' And they could be my mother or my grandmother, my aunt or my uncle, sitting outside their house in Bandung fifty years ago, asking the same question.

The parallels only go so far; my mother's family were free to move around Indonesia, run gold shops and trading businesses and, ultimately, obtain Indonesian citizenship. My mother went to proper schools and had proper enough documents and wealthy enough parents to go to university in Australia. Were Chinese Indonesians victims of institutional discrimination? Yes. Did they suffer as much as the Rohingya do today? Not even close.

More to the point, my family's old documents, that paperwork of racism, are fifty, sixty, seventy years old. And even those – birth certificates, school transcripts, visas – elude the Rohingya today. In 2017. Most Rohingya children have no record of their births. They are not eligible to apply for passports, from Myanmar or any other country. The visa my grandmother obtained at the Dutch consulate in Amoy in 1947 is what Hasina, the Rohingya child bride, could only dream of seven decades later, as she vomited without end and drifted in and out of consciousness in the Andaman Sea.

*

Hasina made it to land in a relatively uneventful fashion. After being turned back by the Malaysian navy, her boat fortuitously drifted almost right to the shore of northern Aceh, in Indonesia. On 13 May 2015, Acehnese fishermen helped disembark the boat's 578 passengers, and they were eventually sheltered in a kind of refugee camp outside the city of Lhokseumawe, which is where I met Hasina.

Understanding what happened to the other ship, the one that sailed 220 degrees to nowhere, is a *Rashomon*-like exercise of conflicting interests and narratives – though it also ended up in Indonesia. To start with, it is impossible to know how many people were on the ship. Most estimates range between 800 and 1000, but there is no passenger manifest, just best guesses by starved individuals who had been at sea for months. Because the smugglers were treating the passengers as sunk costs, there was no need for a passenger count.

There are some things most of the passengers agree on. Other than about forty people who were on the ship from the time it set out from the Bay of Bengal in March 2015, everyone else was transferred to it from one of three different boats. The ship was dark grey, with at least two levels each above and below deck. And not long after the transfers were complete, the captain shot dead a Rohingya man sitting near the ship's bow. He was wrapped in a *longyi*, given funeral rites and thrown overboard. No-one really knew why, but some Rohingya told us it was superstition: an offering to the sea to indulge its mercy.

The captain and crew abandoned ship several days after the shooting. That is when a scramble for what little drinking water remained erupted into a fight to the death between Rohingya and Bangladeshis, who began slicing crowbars and axes at each other and at the ship. The Bangladeshis acknowledged that some of them punctured a hole in the hull, but accused the Rohingya of keeping all the water for themselves; Rohingya said they were saving it for the children. Some said the Bangladeshis sabotaged the boat because they wanted to bring everyone down with them. Others said the Bangladeshis were irate that the Rohingya had told naval authorities there were Bangladeshis on board, which the Bangladeshis believed ruined their chances of being rescued. Rohingya said only Rohingya were killed. Bangladeshis said Bangladeshis were also killed.

The ship was badly damaged in the fight and eventually sank, though Acehnese fishermen again came to the rescue, ultimately bringing 820 Rohingya and Bangladeshis to safety on 15 May 2015. Because no-one knows how many people were on the boat to begin with, there is no way to know how many people died in the fighting or drowned, but based on interviews my team and I conducted, we counted at least fourteen, not including the man shot by the captain.

The survivors were brought to a shelter near the city of Langsa, in eastern Aceh. Many had gaping wounds across their backs and torsos. We registered sixty women and 217 children, some whose parents had drowned. One three-year-old girl, Shahira, was dying from tetanus.

At the time, Tony Abbott was asked about the Rohingya situation. Abbott, who originally came to Australia by boat from Britain, became Australia's twenty-eighth prime minister in 2013 after promising to 'stop the boats' of refugees and asylum seekers attempting to reach Australia by sea. Any who made it to Australian waters were remanded, indefinitely, to 'offshore processing centres' on Manus Island in Papua New Guinea and the tiny island nation of Nauru, 4000 kilometres from Sydney. But the Rohingya rescued in Indonesia had neither come close to nor been on their way to Australian waters. So, Abbott was asked, might Australia resettle some of them?

'Nope,' Abbott said. 'Nope, nope.'

By the time Shahira was taken to a doctor, it was too late, anyway. It was too late also for the Rohingya teenager who showed up at our office in Kuala Lumpur last year past the point of rescue, afraid he would be turned away by a local hospital. It was too late, again, for sixteen-month-old Mohammed Shohayet, fleeing more recent violence in Rakhine State, photographed dead on the banks of the Naf River in December 2016. He lies prostrated like Alan Kurdi, the Syrian boy found on a Turkish beach a year earlier, only Mohammed lies on mud, not sand, with his arms up by his head instead of down by his side, yellow shirt instead of red, shoeless instead of sneakers unstrapped.

*

There are at least 14,000 Rohingya in India, one of the few countries where Rohingya can obtain a kind of legal status in the form of long-term visas. Several thousand have come to Hyderabad, which is 30 per cent Muslim, looking for steady work and a tolerant community. With earnings from scrap-collecting and masonry, they have stitched together a cluster of makeshift settlements – a slum, really – conjoined by the alleyway where I sat on the morning of 9 November 2016, watching the US election returns come in on my iPhone.

I had just come from meeting the leaders of one of the Rohingya settlements and was on my way to meet the leaders of another. My main task was to understand how the most recent Rohingya arrivals to India had made their way from Myanmar, but whenever I have held these meetings with Rohingya communities, everywhere from Bangladesh to Malaysia, they invariably evolve into discussions about what can be done to finally give the Rohingya people a home.

I try to be optimistic. I explain that the United Nations continues to advocate for the Rohingya inside Myanmar and across the region. The international community, I say, is determined to keep Myanmar on the path towards openness, to ensure that the tide has turned for good and will, however slowly, eventually lift the Rohingya in its wake.

I sometimes want to tell Rohingya to look to my family for hope that progress comes, even if it takes seventy years. For the Rohingya who have risked everything and taken to the seas, I want to tell them my grandmother set out on a boat in 1947 and now lives in a care home in Sydney with Chinese-speaking staff serving Chinese meals, funded by the Australian government to provide dignity in old age to a people successive Australian prime ministers once called unequal and inferior.

To the Rohingya who remain in Myanmar, I want to tell them how, even though I look very much Chinese, when I meet Indonesian officials in Jakarta they embrace me with their delighted voices when I tell them my mother is from Bandung. All the anti-Chinese legislation and regulations from my mother's childhood have been repealed. Chinese New Year is now a public holiday. In Jakarta, where 10,000 Chinese were once slaughtered, a Chinese Indonesian became governor in 2014: Basuki Tjahaja Purnama, known more commonly by his Chinese nickname, Ahok.

Some Rohingya accept that line of thought; they have no choice but to be optimistic. Many do not. Not for the first time, an elderly Rohingya man openly wept to me that morning in Hyderabad, presenting his own life, lived entirely on the run, as evidence that the world would never care. I was in no position to disprove his despair, but until that morning I had always believed in what I said, even if many of the Rohingya I spoke to had not. I work for the United Nations; for me, the justice towards which the arc of the moral universe bends is the justice of diversity and inclusion, born of looking out rather than turning in.

But sitting by the side of that alley in Hyderabad, watching as Donald Trump was elected President of the United States – I felt like a hypocrite, like I was lying when I said that things would ever get better for the Rohingya, or that the international community would keep trying to help Muslim refugees like them. Donald Trump is President of the United States because there are millions of Americans who feel forgotten and are fearful of their race being wiped out. Try telling that to the Rohingya.

*

The many Rohingya who have completely and justifiably given up hope would not be convinced by my family's better fortunes in Australia or Indonesia. They would remind me that ethnic Indonesians looted and raped Chinese in the streets of Jakarta in 1998, nineteen short years ago. They would WhatsApp me the conspiracy theories of a Chinese fifth column that have gone viral on Indonesian social media. And they would show me the half a million Indonesians who demonstrated in November 2016, protesting not the policies or politics of governor Ahok but his race and his religion, believing Indonesians should not be ruled by a Chinese Christian. The next month, Ahok went on trial, not for corruption or embezzlement but for blasphemy, accused of insulting the Qur'an.

The last time I was in Jakarta for work, my hotel happened to be around the corner from City Hall, a stately compound that takes up an entire city block. It has been the seat of the Jakarta government for over a century, the official office of Indonesian and Dutch governors alike. As I drove by it one evening, our office driver pointed to it and simply said, 'Ahok', and for a moment what I felt was pride that someone from my mother's community had ascended to the pinnacle of a society that once spurned people who looked like me.

But the next time I am in Jakarta, Ahok will no longer be in office. In April, he was voted out following a race- and religion-baiting gubernatorial campaign that the *Jakarta Post* called 'the biggest political spectacle the country has ever seen'. Ahok's loss, the editorial said, 'shows that a political candidate is now judged by his faith rather than what he has done or will do to improve people's lives.' The blasphemy case against Ahok continued, and on 9 May 2017 he was sentenced to two years in prison.

The next time I drive by the Jakarta City Hall, it will not be my mother or grandmother whom I think about, or the status and happiness they have attained. It will be the Rohingya I have listened to from Maungdaw to Aceh, the pain that has turned an old saying of theirs into a stubborn truism. 'People never change,' they tell me. 'The tamarind is always sour.'

*

The first time a Rohingya told me the tamarind is always sour was a month before the US election. I was sitting in a KFC in Penang, Malaysia, after meeting with a nearby Rohingya refugee community, the 'community' being a few ramshackle lean-tos by the side of a busy thoroughfare. My colleagues and I were discussing what the community had just told us two days earlier: on 9 October 2016, militants had allegedly stormed Myanmar border guard posts in Maungdaw, killing several officers. In response, the Myanmar military unleashed a full-blown clearance operation to apprehend the militants. The Rohingya we met in Penang were frantic, hearing from relatives back home that entire villages were being scorched, women raped and men shot dead on sight.

It was a devastating development. I had been in Maungdaw earlier in 2016, asking Rohingya if they still had any intention of attempting to reach Malaysia by boat. The consensus was that it was no longer possible; they had seen all the boats – and their relatives – adrift in the Andaman Sea in May 2015. Smugglers were no longer confident they could circumvent increased border patrols.

But there was also a smattering of hope, however tenuous, that things at home might soon improve. In early 2016, Aung San Suu Kyi, the Nobel Peace Prize laureate, was just about to assume power after her political party overwhelmingly won Myanmar's first democratic elections in November 2015. One of my Rohingya colleagues, Saw Myint, once told me how he canvassed through Rakhine State in 1988 with young Muslims and Buddhists, spreading the democracy movement spearheaded by Aung San Suu Kyi, shortly before she was placed under house arrest for the better part of two decades. It was a memory Saw Myint recalled with a kind of euphoria, as if it had been a dream, this bygone time when Muslims and Buddhists had shared a common vision for the country.

So when Aung San Suu Kyi came to power in April 2016, though Rohingya had no illusions of instantly being embraced as citizens of Myanmar, they at least felt the tide, so long against them, had turned. I did, too. As a student, I had backpacked around Myanmar when it was still strictly under military rule, and when I returned to law school, I raised money for media outlets exiled from Myanmar and drafted legal briefs contesting the arbitrary detention of Aung San Suu Kyi and other dissidents.

I could not envision then Myanmar's spectacular transformation in the ensuing decade: first the transition to a civilian government and the freeing of Aung San Suu Kyi; then the end of American sanctions, Barack Obama and Hillary Clinton embracing Aung San Suu Kyi on the steps of her house – once her prison – in Yangon; and finally, free and fair elections that gave Aung San Suu Kyi the reins of the Republic of the Union of Myanmar.

When, shortly after coming to power, Aung San Suu Kyi commissioned Kofi Annan, the former UN secretary-general, to find solutions to the issues that beset Rakhine State, there was some optimism that the suffering of the Rohingya might ease. Full citizenship may not have been on the immediate horizon, but at least increased freedom and opportunity, and perhaps an end to segregation.

Then in the small hours of 9 October 2016, a band of armed insurgents no one had ever heard of before carried out a coordinated series of attacks on three border guard posts in

Maungdaw. The military's clearance operation in response has driven 74,000 Rohingya across the border into Bangladesh.

Based on interviews with these refugees, the UN High Commissioner for Human Rights reported 'mass gang-rape, killings – including of babies and young children, brutal beatings, disappearances and other serious human rights violations by Myanmar's security forces', and that 'hundreds of Rohingya houses, schools, markets, shops, madrasas and mosques were burned by the army, police and sometimes civilian mobs.' The Myanmar government has denied any wrongdoing.

At the KFC in Penang two days after the initial attacks, my colleagues and I were discussing what this would all mean for the Rohingya. It was a bleak conversation. At one point, Saw Myint and another Rohingya colleague exchanged a few words in their native dialect. They interpreted for the rest of us: 'The tamarind is always sour,' they said. 'It means what's sour will never be sweet.'

*

In humanitarian work, or maybe just in the ubiquity of everything in our internet age, we are necessarily desensitised by this still-common brutality. But what I can never seem to get over is how medieval, even ancient, it all seems. Shakespeare wrote four centuries ago of our 'mountainish inhumanity' towards refugees and still today, across the Straits of Malacca, human beings are sacrificed and starved men cut each other down on the high seas. Wayfarers seeking new lives in the Antipodes are marooned without end on all but deserted islands thousands of miles from nowhere. The demagogues of North America and Central Europe want to raise great walls to keep intruders at bay. At the crossroads of Europe and Asia, refugees flee war on airplanes but steal away with life vests in preparation for navigating the same whale road Ulysses sailed to Lesbos. And a little boy we lose along that road – or really just at its start – forgets to strap his sneakers but lies softly in repose, his spirit evaporated.

These moments, these movements, are as anachronistic as they are timeless. We are by our nature both territorial and mobile, creatures of comfort and aspiration. And I don't know whether that makes me feel hopeful or hopeless. I don't know if there has been another moment when so much of the world is concurrently wrestling with the same question: to close doors or open them, to turn out to the world or away from it. Germany has answered in one way, and Australia, where I was born, has answered in another. In South-East Asia, where I work, countries trying to open up are constrained by neighbours who have known for so long only how to be closed. And in America, where I was educated, the self-proclaimed Leader of the Free World clamours more (or at least more loudly) than anything else over how free that world should be and who gets to be a part of it.

I thought we would all get to be a part of it. I thought that was the point of freedom, of struggling to improve one's lot: so that the entire world could be your children's. What is wrong with aspiring to be global and elite, to be worldly and the best at what you do? My parents outran the war lords of China and the bigots of Indonesia to seek out somewhere and something better, for themselves and for me. They bussed dishes in Chinatown and faced down lecherous men in boardrooms to raise me in international schools and on three continents, so that I could work for the United Nations, trying to help those who don't have what I had. This was the right trajectory, was it not? My whole life I was led to believe I could feel at home anywhere. My UN passport made it official, but I thought all along I was a citizen of the world.

'But if you believe you're a citizen of the world,' Theresa May said recently, 'you're a citizen of nowhere.'

If that is what I am, if I was not so much a prototype as a fleeting diversion, the last of an experimental line soon to be discontinued, then what was it all for?

The tamarind is always sour, the Rohingya say. They should know. They know better than I do, better than anyone, what it is like to be a citizen of nowhere, in danger of being discontinued.

The views expressed here are the author's and do not necessarily reflect the views of UNHCR or the United Nations.

Bonfire of the Narratives

Richard Cooke

'Novelties', bookmakers call them. That's where you can wager on an Elvis sighting or alien contact event, usually at long odds. 'Donald Trump is elected president' was once a novelty, but not any longer. At first, the Irish betting site Paddy Power rated him a 66 to 1 chance to become the Republican nominee, then a 150 to 1 chance of becoming president. By May that was 2 to 1. What odds would you take now, on some other former novelties? A candidate drops out during the campaign. Mass civil unrest on polling day. Armed insurrection after it. In Pennsylvania, I met a woman who was voting based on the vice-presidential candidates alone. Whoever won the presidency, she believed, would be irrelevant: they would either be impeached or assassinated in their first three months in office. In current conditions, that's starting to seem like a value bet.

After all, so many outside chances have conspired already to get us here. 'Here' is a place where the Republican candidate has not been endorsed by a single major newspaper. He has in fact been disendorsed by more than 160 leaders of his own party, including a third of its sitting senators. The GOP speaker of the US House of Representatives, Paul Ryan, refuses to campaign with him in person. Even two items of confectionary – Skittles and Tic Tac – have made public statements distancing themselves from the nominee.

Donald J. Trump is the most unpopular major political figure in the divined history of politics in the United States. He has been attacked by virtually every establishment institution in the country, and traditional political donors have shunned him as well. And yet he survives, within sight if not striking distance of the presidency, thanks to grassroots donations that broke records and an unshakable bedrock of support that encompasses almost half the country. Even as he slides towards likely defeat, the best estimates are that he will win more votes than any Republican nominee ever. The two 'sides', Republican and Democrat, now occupy not just different positions, but different realities. There is, though, a rare point of concordance: if Trump is here, something has gone disastrously wrong for America.

It's not easy to correctly diagnosis societal decline. We're all mortal, so the prospect of everything flourishing as we age and excelling after we die is a natural one to resist. Besides, like all big, chaotic things, America always seems to be on the brink of some breakdown. It's almost a tradition for writers to tar each Republican presidential candidate as uniquely idiotic and dangerous, someone 'justly famous for his howlers, blind spots, mangled statistics and wishful inaccuracies. Each time he goes up to speak, you sense that the pollsters are reaching for their telephones, the aides for their aspirins.' (That's not some 'On Trump', but Martin Amis talking about Ronald Reagan in 1979.) We forget all the times the doomsday clock was wound back, the peasants who wandered out of St Peter's Basilica on New Year's Day, 1000 AD, unraptured, the bunker merchants tending rusting cans in lieu of Armageddon.

Perhaps things are not as bad as they seem, and we've just forgotten how high and dangerous the social fevers of the '60s and '70s were, when there were 370 bombings in New York in two years, Detroit burned every Devil's Night, convention riots were routine, and Kissinger had to talk Nixon out of dropping an A-bomb on Hanoi. But in more recent history, American political careers were ended by sighing loudly at a debate opponent (Al Gore) and yelling during a speech (Howard Dean). This year, it was possible to watch the second presidential debate, see the moderator directly accuse one candidate of sexual assault, and find that a footnote in the subsequent reporting.

Stories that in any other era would have been definitive – the widespread re-emergence of anti-Semitism, WikiLeaks morphing from darling of the left to darling of the right almost overnight, a former CIA director accusing campaign staff of collusion with Russian intelligence, 'America's Mayor' Rudolph Giuliani saying live on television that everyone commits adultery – became incidental, half-buried subthemes of a rangy, monstrous metanarrative. The 2008 presidential election is often described as the first social media election, but the full toxicity and speed of that mode of communication has taken its time to leach into the political fabric of America. Here we are.

There's an under-subscribed theory that all this is a good thing, well disguised. That underneath the coarseness and vulgarity and strangeness of this election are secret signs of hope, a reality where Trump is not only the most extreme GOP candidate in decades but also the most moderate: anti-war, anti–Wall Street, anti-globalisation. He would have been a different kind of unacceptable candidate not long ago.

It does not feel that way, though, when the cab driver from J.F.K. airport shows you an all-points bulletin text message for a jihadi bomber still at large. (A touching New York detail: the plot was twice foiled by accident, when two separate bags containing bombs were both stolen.) On the ground, this political moment announces itself as the end of something massive, a bonfire of the narratives, where the agreed understandings of how democratic politics should work have disintegrated, replaced by something no-one is in control of, not even the protagonists. No matter how bitter the partisan rift of the past, at least one side had optimism and the other had authority. Both qualities have gone.

'How did this happen?' is a question I hear many times in America, from the candidates, from the press, from voters. Its variation – 'What is happening?' – is something I'm asked all the time, as though a stranger from a foreign land might carry some antidote. 'So, you've been to a Trump rally – what's it like?' I have been to a couple, but attendance doesn't grant any special insight. Just look at the wildly different results across the genre of Trump Rally Anthropology, where liberal writers get sent into deepest, darkest America to find out what the natives think. For Dave Eggers, writing in the US *Guardian*, Trump's choice of Elton John's 'Tiny Dancer' as a theme song reflected the mood, which was 'so gentle, so calm and so welcoming'. Eggers even laced his article with the song's lyrics, as though they contained some gnomic clue to what was going on. For David A. Graham in the *Atlantic*, such events were frighteningly hostile: 'Just below the surface of a Trump rally runs an undercurrent of violence.' These reports describe different people, different places. ('You should have seen Florida,' one reporter told me. 'It was like a rock concert for old people.') But that doesn't explain the discrepancy by itself. After my first Trump event, in a studio southwest of Philadelphia, Pennsylvania, I left with the impression that not a single person there really knew what was going on, including Trump himself.

*

I have to admit – my first impulse on seeing Donald Trump in person was to laugh. He was walking cross-stage, past a statue of Rocky Balboa wearing a 'TRUMP' T-shirt, on his way to a lectern that was bracing itself for gripping. I caught the signature lemon-suck expression on his face, and lost it. I'm not alone in this reaction; other attendant reporters, and even Trump fans, respond the same way. Later, at the first presidential debate, the press-overflow room greeted his arrival with chuckles. One French journalist said, to no-one in particular, 'Donald is an idiot – how the fuck did he get here?' It's like the comedy of streaking: taboo violation and an inappropriate context. How the fuck *did* he get here?

By itself, turning up at a Trump rally is the empirical equivalent of lifting a wetted finger into a tornado. It is too chaotic, too diffuse to understand just by being there. There is a simultaneous impulse to patronise, excuse, exonerate, mansplain, coddle and make fun of the attendees. Here in Pennsylvania, like everywhere else, the Trumpies are pervasively Caucasian, even though the local area, Chester Township, is majority black. In fact, the huge attendance (several thousand) belies a local reality: the counties surrounding Chester Township are exactly the kind of places Trump will need to win. But he is struggling among suburban moderate Republicans, who baulk at things like Muslim internment camps.

The crowd are really from further afield, bus-ins from the surrounding region known as 'Pennsyltucky', a mildly pejorative nickname for the rural areas outside Pittsburgh and Philadelphia. They are people used to being addressed in a mildly pejorative tone. Trump is on a moderating pivot, and has noticeably toned down his racial rhetoric. He's ostensibly making an appeal to African Americans, but it's really for the benefit of those uncomfortable white moderates. 'What do you have to lose?' he says to people who aren't there, repeating the phrase three times in a Marlon-Brando-Is-The-Godfather accent that doesn't quite come across on TV. But there must be something to lose; there are cities where Trump wins 0 per cent of black voters, making him a more unpopular figure than the former Grand Wizard of the Ku Klux Klan, David Duke. (Duke, like most of his ilk, is enthusiastic about The Donald.)

It's Trump's rhetoric and persona that have brought him this far, but hearing him speak is not like witnessing a demagogic doomsday device being unveiled. It's effective, but not ominously so. There are no ums, ahs or hesitations in the whole presentation, partly because he has given it so many times, with only occasional variations and ad libs. Everyone knows this speech. It is the one about the wall, the big beautiful wall that Mexico is going to pay for. It is the one about the way America doesn't make things anymore, about how once upon a time cars were built in Flint and you couldn't drink the water in Mexico, and now the cars are built in Mexico and you can't drink the water in Flint. It is a lament for a country that the crowd no longer recognises, and that no longer achieves greatness. What a relief that someone can finally say it! Trump is controlled, often funny, and extremely vulgar. Parts of the speech are for entertainment purposes only, but you leave not quite sure which parts those are. Stretches about special interests and the media sound a lot like Noam Chomsky.

It might even seem harmless, politics as professional wrestling or pantomime, if it wasn't for the race-baiting and the nauseating level of excitement that accompany it. Not long before, Hillary Clinton had made this charge against Trump's hard core of 'irredeemable' supporters. This 'basket of deplorables' was 'racist, sexist, homophobic, xenophobic, Islamophobic, you name it'. She subsequently walked back from the comment, but it had already become a badge of pride. There are dozens of 'Deplorable for Trump' shirts, and women wearing 'Adorable Deplorable' versions, and when one reporter hears the crowd has an effigy of Hillary Clinton she says, 'Oh, you mean a sex doll?' – like seeing a Clinton-themed sex doll at this stage would just be a matter of routine.

Trump crowds are always described as 'angry', but that's not the first thing apparent in a humid auditorium filled with self-proclaimed 'deplorables'. They don't look livid; they look sick. This time around, America's malaise has become a literal malady. It's not just pallid, marbled, middle-aged people making their way with canes, either; sometimes it's inexplicably young men. There is a long rank of wheelchairs by the wall, full of people who shouldn't be in them. You see these tentatively moving individuals outside the rallies as well, anywhere where private wealth borders on public squalor (a phrase first used about America fifty years ago, and still biting afresh). There's something almost medieval about it, this physical indicator of decline, as though the crops are blighted outside the imperial capital, and the afflicted aggregate to have their scrofula attended to. The phenomenon, when lethal, even has a name: 'deaths of despair'. These are the white suicides and opioid overdoses and cirrhosis cases, seen en masse before only in places like post-Soviet Russia and post-industrial Glasgow, and never on this scale. The *Washington Post* ran a story called 'Death predicts whether people vote for Donald Trump', noting an 'eerie correlation' between this kind of mortality and primary votes for Trump by county.

The obnoxiousness is masking pain, real pain. Trump isn't exactly hiding the fact that he is a braggart and a liar and an ass-hole. As a child he punched his music teacher because he thought the man didn't know anything about music, and we know this because he included the story in his autobiography: 'I'm not proud of that, but it's clear evidence that even early on I had a tendency to stand up and make my opinions known in a very forceful way.' The list of policies outlined at the rally wouldn't fill a Post-it note, and might change without notice. But for Trump's supporters, all of this is a plus.

They have decided the system is a circus, so they are sending in a clown. Trump marks the point at which many Americans decided their politics was so corrupt that they would elect a man already so corrupt he would be incorruptible. No charge the media throws at him will break his candidacy, any more than pointing out that the Dirty Dozen had criminal charges would be germane. He also knows how to run interference – his time inside the popular media means his language solders right onto the brain stem. In Campaignland you start to find yourself thinking in Trumpisms. Sad!

If polling is accurate, most people cheering the big beautiful wall don't believe he'll ever build it, and they don't care. They see it as a negotiating tactic and a symbol. It was mooted at a time when terrorism was the number one concern for Republican voters, and few other politicians seemed capable of meeting that with any kind of determination. In July this year, Islamic State–linked attacks reached a frequency of one every eighty-four hours, not including those in the war zones of Iraq and Syria. There was also an embarrassing sense that mainstream governance had absolutely no idea what to do about this. Trump's wall is questionable as a policy. But as a statement? It is unmistakable.

Some of those here in Pennsylvania are quite open about misgivings. They cheerily admit they have no idea what Trump will actually *do* if he's elected, just that he must be elected. I speak with a man called Harry Dugan. He has a greying five-day growth and is wearing a T-shirt that says 'Crooked Hillary for Prison'. It is his fifty-eighth birthday today, and he is attending the rally with his son. Dugan is the kind of voter pundits are drawn to: a former registered Democrat in an important swing state, who switched sides the moment Trump began his run through the primaries. Why? 'ISIS and the borders and the economy. And [Clinton is] just going to make both of those things worse.' Two of those things are so closely linked as to be one, but which two it's hard to say. Dugan is not stupid. He does not seem especially motivated by racial animosity. He seems to be someone in somewhat reduced circumstances, willing to bear that personally, but unwilling to see his country humiliated as well. 'A lot of people don't even know what's going to happen with Trump. They just want a change from business as usual. It's a gamble. They don't even know where it's going.' Trump is an unknown – a danger-ous unknown, even for many of his supporters. But they have given up on the status quo changing any other way.

It's exactly the hollowness of the Trump campaign, the light-ness on detail, the shoddy composition, that makes this hope possible. It's a melange that can't be unified by logic, but can be unified by style. Trumpies talk about World War Two, and the flag, and how *important* Trump is, sometimes while clutching my hand. Special hatred is reserved for the media, at least the American media. Soon, CNN and MSNBC will give their anchors security guards at these events.

One young man, a navy veteran, yells 'You're liars' at the press pen, and a city reporter tries a handshake to cool things off, but it's refused. On leaving, a phalanx of Trumpies gives the assem-bled reporters the finger, almost ceremonially. Afterwards, I speak with the navy man. What was all that about? He talks to me passionately, lucidly, articulately, but in his argument the stakes and the bedrock beliefs are all wrong, and his pupils are getting pinny. His views have that graduate-of-bong-university feel, where someone has self-educated online too deeply, starting with the wrong set of premises. Why would the media want to destroy society? I ask him. Freemasons.

The persistent thread linking those I speak to is humiliation. Where are their meagre pieces of patriotism now? They can't even get pride by proxy. An honest day's manual work, commu-nity self-reliance, the meaning of America, military service, belief, strength – it was all supposed to pay off, and it has turned out to be just another bum pension plan, being shorted the whole time. Belief in their country has turned out to be a kind of scam, just like everything else has turned out to be a scam, and that belief has curdled into a crisis of faith. Overwhelmingly, they want some sort of revenge. On those who told them other-wise. On those who should know their place. On those who don't belong here. And they have chosen a bully to enact that revenge.

Imagine, for a moment, being on Ted Cruz's campaign staff. Preparing for Trump in the Republican primaries. Carefully war-gaming your team positions, strategies, tactics. And then a few short months later, having to prepare a statement in which the senator denies his dad assassinated J.F.K. I mean, no-one believed, genuinely believed, that Ted Cruz was the Zodiac Killer when that claim did the rounds. But didn't people get a kick out of seeing that cardboard man up there, humiliated, sweating, human? I mean, what's inexplicable, in current conditions, about the appeal of a Disney-villain cartoon boss turning his catch-phrase – 'You're fired' – on his fellow elites?

Those elites are different from their forerunners as well. At least the robber barons built Carnegie Hall and garnered the Frick Collection, even if it was the threat of pitchforks that prompted them. Today tech billionaires are not just occupying different strata from the rest of us, they are trying to occupy a whole other world. PayPal co-founder Peter Thiel (himself a Trump supporter, because 'disruption') has invested in immortality, and wants to be given blood transfusions from the young. He once investigated building a lawless, artificial micronation off the coast of San Francisco. Elon Musk (PayPal, Tesla Motors, Hyperloop) wants to die on Mars. There is an unnamed consortium of billionaires trying to prove that we are living in a simulation, and they're paying scientists to break us out of it. Or some of us out.

In a sense, trying to understand Trumpism at a Trump rally is looking in the wrong place. The rallies are familiar, but not because they supposedly resemble Nazi rallies or lynch mobs, or any of the other retrofits people try on. These events are manifestations of the comments section, the anonymous Twitter egg, the hate email and 'shit-post' made flesh. The Swedish police recently did a study about the kind of people who make death threats against the media (often the same ones who make death threats against women). They are usually marginalised men, unsuccessful in school and work, who enjoy poor relationships with women. Here in the United States, these men are now more numerous than ever before. If the vote were restricted to white men only, as it used to be, Trump would win in a landslide. It is not a coincidence that in the first year a woman contends for the presidency the GOP base has nominated a class-A misogynist to oppose her.

This political reality was gestated within digital confines, but has now broken loose. We are living in a simulation, in a way. Only it's not simulation anymore.

*

Like everyone else, Thomas Edison got most of his predictions about the future wrong. In 1911, he tried to describe the world of 2011 to *Cosmopolitan* magazine. It would be full of pneumatic tubes and free gold, and machines that could make everything except hats. But Edison was accidentally prescient about one thing. He believed writing would be distributed on vast compendia of extremely thin slices of nickel, 40,000 leaves thick. 'What a library might be placed between two steel covers and sold for, perhaps, two dollars! History, science, fiction, poetry – everything.' Distracted by the lure of knowledge, the great inventor didn't realise he was describing books made out of razor blades.

We have Edison's promised library now, all that history, science, fiction, poetry, along with everything else, just about universally accessible and for free. This dawn of knowledge didn't arrive accompanied by any great sense of optimism. But who would have anticipated, less than a generation later, an American election contested between two of the most widely despised politicians in the land? And one of those politicians not being a politician at all but a casino mogul, real-estate tycoon, one-time professional wrestler, beauty-pageant impresario and reality-TV show host, whose own runner-up for the nomination called him a narcissist and a pathological liar; also an adulterer and a bill-skipper and a draft dodger (this list can keep going), who simply walked into the 162-year-old Republican Party and broke it to pieces in a few months.

That's a single-layer irony – the president is supposed to be good, and Donald Trump is not good. Politics, especially American politics, is replete with these ironies. We can give some of them significance: for example, if you go to the September 11 memorial in New York, and visit its adjacent shopping mall, it's the mall that feels like the sacral space, and the queue for the iPhone 7 is longer than the one for the memorial museum. A kind of resilience or an accidental show of human priorities, depending on how you look at it.

The scenario outside the first presidential debate, at Hofstra University in New York, is a single-layer irony. There is an area called Broadcast Alley, where media set up their desks in front of students waving signs, and do pieces to camera with a bad brass band. It is modelled on a sideshow, complete with a jumping castle and balloons. There is a virtual-reality booth where voters, either GOP or Dem, must try to solve 'extreme poverty'. Voters are ushered into this bogus little environment through two carefully demarcated doors, to 'see' extreme poverty they could see in analogue reality just a few blocks away.

Nearby is a Black Lives Matter protest, where college students link arms in silent tribute to yet another man killed by police. Other students, not part of the protest, have signs saying 'Killer Bees 2016' and 'Trump for Harambe' (a then-trending reference to the Cincinnati Zoo gorilla, shot dead when a child fell into its enclosure).

'They think it's a joke,' says one of the Black Lives Matter protesters. 'That's the epitome of white privilege, to be going around with a "Trump for Harambe" sign, when our lives are on the line.' Only one of the Black Lives Matter protesters has been admitted to the debate hall; the others, who have more African American–sounding names, seem to have been weeded out in case of protest. Another asks me about Australia, already planning an escape route if Trump is elected.

Conservative figures routinely describe Black Lives Matter as a terrorist organisation, even though it has been an almost exclusively peaceful movement. Another single-layer irony: inside the debate area, known as Spin Alley, where the media interview campaign surrogates (they have their names on giant sticks so they're easy to find), is Peter King, a Republican congressman from New York. King has been a leading critic of Black Lives Matter. He was also described by a judge in Northern Ireland as an 'obvious collaborator with the IRA'. But he doesn't see the contradiction in condemning one organisation that criticises police, while supporting another that assassinated them. 'Ask Tony Blair,' he says, when I ask him about it. Who does what means a lot in American politics – perhaps everything, it turns out. Running down the country, attacking big business, denigrating military allies, bragging about sex crimes, killing police. It's the difference between braggadocio and whining. 'Better to Grab a Pussy than to Be One', as one Trump rally sign put it.

These hypocrisies are what we are used to, and what satirists use for their work. But the influence of technology on reality is creating phenomena that aren't so much contradictions, but tangled threads of competing narratives. Pull a thread, and the knot tightens instead of unravelling. For example, the world's leading virtual-reality mogul is a man named Palmer Luckey. He is twenty-four years old, and often has black feet because he refuses to wear shoes, and his girlfriend dresses up as characters from video games, and he is worth $700 million. He has spent some of this money on an anonymous pro-Trump meme-creation group – hackers? teenagers? – who produce viral pictures, some of which feature a cartoon frog called Pepe.

Pepe has already enjoyed an expansive online life, but has now been repurposed as a neo-Nazi symbol. Luckey's funding for this 'shit-posting' led him to semi-apologise. It also led to two anti-hate groups arguing about whether Pepe really was a Nazi symbol, and to the Clinton campaign denouncing Trump's closeness to Pepe. Do you get a sense of the problem here? How do you interpret an event where a common sense of meaning, or even a structure in which that meaning can be demarcated and slowed down, has collapsed almost completely?

*

In a campaign about what America means, Hillary Clinton's main argument is that it means 'Not Trump'. It might even be a sign of sexism, some strain of marginalisation, that Clinton can feel like an observer to her own likely election. But if Trump is inexplicable, she is also something of a mystery. And for someone so emblematic of an era – the Third Way triumphalism of the 1990s – Clinton has a knack for getting her timing wrong. As the counterculture flourished in the 1960s, she was a young Republican, a Goldwater girl. It was the only time she did anything radical, and in the wrong direction, so she tacked. 'True to my nature and upbringing, I advocated changing the system from within and decided to go to law school,' she writes in her 2003 memoir *Living History*, a story of hedges, accommodations and measured political considerations that often occlude or overwhelm the personal impulse. She explains:

> I could get away with 'eccentricities' as wife of the Attorney General, but as First Lady of Arkansas, I was thrown into the

spotlight. For the first time, I came to realize the impact of my
personal choices on my husband's political future. Many
Arkansas voters were offended when I kept my maiden name,
Rodham. I later added Clinton.

Even her name – Hillary Rodham Clinton – is a calculated political decision.

She is a seasoned campaigner, but not an especially effective
one. In 2007, she began the primaries strongly favoured against
Barack Obama, and lost. Bernie Sanders, a bright-red Vermont
socialist throwback who sounds like the dad from the TV series
ALF, keelhauled her through the fight for this nomination. It was
supposed to be easy, and instead she was reframed again, for anyone who had missed it, as an agent of the status quo.

Midway through the campaign, she even hit a patch of unexpected trouble. I caught up with her in New Hampshire, a place
that should now be an easy Democratic win. But then, after a
week of bad polling, it was in play. Clinton collapsing with pneu-
monia (remember that?) hadn't helped. Her defenders tried to
cast this as an omen of her fitness for the presidency: wasn't
working too hard a good thing? Still, even the candidate herself
was asking the question: 'Why aren't I fifty points ahead?' She
was barely ahead by three, and in New Hampshire that margin
had shrivelled to less than 1 per cent.

*

New Hampshire is one of those jarring contradictions America
specialises in, a slow, forested state that retains the death penalty and the motto 'Live free or die'. Here at the University of
New Hampshire in Durham, Sanders and Clinton are appear-
ing together, partly so Clinton can garner some extra enthusi-
asm from the student crowd. Not a good sign: the presumptive
first female president has to turn to a seventy-five-year-old
grandpa for youth appeal. There are queues of wellwishers
here, but most will be turned away from the neatly ordered
chairs and bleachers inside. This is really a speech, not a rally,
and panicked volunteers have called in too many reserves.
There are also a handful of protesters, supporters of Dr Jill

Stein, a Green Party candidate who is shaving a point or two of support off the Democrats.

'Right now you've got four people running, and the two top choices are the most hated people in the world,' says Jordan, one of the protesters. He is a former electrician who was energised by the Sanders insurgency and now can't bring himself to vote for 'whatshername'. After Ralph Nader allegedly cost Al Gore the presidency and ushered in the Dubya Bush era, triangulating the progressive vote is a site of past trauma. But Jordan has a retort. 'I keep hearing about the Nader factor in 2000, when there was three people running. Well, there's four people running this time.'

The fourth is Gary Johnson, the Libertarian Party candidate. Johnson is so unprepared for the presidency that even he seems to look on his own entry as comic relief, but he still polls around 5 per cent nationally. (A measure of American battle-sickness: among active-duty military personnel, who usually lean hard Republican, this isolationist – 'What is Aleppo?' – sometimes hits the lead.) Jordan really seems to believe Jill Stein can win. 'She's honest. She's healthy. She's not corrupt. She's not being bought by big money, super PACs, things like that.' His disillusionment is so deep that he would rather Trump than Clinton, even though he loathes the prospect.

'The only reason people would support him is racism. Just people that are uninformed and full of hate ... He talks a lot, but they're not going to let him do half the stuff he's saying. I think we're better off with four years of him than eight years of Clinton. She's going to start a war [because] she owes a lot of people who gave her money for big favours.' It's becoming familiar, this idea of the presidency as a puppet show, working from the assumption that the real people running the country are somewhere else.

Clinton may be one of the most hated women in the world, but pinpointing what grates about her persona isn't easy. Ask supporters why her poll position is so timorous, and they will sometimes blame sexism. A Caribbean woman with green eyes bangs on the metal barrier outside the rally, saying, 'Because there are too many men in this country who don't want to be led by a woman.' That's true among Trumpies, where misogyny is all part of the sneering, alpha-dog attraction. There are also deficiencies that show sexism's second-hand effect: to survive in politics as a woman, Clinton was forced to eschew exactly the emotions the public now hanker for. But college students and Stein voters aren't primarily sexists; they're left cold by something else.

Clinton sits alongside Sanders onstage, and she listens to Sanders talk, nodding along in a lolling, incessant movement that doesn't seem to bear much relationship to what is being said. She doesn't look too awkward or phoney. She's an engaging listener who seems to fulfil the suite of emotional qualities, or their simulation, that we ask for in television-era politicians. But there's something inert about her, something that after a few minutes sets some students chewing their fingers.

'Think big, not small – we need to have the best-educated workforce in the world,' says Sanders. 'Thing big, not small' could be the inversion of the Clinton motto, and her long period at the top has cemented a belief in slow change. Consensus. The best progressives can hope for. Obamacare, the signature achievement of the current president, and perhaps the American Left in the last quarter-century, is running into trouble already. Even this measure, realised decades after the rest of the world rejected market-based health care, may have been too soon.

One of the least mentioned facts of the 2016 campaign is this: Clinton is also a dynastic politician. She's a former first lady and secretary of state, and after Bush II, presidential candidates with familiar names are on the nose in America. Most recently, Clinton's focus has been the projection of American power internationally, as well as the projection of foreign power within America, through speaking deals and the like. ('Those millions in speaking fees – let me tell you, it's not because she's a good speaker,' says Trump, in one of his better lines of attack.) Foreign policy is at the heart of America's decline, and burning $6 trillion in Iraq and Afghanistan instead of spending it on domestic bridges and schools is her policy as well.

Her speech starts to ginned-up applause and the waving of machine-made banners, all much more decorous than Trumpland. 'Debt Free College', say the signs behind her, and that's all she has to repeat. Even in a country defined by grotesque inequalities and rampant financial predation, the structuring of American college debt is an outlier madness: more than a trillion dollars' worth, much held by the government, some at an interest rate of 10 per cent, which cannot be renegotiated. In 2013, the average cost of a medical degree was $278,455. Sanders points out that this absurd expense means not only that the road to the middle class is closed, but also that well-to-do doctors and dentists have to forget about working in disadvantaged communities. All Clinton has to do is hit these same notes, bash Trump a little, not fall over, and she'll be fine. For once, this is not a popularity contest.

It's an unusual choice, then, to name-check the endorsement of the Republican former secretary of the navy. John Warner – 'a World War Two veteran' – is on Team Clinton, the first time he's ever backed a Democrat for the White House. That's the same John Warner whose name appears on the 2007 *National Defense Authorization Act* (a multi-billion-dollar increase in defence spending, broadening the powers of the president to declare martial law, eliminating the auditing of expenditure in Iraq), as well as the USS *John Warner*, the navy's 'most lethal' submarine. Not natural catnip for a college crowd.

This turns out to be one of the last times that Sanders and Clinton will campaign together. Audio emerges of Clinton trying to explain the Sanders phenomenon, a leak that the opposition tries to confect into an attack. In reality, Clinton sounds sympathetic on the tape. 'So, as a friend of mine said the other day, I am occupying from the centre-left to the centre-right,' she said. 'And I don't have much company there. Because it is difficult when you're running to be president, and you understand how hard the job is – I don't want to over-promise. I don't want to tell people things that I know we cannot do.' This is the enigma of Hillary Clinton: that after thirty years it is still not clear what she believes she cannot do. But it seems to be a lot.

She doesn't sound angry when she says she is angry. She doesn't sound hopeful when she says she has hope. When she tries to render her policies down to personal anecdotes, they feel somehow abstract, like they happened to someone else a long time ago. She is now unimaginable as a non-political figure, and faces an impossible task if elected, of restoring faith in the system that has made her who she is.

*

Outside the hall, the merchandise stands are packing up. One of the vendors has had a slow sales day, his table still piled with Clintonware. He usually sells ice-creams, which is how he got his nickname, Icee Don.

'At the beginning of the election during the primaries, everything was really kind of smooth,' says Don. 'Everybody was excited by it. It seems like it's kind of dwindled now that the primaries are over. I don't know why. I mean, Bernie Sanders, he had a big wave going. Now the two candidates are Hillary and Trump, it seems the excitement is pretty low now. I'm a merchant, and I sell product, and sales are down. The momentum is down. Morale is not as it was.'

Usually he would pack up his Clinton and Sanders gear and then head to the next Trump rally, where the market is for 'Hillary Sucks – But Not Like Monica' stickers, and T-shirts invoking the size of Trump's balls. Instead he has to be in court in New York, an unfortunate piece of timing that might cost him a few thousand dollars in sales. Eight dozen Trump shirts are in his van. 'His product *moves*.'

'Honestly, it's funny, I thought I was a Democrat – [but] the one that really could bring change is Donald Trump. Because he's a gambler. He's new to the field. He has nothing to do but to change everything around. If any kind of change were to come, even if it's change for the worse, it would be Donald. A spark is needed. Even if it's just for six months, seven months. There's an energy that's needed. I never thought I would be selling Republican products – ever. But Donald Trump has actually brought revenue to me, because he's a spark. And that's what America's looking for.'

Icee Don is something of a 'quiet political activist' himself, someone with an economic revolution in mind, something that would reduce the violence he sees in the street. That's his product. But what is America's?

'America's product is reality … What's it based on now? Embarrassment. If you watch TV, it's based on embarrassment. And who can embarrass themselves the most.'

'America's product,' says Icee Don, 'is bullshit.'

Icee Don must be one of the last truly bipartisan men in America, able to mix with Trump fans one day and Clinton fans

the next, both assuming he's onside because of all the paraphernalia. It seems like a perverse version of Obama's 'Red State,
Blue State' speech: 'The pundits like to slice and dice our country into red states and blue states. Red states for Republicans,
blue states for Democrats. But I've got news for them, too. We
worship an awesome God in the blue states, and we don't like
federal agents poking around in our libraries in the red states.
We coach Little League in the blue states and, yes, we've got
some gay friends in the red states.'

But the acrimony captured in that speech now seems quaint,
a golden age of harmony in comparison to what is happening
now. And what is coming next.

Killing Our Media

Nick Feik

'Today I want to focus on the most important question of all,' wrote Facebook CEO Mark Zuckerberg. 'Are we building the world we all want?'

The 'social infrastructure' built by the company Zuckerberg founded is now regularly used by almost two billion people. His 'Building Global Community' essay, which he posted on Facebook in February, is an ode to the virtues of connectivity. Joining up the world and empowering 'us', Facebook is connecting people more regularly and intricately than anything that's ever come before, and Zuckerberg intends it to become synonymous with human progress.

'Progress now requires humanity coming together not just as cities or nations, but also as a global community.'

Reasons for optimism abound. 'We had a good start to 2017,' Zuckerberg said in May, on the release of Facebook's latest financial figures. Total revenue had soared by 49 per cent in the past year and profits topped $1 billion per month.

*

In April, Melbourne schoolgirl Ariella, sixteen, joined a Facebook group '16+ hangouts' to chat with other teens. As Rachel Baxendale reported in the *Australian*, when another member realised Ariella was Jewish, he and more than a dozen other teenagers began abusing her. 'All aboard Jew express next stop Auschwitz gassing chambers, I hear there is a lovely shower aboard, Exterminate, Exterminate,' wrote one. 'I'll make u proud,' wrote another. 'I'll f*** her in the gas chambers.'

By the time Ariella left the group twenty-four hours after joining, she had compiled almost fifty pages of screenshots of abusive messages. She reported the abuse to Facebook.

'Thanks for your report,' Facebook replied. 'You did the right thing by letting us know about this. We looked over the profile you reported, and though it doesn't go against one of our specific community standards, we understand that the profile may still be offensive to you.'

Facebook's Statement of Rights and Responsibilities prohibits 'hate speech', and it has previously said that 'while there is no universally accepted definition of hate speech, as a platform we define the term to mean direct and serious attacks on any protected category of people based on their race, ethnicity, national origin, religion, sex, gender, sexual orientation, disability or disease'.

Not that any of that was helpful to Ariella. Was this the world Zuckerberg talked about building?

*

In May, on the same day Facebook announced its first-quarter earnings, Fairfax Media employees across Australia went on strike after the company decided to cut 125 editorial staff in a bid to save $30 million.

The staff cut was greeted with great public anger and frustration. Most of it was directed at Fairfax management, particularly CEO Greg Hywood, who'd landed a $2.5 million share bonus a couple of months earlier. (Some reports suggested he may have earned as much as $7.2 million in 2016.) Fairfax's management has not excelled over the past decade, and Hywood was never going to please many outside his family for accepting the bonus while shedding workers. But the problems Fairfax faced were much greater than those stemming from its management, and have been growing for years, just as they have at News Corp, the *Guardian* and almost every other major news organisation not funded by government.

It's self-evident that news doesn't report itself, but the economic model that has traditionally supported quality journalism is mid-collapse. Newspaper revenue has been falling by 5 per cent per year worldwide since 2009, according to Bloomberg. Print circulation has been falling, as has print advertising.

In Australia, newspaper advertising revenue has dropped 40 per cent, to $2.4 billion, in just five years, according to PricewaterhouseCoopers. By contrast, the online advertising market is growing at 25 per cent a year and on various estimates will be worth $6 billion this year. According to Morgan Stanley, Google and Facebook would generate the lion's share of this, between $4 and $5 billion – around 40 per cent of our total advertising market and rising fast.

Globally, these two tech companies account for approximately half the entire digital advertising market. Estimates vary, but it's widely accepted that they are picking up 80 to 90 per cent of all new digital advertising.

By now these trends are reported with a degree of resignation. The leak of advertising to the tech giants seems inexorable. It's not that readers are deserting the mastheads: the number of people who read them either in print or online has never been higher. It's simply that 'print dollars turned into digital cents'.

The *New York Times* recently added more digital-only subscriptions than in any quarter in its history: 300,000 for a total of 2.2 million. Yet its advertising revenue in the same quarter fell by 7 per cent, driven by an 18 per cent drop in print advertising.

There hasn't been a Trump bump in Australia. And major news outlets here don't have a potential audience of a billion people.

In May, Greg Hywood told the Senate select committee inquiry into the future of public interest journalism that in the 'good old days' 85 per cent of newspaper revenue was from advertising revenue and 15 per cent from subscriptions. Now it's more like 50/50 – and not because of rising subscriptions.

*

While Facebook, Google and 'the internet' may be responsible for the collapse of the traditional media business, blaming them is like holding a shark responsible for biting. Technology was always going to reveal mass-market advertising as a blunt instrument. Printing every single advertisement for a second-hand car, and attempting to distribute this to every single person in the market, may have seemed great at the time, but time makes fools of all of us, especially if we're Fairfax executives. Spraying ads for holidays to Fiji across the media was never going to be as effective as simply catching those who googled 'flights to Fiji'.

Facebook allows advertisers to target consumers by age range, gender, location, education level, political leanings, interests, habits, beliefs, digital activities and purchase behaviour; by what they 'like' and share, and who their friends are; by what device they use. It can shoot an advertisement directly into your hand because you're a middle-aged male who searched online for a hardware product and you're near the new Bunnings on a Saturday afternoon.

It knows when you're having anniversaries, when you're pregnant, when you're planning a bar mitzvah, and when you're watching a sad film and might feel like chocolate. What's more, it's getting smarter at pegging your interests and vulnerabilities every time you log in. Its natural-language processing and machine-learning algorithms are building a profile based on what you look at and for how long, what your friends shared and what you commented on. Its systems are gauging why you chose to comment on this but not that, and are comparing what you looked at versus what you typed.

According to its own Data Policy, Facebook receives information about your activities on and off Facebook (loyalty cards, mailing lists, browser cookies, receipts, apps, mobile phone permissions and the like) from hundreds of third-party partners. Additionally, 'we may share information about you within our family of companies to facilitate, support and integrate their activities and improve our services'. If you're using Instagram, WhatsApp or Atlas, just to give a few examples, the data belongs to Facebook. Or anyone it chooses to share with.

It may have been set up with the best of intentions – to build communities – but its corporate aim now is to build an unparalleled and irresistible machine with which to know you and influence you.

'It's a commercial space; it's like a shopping mall' is how Greens senator Scott Ludlam, deputy chair of the inquiry into the future of public interest journalism, describes it to me. '[And] the people who use Facebook are the commodities. It's us that's being sold to advertisers. I don't know if that's really sunk in.'

We're discussing the implications of a cavalier attitude towards users' data and privacy.

'I don't know if I'd even say they're cavalier with privacy. They're *mining* our privacy on a massive scale and that's the product: that's what they sell.

'Their values are somewhat arbitrary, and they're not really contestable because it's a commercial space. "If you don't like shopping in our shopping mall, you're free to go sit in the car park."'

Which might be a reasonable argument were it not for the ubiquity – the platform monopoly – of the online giants, and the impact two companies in particular are having on the rest of society. When it comes to collecting and employing data, they have demonstrated an inconsistent regard for users' rights.

In 2012, Facebook supported an experiment in which researchers manipulated the News Feed of almost 700,000 users to find out if they could alter people's emotional states. By hiding certain words, it was discovered, unsurprisingly, that they could. 'We show,' researchers announced, 'via a massive experiment on Facebook, that emotional states can be transferred to others via emotional contagion, leading people to experience the same emotions without their awareness.' The experiment was done without user knowledge or consent. When it became the subject of controversy in 2014, the researchers first claimed that they *did have* people's consent, because it was 'consistent with Facebook's Data Use Policy, to which all users agree prior to creating an account on Facebook, constituting informed consent for this research'. The Facebook data scientist who led the research claimed it was carried out 'because we care about the emotional impact of Facebook and the people that use our product'. Finally the company's chief technology officer apologised, adding that the company had been 'unprepared' for the anger it stirred up, which suggests that perhaps it was the backlash rather than the experiment itself that caused remorse.

In 2015, it was revealed that Facebook tracks the web browsing of everyone who visits a page on its site, even if the user doesn't have an account or has explicitly opted out of tracking, and even after a user has logged out.

The *Guardian* reported on the research commissioned by a Belgian data protection agency, which argued that Facebook's data collection processes were unlawful.

'European legislation is really quite clear on this point. To be legally valid, an individual's consent towards online behavioural advertising must be opt-in,' explained Brendan Van Alsenoy, one of the report's authors. 'Facebook cannot rely on users' inaction to infer consent. As far as non-users are concerned, Facebook really has no legal basis whatsoever to justify its current tracking practices.'

In May this year, European regulators announced that Facebook was breaking data privacy laws in France, Belgium and the Netherlands, and faces investigations in Spain and Germany. French regulator CNIL announced that that it was applying the maximum fine that had been allowed under French privacy law when its investigation began: a grand total of 150,000. CNIL had last year issued an order that Facebook stop tracking non-users' web activity without their consent, and stop some transfers of personal data to the US.

'We take note of the CNIL's decision with which we respectfully disagree,' replied Facebook. It has argued that it should only be subject to rulings from the Irish data protection authority because its European headquarters are in Dublin. In Europe, though, new personal data protection regulations will come into force mid next year, potentially allowing regulators to impose fines of up to 4 per cent of Facebook's revenues.

Also in May, the *Australian* uncovered a document outlining how the social network can pinpoint 'moments when young people need a confidence boost'. By monitoring posts, pictures, interactions and internet activity in real time, Facebook can determine when people as young as fourteen feel 'stressed', 'defeated', 'overwhelmed', 'anxious', 'nervous', 'stupid', 'silly', 'useless' and a 'failure'. The confidential presentation was intended to show how well Facebook knows its users, and by implication how willing it is to use this knowledge on behalf of advertisers. Privacy laws in Australia are nowhere near as stringent as in Europe, and not enforced with any great vigour.

In the US, the Trump administration recently repealed data protection rules, meaning browser histories could be sold to advertisers without user consent. According to research from Princeton University published last year, Google and Facebook together own all of the top ten third-party data collectors.

Not that any of this has so far caused any great public outcry, either here or in the States, perhaps because it all appears to be in the service of giving people exactly what they want. Nothing seems to interest the public less than debates about privacy laws and metadata collection. Until recently, it didn't seem to be a major issue.

*

In June 2007, David Stillwell, a PhD student at the University of Cambridge, created a new Facebook app called myPersonality. Volunteer users filled out different psychometric questionnaires, including a handful of psychological questions, and in return received a 'personality profile'. They could also opt to share their Facebook profile data with the researchers. Stillwell was soon joined by another researcher, Michal Kosinski, and their project took off. People were happy to share intimate details, their likes and dislikes (both online and off), their age, marital status and place of residence. Before long, the two doctoral candidates owned the largest ever dataset combining Facebook profiles and psychometric scores.

In 2012, wrote Hannes Grassegger and Mikael Krogerus in an article for *Das Magasin* and *Motherboard*, Kosinski proved that, on the basis of an average of sixty-eight Facebook 'likes' by a user, it was possible to predict their skin colour (with 95 per cent accuracy), their sexual orientation (88 per cent accuracy), and their affiliation to the Democratic or Republican party (85 per cent) ... Seventy 'likes' were enough to outdo what a person's friends knew, 150 what their parents knew, and 300 'likes' what their partner knew. More 'likes' could even surpass what a person thought they knew about themselves.

On the day Kosinski published these findings, 'he received two phone calls', reported Grassegger and Krogerus. 'The threat of a lawsuit and a job offer. Both from Facebook.'

Shortly afterwards, Facebook made 'likes' private by default. The personal information users put on Facebook had always been owned by the company, to analyse or sell, but what it was worth was only just becoming clear. (It has a long history of changing privacy settings without much notice or explanation.)

Facebook wasn't the only one to register the potential of this tool. A young assistant professor from the Cambridge psychology department, Aleksandr Kogan, soon approached Kosinski on behalf of another company that was interested in the myPersonality database. Kogan initially refused to divulge the name of this company, or why and how it planned to use the information, but eventually revealed it was Strategic Communication Laboratories. SCL is a communications group whose 'election management agency' does marketing based on psychological modelling; its offshoots, one of which was named Cambridge Analytica, had been involved in dozens of election campaigns around the world. The company's ownership structure was opaque, and Kosinski, who by this stage had become deeply suspicious of its motives, eventually broke off contact.

Kosinski was therefore dismayed, if not altogether surprised, to learn of Cambridge Analytica's role in last year's election of Donald Trump.

'We are thrilled that our revolutionary approach to data-driven communication has played such an integral part in President-elect Trump's extraordinary win,' said Cambridge Analytica's forty-one-year-old CEO, Alexander Nix, in a press release.

In September 2016, speaking at the Concordia Summit in New York, Nix had explained how Cambridge Analytica acquires massive amounts of personal information (legally) – from shopping data to bonus cards, club memberships to land registries, along with Facebook information and other online data – and combines it (including phone numbers and addresses) with party electoral rolls into personality profiles.

'We have profiled the personality of every adult in the United States of America – 220 million people,' Nix boasted.

According to Mattathias Schwartz, writing in the *Intercept*, Kogan and another SCL affiliate paid 100,000 people a dollar or two to fill out an online survey and download an app that gave them access to the profiles of their unwitting Facebook friends, including their 'likes' and contact lists. Data was also obtained from a further 185,000 survey participants via a different unnamed company, yielding thirty million usable profiles. No-one in this larger group of thirty million knew that their Facebook profile was being harvested.

It doesn't take a great deal of imagination to see how useful this could be to the Trump campaign. As Grassegger and Krogerus reported:

> On the day of the third presidential debate between Trump and Clinton, Trump's team tested 175,000 different ad variations for his arguments, in order to find the right versions above all via Facebook. The messages differed for the most part only in microscopic details, in order to target the recipients in the optimal psychological way: different headings, colours, captions, with a photo or video.

The Trump campaign, heavily outspent by the Clinton campaign in television, radio and print, relied almost entirely on a digital marketing strategy.

'We can address villages or apartment blocks in a targeted way,' Nix claimed. 'Even individuals.' Advertising messages could be tailored, for instance, to poor and angry white people with racist tendencies, living in rust-belt districts. These would be invisible to anyone but the end user, leaving the process open to abuse.

In February, the communications director of Brexit's Leave. EU campaign team revealed the role Cambridge Analytica had played. The company, reported the *Guardian*, 'had taught [the campaign] how to build profiles, how to target people and how to scoop up masses of data from people's Facebook profiles'. The official Vote Leave campaign, Leave.EU's rival, reportedly spent 98 per cent of its £6.8 million budget on digital media (and most of that on Facebook).

Trump's chief strategist, Stephen Bannon, was once a board member of Cambridge Analytica. The company is owned in large part by Robert Mercer (up to 90 per cent, according to the *Guardian*), whose money enabled Bannon to fund the right-wing news site Breitbart, and who funds climate-change denial think tank the Heartland Institute.

The critical point is not that wealthy conservatives may be manipulating politics – this is hardly new – but that politics has become so vulnerable to covert manipulation, on a scale never before experienced.

There is good reason for the strict regulations around the world on the use and abuse of the media in election campaigns, yet governments have almost completely abrogated responsibility when it comes to social media.

According to Labor senator Sam Dastyari, chair of the future of public interest journalism inquiry, Australia's security agencies 'are very clear that [deliberately misleading news and information] is a real and serious threat … We would be very naive to believe it's not going to happen here.'

*

A BuzzFeed News analysis found that in the three months before the US election the top twenty fake-news stories on Facebook generated more engagement (shares, reactions and comments) than the top twenty real-news stories. The Pope endorsed Donald Trump. An FBI agent suspected of leaking Hillary Clinton's email was FOUND DEAD IN APPARENT MURDER-SUICIDE. In other news, WikiLeaks confirmed that Clinton had sold weapons to ISIS, and Donald Trump dispatched his personal plane to save 200 starving marines.

Facebook's algorithm, designed to engage people, had simply given Americans what they wanted to read.

The criticism was heated and widespread, prompting Mark Zuckerberg's 'Building Global Community' essay.

Sure, there are 'areas where technology and social media can contribute to divisiveness and isolation', Zuckerberg wrote, and there are 'people left behind by globalization, and movements for withdrawing from global connection', but his answer to these problems was consistent and uniform: people need to be more connected (on Facebook). His promises to build a better network – to counter misinformation, for example, in a veiled reference to the US election campaign, or filter out abuse – rely to some extent on our goodwill and credulity. We're denied access to Facebook's internal workings, and that's as Zuckerberg intends it. Which is within his right as chairman and CEO of a business. But a network this large, this influential, this secretive is more than a business. In many ways, it's a test of our belief in the market.

Promises to fix problems ranged from introducing a different system for flagging false content to working with outside fact-checking outfits. Perhaps changes were also made to the News Feed algorithm, but if so they remained confidential. How would the new community standards be applied? Would Facebook ever make changes that crimp its business prospects? Does it accept that social obligations come with such editorial decisions? All this remained obscure, notwithstanding a mess of corporate nonsense posted by both Zuckerberg and company PR figures.

The News Feed algorithm works like this: in order to engage you, it chooses the 'best' content out of several thousand potential stories that could appear in your feed each day. The stories are ranked in order of perceived importance to you (Your best friend's having a party! Trump has bombed North Korea again!), and the News Feed prioritises stories you'll like, comment on, share, click on, and spend time reading. It recognises who posted things and their proximity to you, how other people responded to the post, what type of post it is and when it was posted.

As *TechCrunch* writer Josh Constine puts it, 'The more engaging the content ... the better it can accomplish its mission of connecting people while also earning revenue from ads shown in News Feed.'

Over time, as millions have joined Facebook, the number of potential posts that might populate a feed has multiplied, so the algorithm has become not only increasingly necessary to prevent users from drowning in 'content' but also increasingly subject to human design.

*

Despite this, Facebook insists it's not a media organisation. It's a technology company and a neutral platform for other people's content. It is certainly true that it piggybacks on other companies' content. But it is also constantly testing, surveying and altering its algorithms, and the changes have vast effects. Kurt Gessler, deputy editor for digital news at the *Chicago Tribune*, started noticing significant changes in January, and three months later wrote a post about them, titled 'Facebook's algorithm isn't surfacing one-third of our posts. And it's getting worse', on Medium. The *Tribune*'s numbers of posts hadn't changed over time, nor had the type of posts. The newspaper had a steadily rising number of Facebook fans but the average post reach had fallen precipitously. 'So,' he asked, 'is anyone else experiencing this situation, and if so, does anyone know why and how to compensate? Because if 1 of 3 Facebook posts isn't going to be surfaced by the algorithm to a significant degree, that would change how we play the game.'

Facebook has made it clear that it has been increasingly giving priority to videos in its News Feed. Videos and mobile ads are, not coincidentally, the very things driving Facebook's revenue growth. It has also been rewarding publishers that post directly to Facebook instead of posting links back to their own sites. None of which bodes well for the *Chicago Tribune*.

There is one way to guarantee your articles will be surfaced by Facebook: by paying Facebook. As every social media editor knows, 'boosting' a post with dollars is the surest way to push it up the News Feed. Greg Hywood and *HuffPost Australia* editor-in-chief Tory Maguire pointed out to the Senate's future of public interest journalism inquiry that even the ABC pays Google and Facebook to promote its content. 'Traffic is dollars,' said Hywood, 'and if the ABC takes traffic from us by using taxpayers' money to drive that traffic, it's using taxpayers' money to disadvantage commercial media organisations.'

'This is normal marketing behaviour in the digital space,' replied the ABC, 'and is critical to ensuring audiences find relevant content. It is [also] used by other public broadcasters like the BBC and CBC.' As well as, needless to say, thousands of other media organisations, including Fairfax and Schwartz Media.

This is what passes for normal marketing behaviour in 2017: news organisations, haemorrhaging under the costs of producing news while losing advertising, are paying the very outfits that are killing them. Could there be a more direct expression of the twisted relationship between them? Could the power balance be any more skewed?

Mark Thompson, CEO of the New York Times Company, recently put it like this: 'Advertising revenue goes principally to those who control platforms.' Over time, this will mean they also control the fate of most news organisations. So it is somewhat troubling that one of the few ways to keep a check on the power of Facebook is by maintaining a robust fourth estate.

*

It was on social media that I stumbled across Rachel Baxendale's *Australian* article about the anti-Semitic abuse directed at Ariella on social media. It was also from social media that I acquired Baxendale's contact details, to ask her about the article.

Baxendale had heard of the story through a contact, Dr Dvir Abramovich, chairman of the B'nai B'rith Anti-Defamation Commission. Abramovich had verified the story himself, and Baxendale then went back and forth with the schoolgirl over several days, checking details, looking at the screenshots of the abuse, discussing whether to use a pseudonym and so forth. Baxendale had explained the story to her bureau chief, and it then went to the *Australian*'s main editorial team in Sydney for approval. It was run past the legal team and then subeditors, and Facebook was approached for comment. All of this is routine at a newspaper. If anyone has a complaint, it can be taken to the Australian Press Council, which will study it impartially before making a public ruling. Or readers can, of course, get in contact with the journalist in question or her editors.

By contrast, Facebook has a single email address for all global media enquiries, and its moderators had only moments to deal with the matter of Ariella's abuse. There were fifty pages of screenshots.

The *Guardian* reported in May it had seen more than 100 internal training manuals, spreadsheets and flowcharts used by Facebook in moderating controversial user posts. The *Guardian* also revealed that for almost two billion users and more than 100 million pieces of content to review per month (according to Zuckerberg) there were just 4500 moderators. That is one for every 440,000 users or more. Most work for subcontractors around the world; Facebook won't divulge where. They are trained for two weeks, paid little, and often have 'just 10 seconds' to cast judgement on issues involving child abuse, suicide, animal cruelty, racial discrimination, revenge porn and terrorist threats, and must balance these against the desire to respect freedom of speech. Fake news? Fact-checking would be impossible. To help them, the moderators are provided with instruction manuals, which contain guidelines for dealing with matters from threats and specific issues to live broadcasts and image censorship. Facebook formulates country-specific materials to comply with national laws, and Zuckerberg often refers to the company's attempts to follow community standards, but he really means Facebook's Community Standards, which it determines. ('You can host neo-Nazi content on Facebook but you can't show a nipple' is Scott Ludlam's shorthand characterisation of these standards.)

Examples of this guidance, relayed by the *Guardian*, give some sense of the impossibility of the moderators' task:

> Remarks such as 'Someone shoot Trump' should be deleted, because as a head of state he is in a protected category. But it can be permissible to say: 'To snap a bitch's neck, make sure to apply all your pressure to the middle of her throat', or 'fuck off and die' because they are not regarded as credible threats.
>
> Videos of violent deaths, while marked as disturbing, do not always have to be deleted because they can help create awareness of issues such as mental illness.
>
> Some photos of non-sexual physical abuse and bullying of children do not have to be deleted or 'actioned' unless there is a sadistic or celebratory element.
>
> Photos of animal abuse can be shared, with only extremely upsetting imagery to be marked as 'disturbing' ...
>
> Videos of abortions are allowed, as long as there is no nudity.
>
> Facebook will allow people to livestream attempts to self-harm because it 'doesn't want to censor or punish people in distress'.

In December 2015, Facebook gave a commitment to the German government that it would remove criminal hate speech from the platform within twenty-four hours; however, a yearlong

German government study reported by the *New York Times* recently found that in some months Facebook managed to delete only 39 per cent in the time frame sought by the German authorities, and that its performance had been getting worse in recent months. In March, the German government proposed legislation in this area, with the threat of fines up to 50 million.

Facebook had already announced plans to hire an additional 3000 moderators, and Monika Bickert, Facebook's head of global policy management, told the *Guardian*, 'We feel responsible to our community to keep them safe and we feel very accountable. It's absolutely our responsibility to keep on top of it.' As ever, the community will have to take their word for it – and rely on unauthorised leaks to the media for the details.

*

The inquiry into the future of public interest journalism, driven by senators Sam Dastyari, Scott Ludlam, Nick Xenophon and Jacqui Lambie, was set up to examine 'the impact of search engines, social media and disinformation on journalism in Australia'. At public hearings in May, a parade of speakers explained the adverse effects.

Union representative Paul Murphy explained that 2500 journalism jobs had disappeared in Australia since 2011, and that pay rates for freelancers had also declined significantly. The inquiry heard examples of regulations that applied to the Australian media but not to the tech companies, such as those relating to local content and media ownership, and heard time and again about the lack of tax paid by the tech companies. Local media had obligations, social, legal and cultural; Facebook and Google traded on the local media's content, smashed their business models in the process, and gave little back to the community in return. How to remedy this is what the inquiry was set up to explore.

Facebook reported that it earned $326.9 million of revenue in Australia in 2016. Google reported revenue of $882 million last year. But these figures radically under-represent the total amount they collect from Australia, which is widely regarded as at least three or four times larger. For 2016, Facebook and Google reported tax bills of $3.3 million and $16.6 million respectively.

A pittance. (Perhaps Australia should count itself lucky: in the UK in 2014, Facebook paid £4327 in tax, less than what the average worker paid.)

'Until this year,' wrote journalist Michael West, 'Google and Facebook entertained a corporate structure that booked the billions of dollars of revenue they made in Australia directly offshore.' Facebook sales were booked to an associated entity in Ireland, and referred to as the 'purchase of advertising inventory'. Now, Facebook has declared itself to be a reseller of local advertising inventory, and the federal government has declared that its new Diverted Profits Tax – the 'Google tax' – will reap billions of extra dollars in revenue from multinationals over coming years, though such projections generally rely on multinationals not altering their tax arrangements in response, and not fighting them out in court for the next decade.

Professor Peter Fray, Professor of Journalism Practice at the University of Technology Sydney, summed up the problem for journalism: 'There is no doubt there are issues around tax for Google and Facebook and they should pay their fair share, but I cannot see how publishers, journalists or politicians can blame Google and Facebook for the fact that digital revenue streams did not, do not and will not replace those of print or that in digital environments audiences have multiple choices for content on demand 24/7.'

Put a different way, how could extracting a reasonable amount of tax from Google and Facebook save local journalism and a collapsing business model?

Only by funnelling that tax revenue into journalism. For which no mechanisms yet exist, and to which the objections are obvious. Historically, there's been ample reason to fear government involvement in private media, and little reason to propose or support it. But how quickly things have changed.

'The economic model no longer works,' Sam Dastyari tells me. 'So either government intervenes and finds a way to support it – without going so far as to tip the scales of what is and isn't journalism – or we let it die. There is no third option.'

Independent senator Nick Xenophon is wary of the term 'intervention' when it comes to a government response; nevertheless, he agrees that 'doing nothing is not an option'.

'It's more a case of government levelling a playing field which has been tipped into a state of imbalance and dysfunction by the advent of disruptors,' he clarifies.

'This is not like the horse-and-buggy and automobile argument of 120 years ago. This is a case where they are piggybacking off traditional media to make a quid. And that should be reflected in some way in a compensatory mechanism.

'I don't want us to end up in a world where we just have so-called citizen journalists and a whole range of bloggers, where there are no standards, where anything goes.'

Scott Ludlam concurs. 'There is a public policy role here … because the market's wiping these [media] entities out. The market couldn't give a shit whether there's strong and independent and diverse journalism going on in a society.'

'I don't think we'll have general daily newspapers on a weekday within the next two or three years,' the Greens senator adds. The loss of dedicated professional reporters in health, education, state politics, arts, science, environment or social affairs will have incalculable effects.

*

Do we still have a democracy capable of creatively moderating the worst effects of the market? With just a few exceptions, governments have shown little inclination to take on corporate interests to protect civil society, or to intervene to prevent market oligopolies.

Looking at the operations of Facebook around the world, you could easily conclude that Zuckerberg makes the rules.

Peter Fray, also a former editor and chief publisher of the *Sydney Morning Herald* and editor of the *Canberra Times* and the *Sunday Age,* warned the Senate inquiry that media independence would be at stake under a direct subsidy model, where payments go straight from government to the media. This is a concern shared by the senators, who each stress to me the importance of maintaining the independence and diversity of the media.

'It's not an attempt by the state to control the media,' says Ludlam. 'It's a genuine inquiry into how we can support [it].'

One of the key proposals being canvassed is a levy on Facebook and Google, which will be used to pay for public interest journalism. Dastyari, Xenophon, Ludlam and Lambie are all open to this idea. (Liberal senator James Paterson, also a member of the select committee, is not.)

'That would free up millions of dollars to further public interest journalism,' says Xenophon.

How the proceeds of such a levy might be disbursed will be the subject of considerable debate in coming months. One method that's been raised is a European-style grants council, in which a panel appointed by government decides how money is allocated. However, there are already reservations among the committee members. 'Who determines the grants?' asks Dastyari. 'Why do you get a grant and someone else doesn't? How independent is it?'

The Labor senator believes the tax system is the best way of supporting the industry, whether it's tax breaks for individuals buying news subscriptions or those who make donations or other investments in journalism. The fact that Xenophon, Ludlam and Paterson are also open to such an idea implies broad cross-party acceptance.

'What we're talking about,' Dastyari adds, 'is actually quite a radical rethink of the role of government as it comes to journalism.'

Xenophon is also keen to explore what he calls the 'copyright approach' to supporting media, via the *Competition and Consumer Act*. He says a formula should be developed by which the use and sharing of intellectual property is valued and compensated fairly.

The obvious challenge all are weighing up is how to define public interest journalism. 'Where do you draw the line?' asks Dastyari. 'Is food blogging journalism?' Is opinion a form of journalism? Television news and current affairs?

'I think the organisations likely to take advantage of it are not necessarily the ones that most advocates have in mind,' Paterson also warns. 'I suspect the first people to seek tax-deductible funds to fund a news service are those seeking to promote a particular world view. On the left, I'd expect to see a GetUp! News, Greenpeace News and maybe Asylum Seeker Resource Centre News. On the right I think we'd see an Institute of Public Affairs

News, Australian Christian Lobby News and Business Council of Australia News.'

Any definition, emphasises Xenophon, will need to ensure that an organisation's dominant purpose is to provide news and opinion and that it's not the arm of an advocacy organisation.

The committee has until December to publish its final report, but it's already clear that these are the key questions exercising the minds of committee members – not whether public interest journalism needs saving, or even whether government should play a role.

'I suspect we're going to end up with a whole menu of things that ideally could work well together,' says Ludlam.

Regardless of what happens next, it is a remarkable shift in public debate.

The talk about the collapse of newsrooms in Australia has until recently tended to focus on newspapers and magazines. It's becoming obvious that television broadcasters both free-to-air and cable are under major pressure too. In mid June, Channel Ten went into administration soon after reporting a $232 million loss driven by flagging advertising revenue.

The federal government promises to overhaul media owner-ship laws and scrap some of the constraints on the big media companies, leading to more concentration and presumably greater efficiencies for them. But it voted against the establish-ment of the Senate's journalism inquiry and shows little enthusi-asm for reining in the tech giants. The task of protecting the diversity of the Australian news media remains beyond the scope of its ambition. For the moment, it's up to others.

*

'History,' writes Zuckerberg portentously, 'is the story of how we've learned to come together in ever greater numbers – from tribes to cities to nations. At each step, we built social infrastruc-ture like communities, media and governments to empower us to achieve things we couldn't on our own.'

I return to the Facebook page to read Zuckerberg's essay one last time, and a message pops up on my normally dormant account. Citing security concerns and unusual activity, it requests that I prove – with photo identification – that I am who I say I am. I hesitate.

'Today we are close to taking our next step.'

And as Zuckerberg runs through touted improvements and inspirational innovations, ever so casually he drops this: 'Research suggests the best solutions for improving discourse may come from getting to know each other as whole people instead of just opinions – something Facebook may be uniquely suited to do.' It's so neatly incorporated you barely notice it. We 'whole people' and Facebook are suddenly indivisible.

The Art of Dependency

Micheline Lee

When I was eighteen and my disability had progressed to the stage where I could longer push myself in a manual wheelchair, a man in a van brought me an electric wheelchair. Actually, it was more like a bulky three-wheeled scooter. He slapped a sticker with a serial number on the plastic orange bonnet that covered the front wheel. He told me that it was the property of the state and should only be driven on covered surfaces.

Oh how I loved it the moment I sat in the chair and pressed Go. All the worry and the million steps between my destination and how I would get there disappeared. I couldn't help laughing, zooming along, starting and stopping with a flick of the lever, taking myself where I wanted. People might have thought I was delirious.

I was in first-year law at Monash University and lived in a student college across a seven-lane road from the campus. For the first six months, before I got my electric chair, I was on the constant lookout for people to push me in my manual chair. I had only enough strength in my arms to shift myself a few metres on smooth level ground. At about eight a.m., I would position myself outside my room, waiting to nab some student coming down the corridor to push me to the dining hall. After gulping down breakfast, I would do the rounds, asking who was leaving for the university and whether they could push me on their way.

Once I was on campus, the tough part was finding someone to push me back to the college at the end of my classes. Mostly

I relied on students from my latest class or passers-by. The college was often out of their way, and it could take them thirty minutes to walk there and back. Most of those I waylaid were kind and warm; one even asked me out. Some had another place they had to be. No worries, I said, I'll ask someone else. But it became more difficult each time I had to approach someone else, and I grew more nervous and beggar-like each time I asked.

A rare few clearly felt put-upon. One of these surprised me, a slender woman with blow-waved hair whom I thought I recognised from a law class and saw as a peer. She would not look me in the eye when I asked but immediately stepped behind me, grabbed the handles and started pushing. She let out an annoyed *huff.* I said, it sounds like you might be busy, that's OK, I can ask someone else. But she kept on pushing, fast and, it seemed from the jerking and the huffing, furiously. Arriving at the college, she gave me one last shove, turned around and walked away without saying a word.

That electric wheelchair liberated me – as long as there were no steps in the way, and as long as it didn't break down. But it did break down, often. It sometimes took weeks to fix. I dreaded facing the man from the state government agency. He would shake his head, warn me that a chair can only be replaced every seven years and say, What have you been *doing* with it? I did take it over grass, of course I did. And, yes, I rammed kerbs – it was the only way to get over them.

Every year, more motor neurones died, my muscles wasted, my breathing weakened. With each part of my body that froze, the more my electric chair and other equipment would loom, needed, vital. An anxiety grew in me.

Six months after I got my electric chair, I applied to an international host program. I underplayed my disability and didn't mention I used a wheelchair. A host family in Germany and another in France invited me to stay. I took only the manual wheelchair, leaving the electric chair behind. On seeing me in a wheelchair, the host in Stuttgart still took me in, but the one in Grenoble withdrew. I was left skint, without any supports and with no place to go. It was the position I feared. It was also the position I had put myself into. My lone travels began.

Three years later, back in Australia, I started to go out with David*. He was able-bodied. There was a beach we had discovered with high tides that flowed over the sand, making it firm enough to take my wheelchair. One hot, still afternoon, we were dismayed to find our usually bare beach teeming with people. We weaved our way to a vacant patch of sand, and he spread out our towels and lifted me down from my wheelchair. Too quickly, he let go of me and I nearly toppled backwards. We were out of kilter, aware of all the surrounding eyes on us. Without telling me what he was doing, he pushed my empty wheelchair to the edge of the sand, hid it behind a shrub, and returned to lie down next to me.

Later I asked, Why did you do that, are you ashamed of me being disabled? And he said, I was just putting it out of the way, it was none of their business. Right there and then, though, I said nothing. I wanted only to lie on that crowded beach, one body among many.

With David around, I did not have to worry about how I could get to the toilet next, or whether I had enough energy to pull a dress off over my head, or that I might fall transferring from my electric chair. Not only that, he took me bushwalking on his back. Together we climbed mountains! We were in love. Still, I worried that I needed him more than he needed me.

I told myself that he would come to his senses eventually. It would be natural for him to regret that he had not chosen a woman who was vigorous and able, and only duty and pity would make him stay with me. He would then deserve those looks he only got from people when he was with me, the ones we laughed about, those 'what a good Samaritan you are' looks.

I think we should be more open and go out with other people as well, I said. He flinched. Hurt showed on his face. No, he said. That's not how I want to be with you. My heart was thankful but I had to get away. This time I travelled for two months in Kenya and Tanzania on my own, again taking just the manual chair. There was no reason why I chose those African countries except that they were unknown to me and travel would be hard.

*

That was about twenty-five years ago. Each year my muscles have atrophied further. Now I have barely enough physical strength to hold a book. I became a lawyer. I was also an artist, but when my arms became too weak to handle a brush I took up writing. David is a writer too, as well as a university lecturer. Today he's at work. I'm at home, taking the day off work, because there are problems with my disability supports that need sorting.

Our sixteen-year-old son bursts in, back from school. He gives me a hug, stuffs his face with whatever food is close to hand, grabs his mountain bike and heads out the door again. It's two hours before the winter dark and he's got to get to the bike trail, the one he and his mates dug with spades into a hidden-away side of a hill, because the jumps on the council-made trail were not big enough, and the turns not crazy enough. He asks me if I want to come and watch but I tell him I have to make a call.

I ring the National Disability Insurance Scheme call line. An automated voice comes on and then the hold music. The NDIS was introduced to replace a disability service system that was widely recognised as underfunded, unfair and inefficient. On completion in 2019, it will provide individualised funding to 475,000 persons under the age of sixty-five who have permanent and significant disabilities. The funding can be used for disability-related supports such as personal care, access to the community, therapy services and equipment. After a trial period, the NDIS started rolling out last year by locality and I was one of the first to transition to it. Over the years I have become what is called in disability services a high-needs client, or a 'complex participant', in the latest language of the NDIS.

I joined the chorus of people with disabilities who fought for the introduction of the NDIS. We raised awareness of how people with disabilities have been excluded from a society whose physical and social structures are designed for the non-disabled person. In Australia, people with disabilities have lower levels of income and employment, and less access to health care and housing. Many are isolated and segregated, and prevented from using their skills and talents to benefit their communities. Some remain vulnerable to exploitation and abuse. Australia is ranked lowest of the OECD nations for the relative income of people with disabilities. We called for the supports that people with disabilities need to participate equally in life, supports that would give us control and choice.

The response was unprecedented, the goodwill from Australians heartwarming. I remember thinking that we had made it to the mainstream consciousness when I saw Bill Shorten, who fought for the trapped miners at Beaconsfield, lead our fight. It should have been Rhonda Galbally in the news, of course, or one of the other people with disabilities who spearheaded the cause. But we were grateful for all the support we could get.

The NDIS became law with bipartisan support. It promised to provide choice and control of services to the person using the services. Funding would go to the individual to buy the supports they chose, rather than to the service provider in block form. There would be no more one-size-fits-all supports, no more budgets that varied depending on the economy and the requirements of other portfolios. Replacing all that would be an insurance approach based on need, which recognised that early investments would reap long-term benefits. At full operation, disability services funding would be more than doubled, to $22 billion a year (almost the cost of Medicare). The Productivity Commission found in 2011 that the benefits of the NDIS would outweigh the costs, in terms of community integration, employment and efficiently delivered services, and would add almost 1 per cent to Australia's GDP.

Fifteen minutes have passed on hold. Last time I waited for forty-five minutes. I get out the plan, the NDIS-generated document that lists what disability services I have been given. I don't understand this document. Previous disability services had problems, but this is the first time I have not been able to understand the care plan.

*

About twelve years ago, when the help I needed became too much for David to do alone, I filled in the forms, obtained the required occupational therapy and medical reports, and applied to the relevant Victorian department for personal care funding. An official told me there was a long waiting list and that someone already on the scheme would have to die or go into hospital for a place to become available. I was referred to my local council's disability services. Again I went through a long process filling in forms, and obtaining more OT reports. The council started providing me with a carer two hours per week at a subsidised rate.

Gradually the hours increased. At first David and I had fights about having these carers in our home. David especially hated the intrusion but we could not have kept up our jobs and our health without this help, so we adapted. There was little flexibility in the service. We could not choose our carers or, often, the times they would come. My son was five at the time, and the council would not provide the disability support I needed to care for him. Another time it insisted that two carers were required to operate a hoist to lift me although I clearly only needed one. Then I was told the funding would not stretch to two.

After about a year on the waiting list, the Victorian department accepted me on its program. Eventually, it offered direct payments so recipients could pay for the services with funding deposited into their own accounts.

I enjoyed the autonomy under the evolved Victorian program. However, as I grew weaker the funding was insufficient to pay for the additional personal care that I needed. Three years ago, I applied for more funding. The pressure on David was too much, my ability to maintain my job was being compromised. I was having to skip showers, I couldn't get to the toilet enough, and I had developed a bladder infection. But the budget wasn't there, and all the disabilities officer could do was add me to the waiting list.

Some people on the waiting list did not even have any services. Some were forced to live at home while waiting, depending on their ageing parents for care. An acquaintance of mine only had enough funds for a carer to help her in and out of bed each day. Sometimes she used the funds to pay for a carer to help take her out, and would be forced to spend the night sleeping in her wheelchair.

My reliance on disability equipment increased. My house is full of it – electric, travel and manual wheelchairs, ramps, hoists, lifting beds, braces, commodes and respiratory aids. I also need modifications to my car, home and office, since everything is designed for the average able-bodied person. Something is always breaking down and needing to be fixed. Because the market is small, everything is expensive – at least two or three times the price you would expect for a comparable mainstream item – and I can't pay for it all myself. There have been many times I wished I could, however, because the hoops I have had to jump through are humiliating and stressful, wasting the time and energy I need to get on with life and my job.

Many people with disabilities experience far greater challenges. I have a supportive partner, am educated and employed, and can generally speak up for myself. How can people deal with the system if they don't have all that? Because of communication difficulties or the biases of the institutions providing their care, these people are less likely to be heard or believed. Some have suffered sexual or violent abuse at the hands of carers. Even where complaints were made, the abuse continued because service providers failed to act.

Thirty minutes have passed on hold. I pick up the plan again. When an NDIS officer answers, I will ask them to interpret the bureaucratese for me. It is humiliating. I can't believe the NDIS is treating plans like contracts, when we are not even given the chance to agree to them. The NDIS promised us choice and control, but if a disability support you need is not listed in the plan, you have to go through a lengthy review and make a whole new plan.

*

My entry into the NDIS started with a phone call in May 2016 from an NDIS assessor called Nicole. She said I had to do a screening assessment. She would guide me through a questionnaire about my disability that would take about an hour. I questioned the need for this when reams of current information about me were already available on my Victorian department file. Everyone, she said, has to do this questionnaire to get on the NDIS. Assessments depress me, especially unnecessary ones. I spend all my energy focusing on what I *can* do and suddenly I'm called to define my deficits. It brings to mind the young male physio who assessed my spine. I thought I was looking rather fit in my bathers. He took one look at me and casually said, Yep, the scoliosis sticks out like dogs' balls. But it was the NDIS and I cooperated because I wanted it to work.

Nicole read out the questions one after the other:
Can you stand?
Can you communicate?
Can you feed yourself?
Was there anything you couldn't do in the last two weeks?
How would you rate your quality of life?
The questions went on and on.
Several times I asked her the purpose of the question, or its context. I'm just reading them out, Nicole said. Everybody gets the same questions. At the end of the interview I asked her for a copy. She said that wasn't possible. As a government agency, I said, under information privacy laws, you are required to give me access to my answers as recorded on the form. I'll consult my manager, she said. Later she told me again it wasn't possible.

After six months without word, an NDIS officer called Deirdre rang. She said that the results from my screening assessment had concluded that my disability needs were minimal. However, she had checked my medical and disability information on the Victorian department file, and realised this conclusion was wrong. Deirdre told me I would have to repeat parts of the screening assessment. In answer to my query, she explained that other participants also had to do this, because the initial assessors did not have the training to properly interpret the questions.

She revisited the questions from the screening assessment. You said you had no difficulties managing all household responsibilities, she said. Is that really correct? What the question really meant was, can you actually physically do the housework yourself? No, I said, I mainly supervise. She said, OK, that's what I thought. It wasn't properly interpreted for you. I will change the answer.

She went on. According to the earlier assessment, she said, you had no difficulties socialising. How often do you go out socially? Maybe once in four weeks, I answered, feeling ashamed. Why don't you go out more often? she asked. I said, I'm often sore from sitting, or too tired from work. It's difficult to organise, and friends' houses, transport and many places aren't accessible. I felt even worse. Right, I'll change that answer too, she said. I told her I must have thought at the initial interview that the question was about my social skills!

The next question was about personal hygiene. In the earlier assessment, you said you had no difficulties managing your hygiene, she began. Before she had the chance to start interpreting the question, I blurted out, I know now you're going to say that the question was about whether I could shower myself – I must have thought she was asking me if I was dirty! I started laughing, and when I tried to stop, more sniggers erupted. Deirdre waited patiently. She seemed like a nice woman trying hard to do a good job, and perhaps if we had been face to face she would have seen the joke of it too.

We continued through the questions. At the end, she added up the new scores. Before you got 55.5 out of 100, or minimal needs, she said. Now you have 88.8 – complex needs!

Then came the drafting of my plan. A face-to-face meeting was not necessary or possible, Deirdre said. The plan would go to a delegate. If it followed all the rules and didn't generate a review, it would be approved. What rules? I asked. She told me each disability support I asked for had to be reasonable and necessary, it had to be linked to a goal, it couldn't be a support that was seen as medical or education-related, and it should come under a line item. I asked what a line item was. She said there was an NDIS list of line items that tells you what supports will be funded. I asked for a copy of this. She said she wasn't allowed to give me a copy. Only the NDIS could see this. Do they think we will look at it like a smorgasbord and get greedy?

I asked Deirdre to add to my plan a whole list of equipment needs. Unless it comes under urgent unmet need, it's not going to be included, she said. I'm not saying things won't get funded. Just that government wants to roll out the scheme on schedule, so things that are not urgent will be looked at on review.

Finally she told me I would not be able to see the plan beforehand. Instead I would receive a hard copy of my plan in the mail once it was approved. I drew in my breath. It is not my plan if I haven't had the chance to sign off on it or even see it! The IT system won't allow it, she said. I told her I had no idea what was going on and the least I could do was to see what she was writing in my plan. She was sorry but it was the system. By the end I had hardly any voice left. Deirdre was hoarse and coughing. She must have done this hundreds of times.

*

The front door crashes open, startling me. It's my son. His face is crimson. Mum, you have to come! You have to see the *sick as* jumps! Sorry, hon, I'll come as soon as I get off the phone, I say. He rushes out again and the classical hold music loops on. Forty minutes have passed and I'm still on hold.

I'm trying to understand why my life has seemed out of control since I entered the NDIS. Normally, it takes me at least three times as long and an orchestration of carers and equipment to do the daily things that most people do without thinking – like get out of bed, go to the bathroom or catch a bus. Along with my job and family life, these demands mean that I am always time-stressed. I had hoped that the NDIS would free up some time for me, with its promise of more-efficient and tailored services. Instead, the bureaucratese and problematic administration of the new system have created greater pressure and made it difficult for me to keep up with my work.

One month before my NDIS plan commenced, funding from my old disability services ceased. My carers couldn't be paid. When my plan did start, I still couldn't access the funding, because of technical problems with the NDIS website portal and my plan manager's failure to make payments. My carers were not paid for up to three months. Unable to afford the long payment delays, one of them could not continue working for me. It then took months to find a new carer, because the growth of the workforce has not kept up with the increase in NDIS demand.

Also, my plan had omitted my equipment needs. This meant I couldn't purchase aids I needed or access funds for repairs or maintenance. I am now required to have my plan reviewed to add the equipment I need. Because the NDIS processes are so complex and obscure, I need to employ a professional called a Support Coordinator under the scheme to interpret the plan and the review rules for me. My Support Coordinator told me of one person who had to have a review because there was a typo in her plan. Another had to have a review because she changed her job. The review process could take around three months, or it could go on and on.

Before you can do anything under the NDIS, it seems, you need an OT's report. You are not trusted to make basic decisions on your own. I was told I needed OT approval just to replace the batteries of my electric wheelchair. Another participant reported that a $25 kettle tipper ended up costing about $100 because an OT's report was required.

So much waste occurs where the system is overly bureaucratic and its rules are not clear or reasonable. No real opportunity is given for choice and control, and we are forced to rely on the professionals and administrators.

From reports, the main people who are happy with the NDIS are those who had no access to disability services before. For others, there are improvements such as increased funding and more supports than previously. Each day, however, more are speaking out about problems with the NDIS. Governments are rushing into the privatisation of disability services without adequate quality assurance. They are putting at risk the safety of the most vulnerable. Services that were formerly funded are now being refused on narrow interpretations of what is 'reasonable and necessary'. Staff administering the scheme have had inadequate training. Payments to carers have been stopped as a result of IT problems. And one of the most common sources of complaint: the plans that we did not have the chance to look at or agree to.

I am wondering what has happened to the voice of people with disabilities that called for equality, choice and control. Now the rhetoric is dominated by financial sustainability. It is ironic that the administrators of the NDIS whip out the language of meeting targets and budgetary bottom lines to justify their implementation of the scheme, when it is their mistakes that are causing waste.

I don't think it's just teething issues. It's symptomatic of underlying attitudes that haven't changed. Transformation still has to occur at a cultural level. We come from a long tradition of disability services being delivered as welfare or charity. In this tradition, it's acceptable to apply different standards to people with disabilities. For instance, we expect insurance cover to be given on terms that are understood and agreed to. Why do we think it's acceptable for the NDIS plans to be made without the participants even getting the chance to view them beforehand?

The Productivity Commission's June 2017 position paper on NDIS costs has many laudable recommendations. I was, however, concerned by the statement that 'the ultimate cap – and test of financial sustainability – is taxpayers' continuing willingness to pay for it'. This seems like a harking back to the welfare and charity days. The legislation that created the NDIS recognises the right to disability services that will enable equal participation. It is not a gift that can be offered or taken away.

At the heart of the NDIS is the Australian goal of the fair go. The insurance model and the legislation are underpinned by this goal. If we stay true to this, the structures and the attitudes that disadvantage people with disabilities can be transformed. The mistakes in the implementation of the NDIS can be righted. The first step to bringing the NDIS back on course is to be aware of the deeply entrenched biases that lead people to act in ways that disregard the dignity and equal value of people with disabilities.

*

When I was young, I decided that I would kill myself when my disability progressed to an intolerable stage. I imagined that point would be when I was dependent on help to get out of bed, go to the toilet, shower and dress myself. I'm at that point now. Each time I lose more of my physical strength, first I object, I grieve, and then, like most people do, I adapt. I have no less love, interest and passion in my life. The sun is still marvellous, and the sky blue. Like everyone else, I have my own goals, successes and struggles. Life is normal.

At least it feels normal, until I see people's eyes on me and feel their pity, their admiration that I go on living, their horror, or their thankfulness that they are not me. The thing that they want to deny is that they are me. This stops empathy, and makes it easy for people to treat us with less dignity than they would like for themselves. Dependency or vulnerability is inherent to our humanity. We are born and usually die dependent, and we live with the ever-present possibility of injury or disability.

When I was eighteen, I was nearly overwhelmed by the anxiety of becoming increasingly disabled, and being dependent and without supports. This fear drove me to throw myself into a situation where I was powerless. I travelled in Europe and Africa alone, without any supports. I was spurred on to experience everything, not miss out, *never miss out*, no matter how hard it was.

Paradoxically, by experiencing my own helplessness, the way was opened to discovering my inherent worth and power. I remember Kamanja, a man I met in Kenya. He was one of many people who came my way and helped me through, who pushed me in my wheelchair and carried me when I was at a low ebb and battered. I started to thank him. He held out his hand for me to stop. 'I help you because you need help,' he said.

Names have been changed.

In Defence of the Bad, White Working Class

Shannon Burns

I spent much of my childhood in a north-western suburb of Adelaide that was, for decades, predominantly white and working-class. Waves of eastern European migrants formed the foundation of its initial settlement throughout the 1950s and 1960s, before it underwent a significant transformation in the 1980s, when the new influx of migrants and refugees from Vietnam, Cambodia and China settled there in large numbers. Mansfield Park also boasted an extensive collection of public housing, which ensured that underemployed Anglo-Australians – like my parents – were well represented.

It was here that I became ashamed of my family's racist attitudes. Some on the migrant Greek side felt that anyone who wasn't Greek was a low-life, including Anglo Australians (they called me and my father 'doggas'), while the Anglo side was more selectively racist: for them, it all depended on the context. My father and stepmother used racist language privately, but got along well with our neighbours, all of whom were Vietnamese or Chinese. They referred to these as 'the good ones', while unknowns were not to be trusted. *Slope* and *nip* were not taboo words in our household, yet my parents would have denied that they were racist for using them. To their minds, the language you employed did not define you.

I suspect that the shame I felt about my parents' racism sprang mostly from experience: the bulk of my friends were Vietnamese and Chinese, and their families seemed more admirable than mine. My attitude was, therefore, a product of intimacy and experience rather than abstract notions of morality or equality. I had an opportunity, as a child, that my parents – who had grown up poor among working-class whites – never had.

I also had the chance to see myself through migrant eyes, and what I saw was often confronting. Poor whites were scorned by more than a few of the Chinese and Vietnamese migrants I came to know, especially the hard-working, self-sacrificing parents who were deeply invested in their children's education and upward mobility. They made it clear that I was not the kind of friend they wanted for their sons.

The experience of being deemed undesirable and unworthy even by new Australians is a peculiarly lumpen trial. For me, it was eye-opening. For others, it's an unutterable humiliation.

*

When I was thirteen, my parents began whispering with noticeable regularity. I assumed that I was in some kind of trouble – I had much to feel guilty about – and kept my head down. But instead of summoning me for punishment, they grew oddly concerned about my safety. Violence had broken out, sporadically, in local public areas, including my high school, The Parks, which doubled as a community centre. There my classmates and I watched a lengthy, bloody brawl between dozens of adults – all Asian-Australian – from a few feet away. For us, it was a God-given interruption to a dreary school day, but my parents were distressed to hear about it.

When a young adult male of Asian appearance kicked me off my bicycle as I rode along the footpath near our house – behaviour that I took to be insulting but not especially scary, since I'd already been threatened with knives in the schoolyard – my parents responded in a surprising way. They made appointments with the public housing trust, and lobbied hard to be moved across town. They claimed that hard drugs were being sold by our new neighbours, and that 'Asian gangs' had replaced the predominantly white criminals who had formerly ruled the roost. This, they believed, was reason enough to be terrified.

They were not alone: scores of students of all heritages were pulled out of The Parks, which closed down a few years later. Within a decade much of my old suburb was demolished and redeveloped, including the house we lived in and my primary school. One of the more galling aspects of lower-class life is that your history is routinely erased. Sometimes you wonder if you were ever really there.

My experiences with the migrants and first-generation Australians of Mansfield Park were mostly happy ones, but for many of the white adults, like my parents, 'Asians' had turned their neighbourhood into a frightening and uninhabitable place. It appeared no more dangerous to me than it had ever been, but I enjoyed a comparatively privileged perspective. I grew up in a multicultural world, so its 'alien' aspects barely troubled me. My parents, however, did not grow up in such a world. They had never been wealthy enough to travel or to experience other cultures on their own terms. As a consequence, the creeping advance of a multicultural society – a reality shift that they had no control over – frightened them.

At the time, I was ashamed of my parents' warped hostilities. But after migrating into a middle-class lifestyle I've become less judgemental. Here I've discovered that, unlike my parents, very little is imposed on me. I live in a predominantly white, middle-class suburb. I eat Asian food and attend cultural festivals when it suits me. The people of colour whom I call friends are all university-educated and English-rich, and they share most of my basic interests and concerns. If they are registered as 'other', it is a very diluted form of otherness.

My son goes to a school where multiculturalism is embraced in the spirit of empathy and generosity, and as an extension of the liberal, middle-class values that most of us share, rather than urgent social and economic need. We are *never* confronted by aggressive people as we go about our daily business, and we enjoy a prevailing sense of safety and certainty. For precariously employed, unskilled labourers, the prospect of competing against a recent migrant for a job is inevitable, while for middle-class people it is only a remote possibility – and *our* competitors are typically required to undergo extensive and onerous retraining, which puts them at a significant competitive disadvantage.

In short, our empathy and values are largely untested, and our livelihoods rarely, if ever, come under threat.

Levels of general hostility to migrants are, I suspect, partly contingent on class experiences like the ones I've described. At one end of the spectrum, professional or middle-class migrants enlarge the dimensions of what it means to be a professional or middle-class Australian, in a relatively controlled, seamless and enriching way; at the other end, poor and criminal migrants enlarge the dimensions of what it means to be poor and criminal in Australia, in a relatively chaotic, fragmented and sometimes frightening way. In the first category, these expansions are largely for the better; in the second category, these expansions are just as often for the worse.

Middle-class progressives have no qualms about exercising their natural right to determine the moral values of our world. Yet a fairer approach would surely entail sacrificing *one's own* comfort for a cause. The trickier and scarier consequences of enlightened policies should fall on those who champion them, yet they rarely do.

*

The habits of progressive social and political discourse almost seem calculated to alienate and aggravate lower-class whites. I confess that if a well-dressed, university-educated middle-class person of any gender or ethnicity had so much as hinted at my 'white privilege' while I was a lumpen child, or my 'male privilege' while I was an unskilled labourer who couldn't afford basic necessities, or my 'hetero privilege' while I was a homeless solitary, I'd have taken special pleasure in voting for their nightmare. And I would have been right to do so.

As an aspirational teenage lumpen, I learned to embrace a working-class ethos. It was a simple, experiential lesson: whenever I allowed myself to feel like a victim, I fell into paralysis and deep poverty; whenever I took pride in my capacity to work and endure, things got slightly better. One worldview worked; the other didn't.

Even if I *was* wronged or oppressed or marginalised, claiming victim status seemed absurd (since I often came across people who were more unfortunate than me), limiting (since there were other, enriching aspects of life to focus on), humiliating (because in the working-class world self-pity is reviled) and self-defeating (because if you allow yourself to think and behave like a victim, you quickly fall into lumpen despair).

At university, I discovered that this ethos didn't apply. A season of despair would not send middle-class teens spiralling into a life of drug-addled indigence; they could simply brush themselves off and enrol again next year. Strong, class-enforced safety nets meant that self-pity could be accommodated, and victimhood could even form part of a functional identity.

Indeed, the willingness to expose your wounds is another sign of privilege. Those for whom injury has a use value will display their injuries; those for whom woundedness is a survival risk won't. As a consequence, middle-class grievances now drown out lower-class pain. This is why the wounded lower classes come to embrace conservative discourses that ridicule middle-class anguish. Those who cannot afford to see themselves as disadvantaged are instinctively repulsed by those who harp on about disadvantage.

Language is another site of class conflict. I grew up in violent environments. For people like me, 'symbolic violence' or 'offensive speech' were, if anything, a benign alternative to real violence and real hate. It was often registered as a joke – or yes, banter – because we understood its relative harmlessness. When I first came across someone who reacted to something that was said to him as though something had been done to him, I thought he was insane. But he wasn't. He was from a lower-middle-class family and was unfamiliar with our habits of speech. He'd never been beaten, so the words felt 'violent' enough for him to react in a way that was, in our environment, laughable.

When I was six or seven, a slow-witted uncle held me down and repeatedly spat in my face, because I'd called my stepsister a nasty name. Another time, he savagely beat his disabled wife as we looked on, after she dared to question my stepmother's maternal qualities. I'll never forget the slap-thumping sounds as she cringed in her wheelchair, and the sight of blood streaming from her nose and lips, or her swollen black eyes and laboured breathing in the night. Nor will I forget the image of my father pinning my stepmother to the ground after she bit and scratched and tore at my stepsister, or my mother remorselessly punching and gouging a boyfriend who refused to lay hands on her, or my stepmother breaking wooden spoons over my knuckles (yes, knuckles, not palms), or my father walloping me hard enough to leave perfect, purple, hand-shaped bruises imprinted on my back and chest after hearing me swear, or … That, to me, is what the word 'violent' describes.

By contrast, the act of, say, revealing the true identity of an Italian writer who hoped to remain anonymous cannot seriously be called 'violently' intrusive. Nor can an orange-faced buffoon's practice of hulking impatiently behind a fellow candidate as she speaks during a political debate be considered 'violently' sexist or truly aggressive. From my perspective, these are examples of impoliteness or bad taste – no more and no less – yet they are commonly bundled together with truly despicable behaviour, as though there is no substantial difference. Indeed, the deplorable nature of real violence is exploited to condemn mere idiocy.

Experience has imprinted this sensibility onto me. I know that an extraordinarily low percentage of lower class writers and scholars are represented in literary awards shortlists and university readers, but to be outraged about it conflicts with an ethos that I haven't entirely shed. To me, this form of harm belongs to another dimension of injustice – the relatively benign dimension – whereas physical harm or neglect requires serious attention. I'm not arguing that others should share my sensibility, or even that it is the best or right one. But progressives *might* benefit from considering lower-class points of view, and the experiences that forge them, at least once in a while. They might also find that addressing those sensibilities, instead of ignoring or deriding them, opens up new pathways to mutual understanding and cooperation.

*

Those who hail from the lower classes rarely have relatives or mentors who encourage them to modify or scrutinise received ways of thinking about social issues. Many go to schools that are under-resourced, where behaviour management replaces education, and where punitive controls make learning feel like abuse.

The only people they know who embrace progressive values are the vegetarians down the street, whom nobody talks to, and those who are materially better off than they are. Because of this, those values take on a particular aura: they represent the world view of those who stand above them.

Given this inherent structural problem, progressives must surely seek to *persuade* lower-class people to entertain their ideas – patiently, inventively and persistently – instead of imposing them.

Consider who determines the standards of so-called politically correct speech. Are they primarily negotiated across classes and social groups, or are they determined from above? If the latter is the case, then it would be senseless to deny that political correctness, as it stands, is a form and expression of elitism. When rules of expression are forced on people who have their own peculiar relationship to speech, and who can reasonably be expected to struggle with the constraints, it is not a fair imposition. Political correctness is hardly the evil that conservative commentators make it out to be, but as a moral burden it is clearly weighted against the lower classes, who are smart enough to recognise when they are being set up to fail.

The rules of speech are habitually negotiated in the working-class world, in ways that many of my middle-class friends would find shocking. The factories I worked in typically employed at least a couple of rough speakers who used 'cunt' in the way the rest of us used 'mate'. It was not suitable for me to call my colleagues or foreman or manager 'cunt', since it wasn't consistent with my way of speaking, but it *was* acceptable for those men to do so. They were upbraided whenever they swore within the hearing of customers or clients, but that was the extent of the surveillance. It was also understood that if they performed their job well and behaved decently, their rough manners would not count against them. How is it that middle-class progressives are unwilling or unable to make similar adjustments?

In the working-class context, in particular, it's what you physically *do*, what you *make* – the observable physical impression – that counts. That is the native language, the one they are fluent in and the one they trust. And *that* language often conflicts with working-class speech or attitudes.

I worked in a recycling centre for some years. One of my work-mates was a kid (we were all kids) called Ricky. I regarded him as a low-life brute, and he regarded me as a rule-following sissy. We were both right.

Every week an elderly Chinese man brought his bottles and cans to us. He couldn't speak English, which tends to frustrate racists, and Ricky was duly irritated. One morning the man – who had difficulty walking – accidentally put his car into gear while he was half out the door and still tangled in his seatbelt. His legs went sideways and dragged on the ground as the car took off, and he struggled hopelessly to pull them in, or to reach the brakes, or to loosen his seatbelt to escape. The car was only a few feet away from me, but all I managed was an incoherent shout and an uncertain jog as it picked up speed and headed for the main road.

Ricky dashed past me, jumped into the man's lap, grabbed the steering wheel, and quickly found the brakes. Then he helped the man out of the car, checked that he was uninjured, and knelt with his arm around him as he cried and shook on the ground. When the man was calm enough to stand, Ricky pulled him to his feet, told him to take care, then walked away, muttering, 'Fucken Asian drivers.' It wasn't a perfect performance, but it got the job done.

My parents were racists in private speech but not in action. Did that make them secret racists who hid their racism from the wider world? Or were they non-racists who played with racist speech? Or a bit of both? Who can possibly say? My worry is that by conflating racist or offensive speech or attitudes with racist or offensive actions or activism, we push people like my parents and Ricky (who represent large chunks of every dominant ethnicity or tribe in every country on earth) over to the wrong side of the political fence. By setting unnegotiated limits on attitudes and speech as well as actions, we claim too much territory and thereby risk losing it all.

The desire to create a world devoid of cruelty and unfairness is unquestionably noble, and the *idea* of a racism-free society is rhetorically useful – especially when you are dealing with impres-sionable children – but it is only a happy fantasy. Tribalism is a global phenomenon. Its roots may be evolutionary or cultural or both, but it appears everywhere, and it flares up whenever people fear that their way of life is under threat. When we *believe* our rhetoric and use coddled, middle-class experience as our reference point, we lose sight of practical objectives, and ignore obvious risks as well as genuine social accomplishments.

Perhaps the most dangerous aspect of a middle-class life is the extent to which it shields its beneficiaries from fundamental, brutal realities. Most lower-class people of all ethnicities quickly learn that universal justice doesn't exist, and probably never will, yet unbridled fantasies of fairness are continually thrust upon them from above. Don Quixote rides his workhorse, Rocinante, with the same blind abandon. But the lower classes are not as tolerant as old nags, and they express themselves with actions rather than arguments and complaints. If you direct them to gallop at windmills, they stand still. When you try to whip them forwards, they buck you off. If you then rebuke them, they kick you where it hurts. And they are right to do so.

People Power at the Ponderosa

Mandy Sayer

Take twenty-four single people from diverse backgrounds. Add poverty, disabilities and old age, then house them among drug dealers and creeping mould. A recipe for chaos? Not at all. Here's proof that life, in any circumstances, is what you make it.

Ten days until Christmas
'You know how we can tell that someone has died?' asks Woolley, standing in the corridor of his Department of Housing building.

He nods at the door of the apartment adjacent to his own unit. 'Flies on the door handle. The flies always figure it out before the smell gets going.'

Woolley tells me that last week he noticed the insects buzzing around his neighbour's lock and called the police, who broke into the flat to discover the corpse of Peter, in his early fifties, who hadn't been seen for three days.

'He was a bit of a conspiracy theorist,' adds Woolley, the unofficial caretaker of the building. 'He reckoned J.F.K. was murdered by the Mob.'

Woolley, however, suspects no foul play in the death of his neighbour. Now there is a sign on the door, posted by the authorities, warning that the interior has been contaminated and that no-one should enter until it has been detoxified by forensic cleaners.

'Probably an overdose,' he murmurs.

Residents call the building 'Ponderosa', in reference to the ranch on long-running US TV western *Bonanza*. It's a block of twenty-four studio apartments in Sydney's eastern suburbs, built in the 1970s, filled with single disability and aged pensioners. All but one survive on Centrelink payments and donations from charities. The majority, Woolley tells me, have no family support.

'You don't want to plan too far ahead, because you don't know who's going to die.'

It's now ten days until Christmas, but he is ambivalent about organising the annual party because four of the building's residents are in hospital and the recent passing of his neighbour puts Ponderosa's death toll for the year at three (thus far).

Woolley leads me into his studio filled with clothing racks and his collection of vintage Hawaiian shirts. A three-quarter bed is wedged into an alcove. A flat-screen TV is mounted on the wall, below a small round table. It's a tight squeeze, even for one person. I ask him about the actual size of the unit. He shrugs and replies, 'Nine paces by five paces. That's how I measure it.'

We walk out into his small, private courtyard and he shows me a huge freezer he's installed under the awning, where anyone in the building is welcome to store their frozen goods. In order to provide round-the-clock access, Woolley has removed three palings from his fence so his neighbours can duck in and out without disturbing him.

'Three good square meals a week. That's enough to keep us going.'

As we walk back inside, eighty-four-year-old Don, who lives upstairs, limps through the open door carrying a steaming plate of fish and chips. He delivers it to the kitchen counter. Don is the unofficial chef for six other Ponderosa dwellers who are either too ill or too lazy to cook a hot meal at night.

'Sunday is a baked dinner,' Don says, leaning against the wall and lighting a cigarette. 'Wednesday is spaghetti bolognaise, or lasagne. And Friday is fish and chips.'

Every Friday morning, Don gets up, collects his shopping trolley and limps fifteen minutes to the local outlet of the charity OzHarvest, where he selects donated fruits and vegetables for his various neighbours. 'I know that Jose likes Asian greens. And

Butch loves kiwifruit. I know what everyone wants so I can pick up stuff for them.'

'And on Fridays we do the washing up and return the plates to Don,' adds Woolley. 'And we check his fridge to see what he needs.'

'Do you charge people for the meals?' I ask.

Don smiles and glances at Woolley.

'We've got a kind of bartering system,' says Woolley. 'It's all based on reciprocity.'

He tells me that some years ago the residents of Ponderosa worked out a plan that would benefit them all – and one that would remove the need to constantly borrow and repay money to each other. 'For example, we all buy the same cask wine – Golden Oak, $12 for four litres from the cellars down the road.'

'Sometimes it's $10,' chimes in Don. 'When it's on special.'

'We all smoke the same tobacco – Endless Blue – and use the same papers, Tally Hos.'

'It's an open-door policy ...' adds Don, stubbing out his cigarette.

I glance at Woolley, hoping he'll further explain the scheme. '... So we can walk in and out of each other's apartments. Say, if I run out of wine, I can stroll into someone else's place and help myself. Same with tobacco. And food. And they can let themselves into my place, without having to find me.'

The ninety-year-olds are housed on the second floor, so they have level access to street exits. Woolley also tells me that all the men in the building have swapped three sets of keys, so that no-one is accidentally locked out of his unit.

'And when one of us goes to hospital,' he adds, 'the rest of us sneak into the empty apartment and clean it all up – like a bunch of elves!'

Sixteen years ago, when Woolley and Don first moved in, the side garden was denuded and filled with trash. Drug dealers stalked the security gates. When Woolley called the police, he was referred to the Department of Housing, and when he called the department he was always referred back to the police. So Woolley and his neighbours decided to take matters into their own hands, marshalling sentries at the windows above the security gates. Whenever a dealer was spotted lurking outside, he'd be pelted with rocks and buckets of water. After a month or so, the block was free of both junkies and dealers.

It was then that Woolley, Don and their new friends set about turning the building's common property into a sanctuary. They cleared the garden, planted trees and ferns, and set up tables and chairs in the shade. Now it exudes the cool green light of a tropical rainforest.

'There's a Chinese guy upstairs,' says Woolley. 'He's eighty-six – and we call him Jose.'

'Why do you call him Jose?'

Woolley grins and lights a rollie. ''Cause he's always hosing the garden. We've sort of given him permission to use a fire hose on the third floor. He stands in the corridor and waters the plants from there. You see, we're only supposed to use the hose in the event of a fire. But because Jose is Chinese, we figure that if he ever got into trouble from the authorities he could pretend that he doesn't speak English.'

As Don bids goodbye and disappears into the corridor, Woolley sprinkles his hot dinner with water and pops it into the oven on low.

At night, Ponderosa becomes an amplifier for the many frustrations of the neighbourhood. A guy upstairs has been yelling obscenities over his balcony for five hours. Woolley tells me that he and a neighbour have been warring for days, but no-one can remember how it started exactly. Bottles and glasses shatter on the street; car alarms wail; and, just before midnight, I can hear somebody spewing. Soon, police sirens are howling over the shouts of neighbours.

'Raid,' says Woolley, calmly, topping up his drink. 'The house two doors up – they're always getting busted.'

Nine days until Christmas

The front door swings open. 'You there, Woolley?' cries a man in an urgent voice. 'Woolley, are you there?'

I look up to see a solid, dark-haired man wearing sunglasses peering down at me, sporting a wide, maniacal grin.

Woolley rises from his chair and introduces me to Leo, who at the age of forty-eight is the 'baby' of the building. They've been close friends since Leo moved in to Ponderosa fifteen years ago.

Every morning, he arrives at Woolley's at the same time – 9.30 a.m. – and they walk around to a local pub to buy takeaway coffees.

Today is no different. Woolley grabs his mobile phone and they disappear out the door together. I stay behind to await the arrival of a health inspector. Woolley has told me that five units have been badly affected by mould, and has already shown me a photograph on his phone of an eighty-seven-year-old man slumped on a bed, with the wall behind him furred with mildew.

'Maybe we can paint over it,' says Woolley, as he and Leo return with the coffees.

'You can't paint over mould,' I say. 'It'll make it even worse.'

'Well, it'll look a lot better,' Woolley reasons. 'You know, some of these blokes don't have much time.'

We wait for the health inspector. Leo, who is on the autism spectrum, tells me a little of his life. He was born in Australia to Italian parents who returned to Naples when he was two years old. He grew up speaking fluent Italian. When he was eleven, however, his family moved back to Australia and Leo struggled to adapt both culturally and linguistically. Hence, when he speaks English, he is compelled to state everything twice.

'When he speaks Italian,' says Woolley, 'he only says things once.'

Leo does his bit for the Ponderosa community by repairing second-hand mobile phones and giving them to neighbours.

'Since Junkie John moved in, the cops have been called twice and Bikie Dan has stabbed him once.'

'Everyone gets a basic Nokia when they move in,' explains Woolley. 'And we get them all on the same plan. Thirty bucks a month. It's cheaper than a landline.'

Suddenly, what looks like water or weak tea begins falling past the open door and into the courtyard. It continues for eight or ten seconds and stops as abruptly as it began.

'When we get junkies in here,' announces Leo, 'it wrecks everything.' After repeating the statement, Leo lets Woolley pick up the story.

'Was that just someone pissing over the balcony?' I ask.

Woolley replies by rolling his eyes and shrugging. He goes on to explain that Junkie John supports his habit by stealing luggage from the carousels at Sydney airport. 'The only problem,' he continues, 'is that John's a clean freak. As soon as he moved in, he ripped up the carpet of his unit and dumped it in the garden. And he had his own washer and dryer in his unit going 24/7, laundering all the stolen clothes and luggage before he sold them on.'

Leo chimes in – twice – that John also threw his television from his balcony and damaged the herbs that Jose had planted. And one day, a neighbour grew so tired of the noise of the washer and dryer, he got up in the middle of the night, broke into the power box and secretly turned the junkie's electricity off. So the junkie moved into the communal laundry, sleeping there and monopolising the three available washing machines.

'And he lives off eggs boiled in an electric jug!' adds Woolley, shaking his head.

We hear footsteps outside and turn towards the open door, anticipating the health inspector. But it's only a neighbour on his way upstairs.

'So how else do you cope?' I ask, 'When you're living on such a tight budget?'

'Lowes!' announces Leo enthusiastically. 'Lowes!'

Woolley tells me that all the male residents of Ponderosa have secured a loyalty card from Lowes department store. 'During sales, it's 15 per cent off. You can get a whole new wardrobe for seventy bucks!'

'Tell her about the toilet paper!' enthuses Leo. 'Tell her about the toilet paper!'

Woolley laughs and explains to me that a few years ago, several residents of the building used to raid the expensive restaurants and bars in the area and steal rolls of high-quality Sorbent. They would then meet at a local pub with their bounties and pretend it was an Addicts Anonymous meeting.

Woolley stands up and strikes an embarrassed pose. '"My name is Henry and I'm a spendthrift. It's been six weeks since I bought my last roll of toilet paper."'

Leo laughs and slaps the table. 'So we gotta have a Christmas party this year, Woolley! We'll have it at your place.' Leo gets up and disappears into the bathroom. 'I'll chip in and bring a case of beer!'

Woolley turns to me and lowers his voice. 'Leo says this every year. "I'll bring a case of beer!" But I'm the one who has to buy the food, and I also have to host it.'

Five days until Christmas

It's so hot today that waves of heat rise through Woolley's court-yard like funnels of steam. I open the freezer and briefly stick my head inside to cool off. Since my last visit, the health inspector has been and gone, yet still nothing has been done to remove the life-threatening mould.

'Usually it takes up to fourteen working days for them to fix a problem,' explains Woolley. 'But with Christmas coming on, it won't be done until next year. I don't blame the Department of Housing. They're doing the best they can.'

Trailing cigarette smoke, he leads me through the gap in his paling fence and onto a narrow strip of common property. We spot a heavily tanned man sitting in his undies in the sun, drink-ing yellow liquid from a plastic one-litre Coke bottle.

'That's Butch,' whispers Woolley. We nod a greeting and con-tinue walking.

'What's in the Coke bottle?' I ask, curious.

'Golden Oak,' replies Woolley. 'Butch used to be a two-cask-a-day man. And he lived under the Harbour Bridge. But after he got a home here, he got a job as a cleaner, which he's managed to hang on to for years.'

He points out a honeysuckle tree further ahead. 'Butch is also the building's spotter.'

'What does he look for? The cops?'

Woolley shakes his head. 'The rats.'

At first, I think he is joking. But Woolley tells me that the rats come from three sources: the first is the nearby bay, where naval ships dock; the second and third are an old hotel and a commu-nity centre on the next block, both of which have been recently renovated and re-plumbed.

'They come up through the pipes,' he explains. 'Don nailed chicken wire over our bathroom windows,' – he points up to a mangled screen – 'but the rats ate right through them. For a while there, I thought someone was coming into my unit and stealing my soap all the time. That is, until I saw a cake of

Sunlight on the floor of the shower recess, covered in bite marks! Apparently they like the taste of the fat in the soap.'

We walk up the concrete stairs to the open corridor of the first floor, where the branches of macadamia and umbrella trees form leafy canopies. Woolley knocks on a door and we're soon greeted by Flora, a smiling, petite Peruvian woman in her late sixties.

He begins to discuss Christmas plans with her: if he organised a party on the day, would she care to come along? Flora is more than enthusiastic. 'He good man!' she announces. 'He very good man! He look after me!'

Woolley promises Flora he will be in touch with the details. I can sense that he still doesn't feel motivated to throw a Christmas party, but it's lonely residents like Flora and Butch who will probably change his mind.

'Flora likes to sew,' remarks Woolley, as we walk up the stairs to the second floor. 'She does all my mending for me.'

'Does she charge you for it?'

He glances at me as if I've just asked a silly question. 'When she moved in, we found out she liked to sew. So we sourced a sewing machine for her and hooked her up with the local community centre to take lessons.'

We reach the second landing and are now facing the tops of the many trees. 'There was a neighbour here a couple of years ago, Neil; he had a tumour on his side the size of a basketball.' Woolley pauses and relights his rollie. 'And he couldn't leave his flat because nothing would fit him.'

We continue walking down the corridor. 'So, we went down to Lowes and bought two oversized shirts. Flora cut them up and sewed them into one big shirt. That's how Neil was able to go out when he had cancer.'

Woolley stops in front of a screen door, opens it, and sticks his head in. 'Is it okay to come in?'

''Course it is!' we hear a voice call.

We walk into a unit filled with shelves of books by bestselling author Wilbur Smith. Don's kitchen is equally packed with pots, pans, colanders, utensils and crockery. Don is sitting on a chair in his singlet and shorts, watching the cricket.

'Is it okay if I have a drink?' says Woolley, heading towards the fridge.

"Course you can!' he replies. 'You don't have to ask.'

Woolley returns with a tumbler of Golden Oak and ice and sits across from us. He and Don begin again to discuss the problem with the resident junkie, and how they'll manage him, and the rat and mould problem, over Christmas. They've resorted to buying their own baits and laying them throughout the building.

'The Department of Housing will not respond in a timely manner,' says Woolley in a deliberately mocking tone. 'It's no use putting a bandaid on when the body has already bled out.' He lets out a loud huff and reaches for his tobacco. 'It hurts poor people who have been promised help and don't receive it. It hurts.'

Don mentions that Junkie John keeps leaving the laundry door unlocked, which could result in the theft of the building's washers and dryers. More worryingly, John has also been spotted trying to enter the units of his neighbours early in the mornings, while they're still asleep.

'Just one person can fuck it up for everyone else,' says Don, wagging his head.

Four days until Christmas

Last night, for the first time in sixteen years, Don locked his front door, afraid of Junkie John and his rumoured light fingers. Over his first coffee of the day, Woolley smokes and broods for a while, and soon decides on a plan of action to deal with John over the holidays.

It's midmorning and already the heat inside his unit is stifling. Sitting at the table, he lights a rollie and rings an officer at the Department of Housing. After he greets her with the usual niceties, they discuss the problems of the building. Together, they collaborate on a letter for her to type up, photocopy and send to him, so that he can forward them by hand to all of his neighbours.

By composing the letter, rather than making a general complaint, the matter will be dealt with immediately, rather than lingering on into the following year. 'Dear Residents,' begins Woolley, 'Just a reminder ... that the laundry door is to be kept closed.'

He goes on to cite the reasons why: safety in the event of a fire. He also reminds residents that they must do their washing between the appointed times of six a.m. and eleven p.m.

As Woolley continues to talk, Leo appears in the open door-way, grinning. 'Does this mean we're gonna have a Christmas Party?' Leo asks.

Woolley waves to him to be quiet. He clears his throat: 'Finally, it is important that residents ... dispose of any unwanted house-hold items ... safely.' He draws on his rollie and shifts in his seat. 'Under no circumstances is anything to be thrown from the balconies.'

He winds up the phone call and drops his rollie in the ashtray.

'Does this mean we're gonna have a Christmas party?' Leo repeats.

Woolley stands and smooths down his Hawaiian shirt. 'We're going to have to write up a shopping list,' he announces. 'And a guest list, too.'

'I'll throw in a case of beer!' announces Leo, thrilled with this development. 'I'll throw in a case of beer!'

Three days until Christmas
Multiple copies of the letter that Woolley dictated yesterday have arrived at Ponderosa via Express Post. He rips open the envelope and takes them out. I expect him to begin slipping them under the doors of his neighbours immediately, but first he takes a pencil, turns the letters over, and begins numbering them with a tiny scribble in one corner. Once all twenty-three pages are numbered, he walks out into the corridor and begins making his rounds.

An hour later, with a shopping trolley borrowed from Don, Woolley and Leo make the trek up the hill to Coles. They plan to finance the party through the judicious use of vouchers, which they collect year-round from ATMs and supermarkets.

'Another lurk we've got,' says Woolley, following Leo onto the escalator, 'is we volunteer for scientific experiments.' He explains that only just recently he and four other Ponderosa dwellers signed up for medical research into liver function. 'All we had to do was fill out a questionnaire, have a blood test and a liver scan,' he says.

We step off the escalator and Leo runs towards the meat sec-tion like a kid let loose in a toy shop. 'And for that, we each get a $20 voucher for Coles,' continues Woolley. 'It all adds up, you know.'

We arrive back at Ponderosa, laden with bags of kebabs, bread rolls and frankfurts. As Woolley pulls the shopping trolley along the ground-floor corridor, he spots a balled piece of paper lying in the garden. Shaking his head, he pauses, picks it up and smooths it out. I can see that it has the Housing NSW logo on the upper left-hand side. Woolley turns the piece of paper over and studies the number pencilled in the corner.

'Bloody Sharkey,' he says. 'He's taken a notice about not throwing anything over the balcony – and thrown it over the balcony.'

'Who's Sharkey?' I ask.

'Lives on the third floor,' says Woolley.

'He was once a cellmate with Ronald Ryan!' announces Leo. 'With Robert Ryan! He was once a cellmate with Robert Ryan!'

Woolley notices the puzzled look on my face, and leans in to explain. 'Ronald Ryan was the last man to be hanged in Australia.'

One day until Christmas

We walk outside from Woolley's unit to find someone has tipped white powder all over the trees, the plants, the flowers and the outdoor furniture. Woolley drops to one knee and fingers the coarse, pale granules, lifting a sample to his nose and sniffing expertly, like a forensic scientist analysing a drug sample.

'You reckon it was Sharkey again?' I ask.

'There's only one person in the building who uses this brand of washing powder.' He tilts his head back and gazes up at the third floor.

'Not the junkie again,' I say.

Woolley rests his hands on his hips. 'Maybe he thought it was artificial snow?'

Christmas Day

Today, Ponderosa wakes up to more items that have been tossed over the balcony throughout the night: a tube of toothpaste, biscuit wrappers, and what looks like a large puddle of porridge lying on the walkway. 'But it could be spew,' observes Woolley, leaning closer.

'One day, that cunt threw a drawer over the balcony,' says Don, 'and it crushed a lime tree that I'd just planted.' The avid gardener and chef has been up half the night, marinating and preparing kebabs for the Ponderosa Christmas party, and he is not impressed by his neighbour's attempts to sabotage the celebration.

Meanwhile, I return to Woolley's unit and inspect the tiny courtyard. Overnight the rats, too, have been hard at work. Three holes the size of basketballs have appeared in the ground, with burrows that curve beneath the paling fence. I glimpse Butch the spotter a few yards down, sitting in the sun, his eyes closed.

While Leo fills recycling bins with bags of ice and beer, Woolley prepares salads and nibblies. A table already sits in the rainforest garden outside, surrounded by empty chairs. At around four p.m., the first of the guests begin to arrive, cradling beers in stubby holders. Leo introduces me to eighty-seven-year-old Theo, a pensioner whose unit is rumoured to be the worst affected by the building's mould. As Theo leads me to his door, I notice how impeccably he is dressed on this hot and steamy day: a crisp white shirt, a tie, a waistcoat and matching trousers.

When he opens the door, the spore stench hits me before I even cross the threshold. I follow him inside and am shocked to see a thick grey sludge growing across the walls, ceilings and kitchen floor, like some gigantic toxic blob from the set of a horror film.

Almost gagging, I ask, 'How long has it been like this?'

'Seven years!' he replies, exasperated. 'Seven times they visit to look at the unit. And seven times they do nothing!'

He points to the ceiling of his bathroom, which is sagging so severely it looks as if it's about to collapse. Theo tells me that it's due to a faulty toilet upstairs which, despite many complaints, has never been fixed. He then calls my attention to the shower recess. Sixteen years ago, a former tenant removed the tiled barrier along one side of the recess and so, for the past decade and a half, every time Theo showers, the water runs straight across the floor and into the carpet in the living room.

'I'm eighty-seven years old!' cries Theo, shaking a fist. 'They probably wait until I die before they come to fix the place!'

I take photos of the mould and reassure him that I will try to help in any way I can. I lay a hand on his shoulder and invite him back to the party, but he is too upset to socialise – even on Christmas Day. I leave him standing in his kitchen, arms hanging at his side, bewildered by the conditions in which he is forced to live.

Back outside, someone is strumming a guitar. As I walk along the path, a bar stool comes flying over an upstairs balcony, arcs through the air and crashes onto the paving, barely missing Don. Those who are chatting and drinking pause briefly to look over at the missile and return to their conversations. I pop my head into Woolley's unit and am met by Leo, who has been charged with delivering plates of food to any resident too ill or too shy to join us. I offer to help and follow him down the corridor.

He knocks on Butch's door; the door opens a little and Leo passes the plate to a gnarled hand that quickly disappears before the door is slammed shut. 'Butch is too pissed to come to the party,' explains Leo. 'But he told me he wanted something to eat.'

Our next visit is to eighty-nine-year-old Albert, who opens his door and receives his Christmas meal with gratitude, thanking Leo repeatedly in a soft, strangled voice, before erupting into a coughing fit. For sixteen years, Leo, Woolley and Don have always ensured that Albert has a good, solid meal on Christmas Day.

We climb the stairs to the third floor and stroll along until we come to Sharkey's unit. Leo bangs on the door and suddenly we see the peephole darken.

'Merry Christmas, Sharkey!' cries Leo. He holds up the plate of food.

We can hear Sharkey snorting for a moment, but the eye remains glued to the other side of the peephole.

'Fuck off, Leo!' he shouts.

Leo picks up the last hot dog, flashes his manic grin, leans in close to the peephole and takes a huge bite.

'Merry Christmas!' he announces, laughing. 'Merry Christmas, Sharkey!'

Bad Writer

Michael Mohammed Ahmad

All happy families are alike; each unhappy family is unhappy
in its own way.

> Leo Tolstoy, *Anna Karenina*

Two years ago the British Centre for Literary Translation invited
me to Anhui Province in China to participate as a guest author
in its annual translation program. I was asked to facilitate a creative writing workshop with the English-speaking participants in
the program, which would follow on from a workshop run by
Vietnamese-Australian author of *The Boat*, Nam Le. For two
hours I watched patiently and quietly as Nam worked with twenty
aspirational writers and translators who had come to China from
all over the (Western) world, including Australia, the United
States, Ireland, Scotland and England. Nam wrote six random
words up on a chalkboard, 'shoes', 'man', 'mountain', 'love',
'fear' and 'fingers', and then he told the participants to each
write a short story or poem using these six words. I was disappointed to hear the writers in the group read back the stories
they wrote, which all followed the same thread: *A man wandered
a mountain in a pair of shoes, searching for love and afraid he would
find it.* It did not occur to even one of them that a mountain
could be in love with a man or a shoe could be afraid of a finger,
or more importantly, that the mountain, the man, the shoes and
the finger could all have a specific identity. After all, we were in

view of China's Sacred Yellow Mountain, and with so much diversity in the room, participants had dirt on their shoes and under their fingernails from places no-one else in the group could have imagined. It was at this point that I realised the universality of bad writing: the bad writing that this international collective of writers produced was no different from the bad writing I had dealt with as a writer, editor, publisher and teacher in Western Sydney for over fifteen years.

Although this essay deals specifically with the bad writing I have encountered in Western Sydney, my argument is that bad writing can never actually be distinctive of one place. Any distinction writing makes for itself is inherently good, which is why there has always been so much potential for good writing to be from and about Western Sydney. What makes bad writing universal is that it lacks detail, originality, specificity and a sense of character and place, it depends on generalisations and clichés (both in terms of language and story), and it only reproduces common tropes and ideas which are propagated in mainstream literature, film, television, music and radio, making it so unremarkable that it could have been written anywhere by anyone at any time. Therefore, while bad writing in Western Sydney has everything in common with bad writing everywhere else, good writing in Western Sydney, and good writing everywhere else, has nothing in common with good writing anywhere else – it is good as an unhappy family is unhappy, in its own way.

Since 2006 I have been running a literacy movement in Western Sydney now called Sweatshop, which is devoted to empowering people from socio-economically challenged and culturally and linguistically diverse backgrounds through reading, writing, critical thinking, creative expression and creative outcomes. The principles of Sweatshop are built on the ideas of African-American feminist, scholar and activist bell hooks, who in an interview with the Media Education Foundation in 1997 argued that all steps towards freedom and justice in any culture depend on mass-based literacy movements because degrees of literacy determine how we see what we see. I have always found this to be a significant alternative to the usual way that Australian parents, carers, teachers and politicians discuss the importance of literacy to young people – in the romantic sense that it is important simply because it is a good in itself or the capitalist sense that it is important because it will give you access to a good job. For hooks, degrees of literacy define our ability to be critical of social systems (which may be racist, sexist, homophobic and/or classist) and to create alternatives to these systems, specifically through critical consciousness, critical discussion and artistic self-representation. Unfortunately, while I've used this model over the years to witness the development of many bad writers who want to become good writers, my general experience is that most aspirational writers I've had to work with are no good, do not know it, do not want to find out, and are not interested in improving.

*

But creative writing is subjective! This is the most obvious and common response that bad writers throw at me when I tell them that their work needs revision. Ironically, my issue with bad writing is always the same: it is not subjective. What these people are writing is consumed with clichés, vague images (or no images), no detail and no specificity, no sense of place, no sense of character and no distinction of voice. Take, for example, Christopher, a thirty-nine-year-old bad writer from Yagoona who sent me a piece of writing that started like this: *The following story is about love, the love between a man and his bitch.*

I agreed to meet Christopher to discuss his story at the reading garden of the new Bankstown library, a building with so much glass that you can see right through it to the old library across the road, which is by contrast a concrete slab with no visible windows at all. Christopher sat in front of a statue of the Lebanese writer Kahlil Gibran that was erected to celebrate the contributions of the Lebanese community to the Bankstown area, and stared at me with an unsettling blue-eyed gaze as he awaited my response to his work. I told him that he could delete the first line, because the story he wanted to tell hadn't actually started yet, but that even if he wanted to keep the line, I had heard other writers attempt to produce this exact same effect with this exact same wording many times before. He raised his eyebrows at me and responded, 'But how would you know if you've heard these words before, English isn't even your first language.' Aside from the fact that English *is* my first language, my concern here is the White belief that bilingual writers and editors from non-English-speaking backgrounds are less capable of identifying subjectivity in English writing than White writers. I told Christopher that being multilingual enhances the ability to imagine, create and critically engage with works of literature because it diversifies modes of thinking, which according to Noam Chomsky is the primary purpose of language, but that the problems with his piece were so fundamental, even a literary critic who did not speak a word of English would probably recognise them. As I spoke, Christopher had a smug smile on his shabby Ed Sheeran face as if all he could hear was, *Ah durka durka Allahu-akbar.*

While some bad writers use 'subjectivity' to argue that I am underqualified to assess their work, there are those who use 'subjectivity' to argue that I am *over-qualified* to assess their work. I was invited to facilitate a workshop for a multicultural writers' group that regularly meets on the second level of a kebab shop in Auburn. The room was dim and on one wall there was a picture of Hassan Nasrallah standing in front of a microphone with his mouth wide open and his fingers making the A-OK hand gesture and on the other side was a picture of the Ayatollah Khomeini with a deep-set frown and his hands out in front of him as though he were holding a Qur'an. This seemed like the perfect environment to wrest some kind of Auburn-esque literature from a group of twelve ethnic writers who were so mixed they looked like a bag of Skittles. The first person to share her writing with the group was a Maltese woman named Tanika. She wore a beret and, I swear on Allah, was holding a feather pen. In a tight bogan accent she read out a story that started like this: *'Fuck you!' the boy roars, spitting venom. A look of disbelief washed over my face, an illusion of compassion that really wasn't there.*

I told Tanika that this sentence was simply a compilation of common images. She was imposing them on us rather than revealing anything through sensory experiences, descriptions of the setting or characters, or anything that is literally or figuratively happening in the scene. Bad writers use this type of exposition after a quotation to elaborate the offensiveness of a comment – but either comments like 'fuck you' are sufficiently offensive that a writer/narrator does not need to stress how offensive they are by saying they are 'roars' or 'spits of venom', or the comments are simply not offensive and the writer is just forcing the idea that they are offensive on us because the comment and the reaction to the comment don't carry their own weight.

As for the *look of disbelief that washed over her face*, I told Tanika that here she had stepped outside of herself to give us yet another cliché – and even if these words weren't old and tired, how can a writer know that a look of disbelief had washed over her face if she's writing from the first-person perspective? On a technical level it is only possible for the first-person narrator to describe how the comment made her feel, and how she imagines her reaction to the comment made her look, example, *Tanika's bad writing made me wish I was wrapped in white sheets and stoned to death.* Then I told Tanika that she finished this sentence with a technique I call the anti-image: *an illusion of compassion that really wasn't there.* Here the bad writer identifies and describes the *absence* of a setting, characteristic or emotion because, I presume, she thinks it will make her sound more 'literary'. 'But if the feeling or image you are describing is not there, then why waste time, words and space discussing it?' I asked her. 'Why aren't you telling us what is there rather than what isn't?'

Tanika didn't give me the smug grin that I spotted on Christopher. Instead she stared at me as if I had smashed the Ten Commandments, completely bewildered and confused. Then she said, 'It's like you're trying to teach me university stuff, but creativity isn't something you can learn.' Such bad writers often pigeonhole me as the narrow-minded snob who cannot appreciate the uniqueness of individual voice because I'm so academically educated that I now have a conservative and restricted understanding and expectation of great literature. But rather than insisting that creative writing was her God-given talent, if Tanika was even slightly interested in learning about creative writing as an academic skill and vocation (which Auburn Council was paying me to teach her), she might not have strutted out of the room like the Queen of Sheba before I could show her the following piece, which was written by a student at Lurnea High School and published in a Sweatshop anthology called *Violence*:

We like to bully Mohamed and Yousif
because they are gay and ugly
because they are show off
because they are bitch
because they are ass holes.

When I share this piece with participants in my creative writing workshops, I ask them two questions, for which I usually get the same answers:

'What is it?'

'Graffiti.'

'Is it good?'

'It's rubbish.'

I then explain that I had published the piece under the assumption that it was in fact a poem, not graffiti (even though I am well aware that graffiti can be poetry), and that it displays many of the features of poetic language that writers are expected to identify and appreciate in the classroom – metaphor, since the author does not literally mean that Mohamed and Yousif are homosexuals or female dogs, and repetition, because because because ... The poem is untitled and the writer is anonymous but when I ask participants in my workshops what they can uncover about the writer's identity from the writing itself, they can often work out that it was written by someone young, male, from a non-English-speaking background (migrant or refugee) from Western Sydney and who is influenced by both Australian-English and American-English vernacular and popular culture. That is an impressive amount of detail to be able to extract about an anonymous writer from what they had deemed 'graffiti' and 'rubbish'. Secondly I ask the students what this poem is about and they always interpret it literally. They say, 'It's about bullying.' The ones who see themselves as cleverer and are trying a little harder, like the Chinese and Indian kids in the Gifted and Talented class at Parramatta's Saint Blah Blah High School say, 'It's about two or more people being racist to Mohamed and Yousif.' Never in five years of teaching this poem has any participant realised the unique sense of irony that is being evoked in the words, that the writer was sitting in the classroom in front of his friends Mohamed and Yousif and was using my writing exercise to make fun of them, who laughed along with him when he read the piece back to me. Analysis of this poem serves two purposes: to identify first that good writing is always unconventional, unique and complex (even in its simplicity), and second that education and training specific to creative writing enhance any writer's ability to read and write creatively, rather than diminish or limit a 'natural' ability to do so.

Of course for bad writers the idea of learning creative writing through education and training is unheard of. *Learn? What do you mean learn? Good writing comes from the heart.* This would be a completely unacceptable attitude in any other discipline. Would you try to perform brain surgery or replace a car engine or get into a professional boxing ring because you have heart? Nobody is denying that to be good at one of these professions you need to have a passion for them – but this is not supposed to be a substitute for education and training. Boxing is a particular area where I can draw some useful analogies because I was a fighter before I was a writer. I strode into the Belmore PCYC like every other Lebo in Bankstown, with my chin high and my chest cocked and a cigarette wedged between my left ear and my razored head. I peered over the boxing ring at a Lebanese boxer shorter and skinnier than me – five foot five and fifty-five kilos max. 'I can knock you,' I said to him, and straightaway he stepped over and spread apart the ropes, inviting me into the ring. I proceeded to throw straight jabs at his head and every time he'd roll under them and give me a roundhouser into the rib, sucking the air from my lungs and my loins, until finally, not even one minute into the fight, he stung me so hard with a right uppercut in the stomach that I went down on the canvas and began to spew up that night's dinner (potato and gravy and two pieces of fried chicken from KFC). Then the Leb called everyone in the gym to come over and have a look at me, and he said out loud while I continued to spew, 'You see, that's what happens when you act like a hard cunt!'

The Leb taught me quickly and painfully and embarrassingly that to be a great boxer, I needed a qualified trainer, someone to watch me from the outside and advise me on my technique – the speed, power, procession and combinations of my punches, my stance and footwork, my defence, my fitness, my stamina and my endurance. I needed the right diet, to put the right food in my body and to keep drugs, alcohol, cigarettes and hubbly bubbly out; and I needed fellow boxers around me, who would get in the ring with me and spar regularly, enabling me to apply the theoretical skills I was learning on pads and bags.

Now, as a teacher of creative writing, every day I have bad writers waltz into my office the way I waltzed into that gym, confidently handing me their work and expecting me to be knocked out by their creative genius, unaware that they are about to hit the canvas. Just like I learned in boxing, I tell them that if they want to be great writers, they need a qualified trainer, what we call in the industry an editor, someone who is watching them from the outside and keeping an eye on their form, technique, development of characters, settings, details and voice, someone who is providing them with critical feedback on an ongoing basis. It is often difficult for me as an editor to convince bad writers that this is a healthy and normal part of the business, which should be accepted without taking personal offence. Next I tell them they need the right diet, not necessarily what they put into their bodies (though I often think a lot of these bad writers need to cut back on the snacks and alcohol and do some sit-ups and push-ups), but what they are putting into their minds: what are they reading, watching and listening to? Here's a scale I use to measure the quality of a writer's diet: *Fifty Shades of Grey* is KFC and *The Swan Book* is the vegetables you grow in your backyard.

Then of course there is sparring for a writer. In boxing this requires a fighter to step into the boxing ring with his or her peers and throw hands, not to hurt one another but to learn from one another and refine technique through one another. With the exception of the writers' collective I have been running at Sweatshop, I have not found another group that has been able to achieve a serious culture of sparring. Usually I attend one of these groups as a guest author and witness bad writers who exchange stories, which they read from start to finish, only to be praised by their fellow writers' group members with perhaps a light tweak or criticism here or there regardless of how unoriginal, unsophisticated and undeveloped the work might be. At Sweatshop nobody is allowed to pull their punches; we train the members to listen to each other's work, find every opening available and strike. Sometimes we will do a stop-and-start edit, in which we will interrupt the writer as they read to offer suggestions specific to each line or paragraph or scene, sometimes we will listen to an entire piece and give an overview of where the piece could improve (though this is rare), and sometimes we will ask the writer to read the piece a few times over (especially if it is a poem by a good poet) because there are particular details that need clarifying.

On multiple occasions bad writers who have attended the Western Sydney Writers' Group for the first time find our feedback extremely confronting and offensive and don't ever return, assured that we simply do not know what we are talking about. To these people I say, *Salaam alaikum!* I don't want to work with anyone who cannot take constructive criticism, who cannot rewrite, and who cannot separate the personal pain of writing about their dead grandmother from the professional craft of conveying the story about their dead grandmother in an effective and original way (and I have also found that it is extremely difficult to help these kinds of people anyway). Take, for example, this Palestinian-Australian girl that once attended our writers' group named Leila, who had an American accent because she learned English at an international school in Abu Dhabi. Of course it was confronting and upsetting to be told that a story about her four-year-old cousin who died in a crossfire on the Gaza Strip is no good, but in all fairness no-one had actually questioned the degree to which she loved her dead cousin, we had simply pointed out that it was lacking in detail and characterisation, preventing us from feeling and understanding the experience of her loss, to write: *I woke up to the news that my sweet beautiful gorgeous baby cousin was deceased and the rest of the day was a blur.* Leila argued that my heartless feedback proved I had Asperger's syndrome. She even recommended that I see a doctor called Jamal Rifi about it, who by coincidence has been my family physician since 1996.

On another occasion I made a bad writer cry because I stopped her while she was still reading so our writers' group could begin discussing her work. This woman told us she had nine children, which I believed because the sleep bags under her eyes looked like onion rings, and that she was Indian, which I did not believe because she was fairer than a snowflake and kept wobbling her head as though she had something to prove. For three minutes my writers' group listened as she read a five-page poem called 'Africa', in which she listed generic and clichéd images about starving black children in a Third World 'country' she'd undoubtedly seen on television, with lines such as: *Africa, a country of wonder in my eye. Hunger, to live and die.* Then finally, after we had heard more than enough to offer an analysis, I interrupted her and began to explain that if she'd actually been to some countries in Africa, then she should speak specifically about herself in relation to those places, or if she was simply writing about her impression of the continent of Africa based on what she'd seen on television, then this was fine too, but only if she came clean and framed the poem in such a way. Indeed, a fair-skinned wannabe-Indian mother of nine living in Harris Park and making judgements about the Third World based on what she sees on the television is more interesting than any of her white saviour fantasies. Straightaway her eyes began to swell and her head began to wobble out of control. She said, 'How can you know if it's good or bad without having heard all of it?' Usually at the core of this response is that the bad writer wants an audience rather than a critic – someone to listen to their story and their pain and show them compassion as though we are offering a free group therapy session (which is what most writers' groups actually become). Nonetheless, to answer the question of 'how do you know?' at face value, the truth is that if a bad writer doesn't know what good writing is on the first page, it's impossible that they have worked it out on the fifth page, and a good editor will pick this up straightaway – especially when the title of the piece is 'Life Happens'.

While some bad writers are not interested in any education and training, there are those who conduct what I call pseudo education and training. These bad writers respond to criticism of their work by claiming that they are emulating or drawing from the techniques and style of a good writer they have been reading. For example, we had a bad Croatian writer named Victor (after a lawnmower) who attended our writers' group for over eight years. This was a middle-aged father of four who only ever wore bland-coloured trousers and checked shirts from

Lowes and had a monotonous reading voice that sounded like Stephen Hawking's speech synthesiser (which is rare because most writers in Western Sydney, even the bad writers, come from cultural backgrounds with developed oral storytelling systems and can perform their writing pretty well). At every workshop Victor attended, instead of taking any notes about his writing, which were always based on the fact that he was not being specific enough about who his characters were and where they were from, he argued that we were burdening him with cultural representation and that he simply wanted to write 'the universal man' and 'the universal place'.

'There is no universal man and place in literature,' I told Victor week after week and year after year, even though I was well aware from his conventional family life, computer voice and plain outfits that he saw *himself* as the universal man.

'But that's how James Joyce writes,' he responded.

Only a clumsy illiterate halfwit might think there is something universal about Leopold Bloom and Dublin on 16 June 1904 – and the problem is that such responses are predicated on the assumption that reading your favourite writer means you can now write like your favourite writer. I have no doubt that bad writers *think* they are writing the way James Joyce was writing but this is as absurd as a bad fighter thinking they can now fight like Muhammad Ali because they watched a video of him floating like a butterfly and stinging like a bee. Imagine this bad fighter then went to a boxing gym and displayed his Muhammad Ali fighting style to a trainer, only to be told that his footwork is a fumbling mess, his defence has major holes in it, and his punches are slow, sloppy and weak. 'But that's how Muhammad Ali fights!' the bad fighter responds.

To adopt the style of a favourite boxer, bad fighters need to start from the ground up, learn how to stand before they learn how to float, learn how to jab before they learn how to sting. Similarly, to adopt the style of a favourite writer, bad writers need to start from the word up, learn how to manage a three-line sentence before learning how to manage a four-page sentence, learn how to write a short story before trying to write a novel – it's unbelievable the number of bad writers who decide one day that they are going to write a novel and turn over

100,000 words before having had any confirmation from an editor, critic, publisher or accomplished writer that they can even write 1000 words.

A more embarrassing response than 'But that's how James Joyce writes' is what I call the Milhouse defence – which draws reference to a moment in *The Simpsons* where Milhouse is criticised by Mr Burns and responds, 'But my mom says I'm cool.' Bad writers use this rhetoric to rebut criticism offered by an editor or literary critic or creative writing teacher; they claim that some well-known writer, who was clearly patronising them like a blind mother, said their writing is good. For example, during a writers' workshop I was facilitating at the Blacktown Arts Centre, I met a young woman named Belle, the daughter of a plastic surgeon who adventured all the way over from North Sydney to show me a personal essay about how she envied the poverty-stricken kids she encountered in Mumbai: *It didn't matter that I was staying at a five-star hotel, brown kids just seemed to know how to laugh on the streets.* I told her that this piece lacked a certain humour and irony about herself which was needed to distance it from yet another case of Poor White Girl syndrome. 'Well, I did a workshop in Bangalore with Arundhati Roy and she said my work was pretty damn great,' Belle shot back. This is a pathetic and disrespectful approach to the maternal and paternal figures we adopt in our writing lives. First, Arundhati Roy wasn't at the workshop in Blacktown to defend such a claim, so I guess we just had to take Belle's word for it; second, even if Arundhati Roy thought Belle's essay was good, that did not mean she would have disagreed with my criticisms and discouraged Belle from any revisions; and third, even if Arundhati Roy once told Belle that she was God's gift to literature, how does that change the fact that I spotted a serious flaw in her work?

*

So now that I have detailed some bad attitudes towards writing, what are good attitudes towards writing? Unfortunately, there are some aspects of creative writing, like in all creative arts, that simply cannot be learned. No-one can just give you the identity or experiences to tell an interesting, new, important or worthwhile story (which explains why so many writers steal them) and no-one can just give you a unique voice or a unique method of evoking, manipulating and evolving the English language, or any other language for that matter. This is why I have always believed that writers from Western Sydney have a particular advantage for creating new Australian literature. It is a region where culture is an orgy of Leb, fob, nip, skip, wog and curry-muncher; where gender is a lawyer in a burka living next door to a Thai masseuse who gives Muslim boys hand jobs; where class is the great-grandchild of Ataturk who is stalking his second cousin on welfare at Auburn Japanese Gardens; and where sexuality is a clash between the Suzuki-driving hausfrau suburban gays of the south-west and the herds of transgender sex workers soliciting truckers in Mount Druitt.

Fortunately, however, for everyone there are some aspects of creative writing that can and must be learned. This involves *research*. To produce a great piece of literature a writer needs to engage in creative writing with the same degree of study, investigation and examination that one would need to engage in academic writing, or any other discipline. And while there are plenty of methods of research for creative writing, in this essay I will summarise them within four distinct categories:

1. Technique
Writers need to develop an understanding of the linguistics of the English language, including a practical knowledge of all the language tools, such as commas, full stops, quotation marks, ellipses, italics, section breaks, colons and semicolons, in order to effectively convey what they are trying to communicate. We can learn about spelling and grammar in texts like Bill Bryson's *Troublesome Words* (1984). For example, Bryson explains that the comma is the most abused and overused of punctuation marks in the English language, which is why, as a copyeditor, and proofreader, I have spent, half my career, just, deleting, them. Another example Bryson discusses is the ellipsis, which in spite of the fact that it can indicate any given length of time is only ever supposed to be three stops. (Some do argue that it is four stops if you use it at the end of a sentence because you also need to include the full stop.) The fact that so many bad writers think the number of stops that form an ellipsis is determined by the length of time

that has passed is the reason editors always have to deal with one
of these ....

Furthermore, technique refers to how a writer might handle
literary systems in creative writing such as tense, perspective,
voice, pace, time, and if a writer is multilingual, how to negoti-
ate the use of two or more languages in Australian English. One
time I tried to explain this to the monotoned universalist, Victor,
whose latest story was constantly moving in and out of the past
and present tense by accident. By this point Victor was a self-
proclaimed Joycean scholar and quickly spat back, 'James Joyce
doesn't follow any of these rules in *Finnegans Wake*.' This was a
total and typical misreading of what Joyce was doing – he was not
misusing the language because he didn't understand it, he was
manipulating language to his will because he understood it so
well. Indeed, the stronger one's grasp of a language, the more
one can bend the language, transform it, and reintroduce it as
new language. To Victor I said, 'Please don't mix up your ignorance with Joyce's genius.' And that was the last time I saw him,
a way a lone a last a loved a long the riverrun ...

2. Subject matter

If a writer is producing a work of fiction which concerns horseracing or mountain climbing or in my case boxing, it stands that the
writer needs to do some research into the subject. This kind of
research might involve practical application, as in you actually
do some horseracing or mountain climbing or boxing, as well as
some theoretical research into the field, for example investigating what mountaineers have said about mountain climbing or
sports historians have said about boxing. If you are writing about
people, then of course you need to do some research about these
people. Now you've already done half the research if you're writing about your own people, which is why writers are always
encouraged to write what they know, not to mention that this is
steeped in the politics of decolonisation, self-determination and
empowerment, so hands off our stories, Whitie! But even if you
are writing about an identity that is your own, you could investigate some of the creative and academic texts on your identity
that are already out there. In Tamar Chnorhokian's case it was
certainly to her advantage that her novel *The Diet Starts on Monday*

(Sweatshop, 2014), was about a physically and mentally challenged Armenian-Australian Apostolic girl from Fairfield and
that she was a physically and mentally challenged Armenian-
Australian Apostolic girl from Fairfield. However, after I read the
original manuscript I said to Tamar, 'What is your malfunction,
numbnuts?' Then I deleted two-thirds of the book in one reading, 40,000 words in total, and as she started over on an Apple
computer so old it still had 'Macintosh' in the logo, I stood over
her right shoulder and screamed into her ear: 'Research food
groups and how they each impact and shape our bodies, you
worm! Research dieting programs that actually work and the
technical processes involved in undertaking them, you slob!
Research socio-economic and cultural factors that directly
impact people's health in Western Sydney, you loser!' And while
Tamar sobbed and read and typed, I continued shouting until I
could feel the veins in my neck throbbing and my voice straining,
'Read some literary criticism about Armenian literature, you sad
case! Read creative fiction about fat people, you maggot!' Finally,
the manuscript was ready and Tamar was standing upright outside my office. Her eyes tipped back into her skull, her teeth
bared, she held the new draft to her chest and said, 'This manuscript is mine, there are many just like it, but this one is mine.'

Even if a writer's subject matter is based on fantasy or science
fiction it still requires a serious degree of research in order to
create a convincing fictional realm. Stories about space travel
need some understanding of orbital mechanics, which were
developed and written about with detailed scientific accuracy
and language in texts such as Arthur C. Clarke's *2001: A Space
Odyssey* (1968). Stories about aliens or monsters need some
understanding of the laws of nature, biology and anatomy,
which were stitched together with disturbing consequences in
Mary Shelley's *Frankenstein* (1818). (It is worth noting that Mary
Shelley also drew from the most advanced scientific understanding of electricity and chemistry available in the early nine-
teenth century in order for Victor Frankenstein to bring his
monster to life.) And stories about robots need some technical
understanding of electronics, mechanics and robotics, which
became a standard in the prolific number of short stories and
novels written by science fiction writer and scientist Isaac

Asimov throughout the last century, including most famously his collection of nine short stories called *I, Robot* (1950) (though claiming Asimov conducted research into robotics is an oxymoron since he was the one that invented the term 'robotics' while thinking it already existed).

3. Genre

This is the category of writing a writer chooses to work in, be it autobiography or autobiographical fiction or magic realism or romance or satire, or even a new, experimental or hybrid category. In addition to reading extensively within the genre you would like to write in, this also requires researching the academic and literary tradition of that genre – for example, understanding the history of the Gothic plays just as an important role in how a writer deals with the subject of vampires as does reading vampire novels, even if it is only to subvert the tradition. Vampires are a particularly relevant topic for me because every time I have taught creative writing in a girls' high school since the *Twilight* series entered our global consciousness, I have been swamped with stories about some misogynist named Edward Cullen. My tolerance for this fad notwithstanding, I've often argued to these teenage girls that if they are in fact interested in producing creative writing about vampires they ought to do some research about the history of the vampire in literature: what does the vampire represent, what are the rules of the world in which the vampire exists and why. During my last workshop at Auburn Girls High School I said, 'You need to know these rules even if it's just to break them.' One girl in a pink hijab responded, 'Sir, do you mean like how Stephenie Meyer decided in *Twilight* that her vampires can go out into the sunlight?'

'Exactly,' I responded, 'exactly.'

4. Form

What kind of text does a writer want to produce – is it a novel, novella or novelette? Is it a vignette or a short story? Is it a hybrid form, a short story written in limericks perhaps? Is it a poem, a prose poem, a slam poem? If, for example, you are interested in writing poetry, then before you start rhyming and rambling on about the moon and the stars, love and hate, life and death – the gospels of bad poetry – ask yourself, 'What is a poem?' Investigate the history of the poem from the root of the word to the day the word was rooted by hip-hop and rap music. I was a teenager when I discovered that the ancient philosophers and the contemporary gangsta rappers on each end of this spectrum had come together to create the poetry of Punchbowl Boys High School. Etched into my English desk like rust and stardust were the words: *Jesus and Tupac are Muslim.*

Next we need to get specific about the kind of poetry and poems a writer wants to produce. Let us say, for example, you are going to write a collection of sonnets. Obviously you need to read a variety of sonnets, but it would also help to examine the context of the sonnet, where it came from and what purposes it serves. You need to learn about the technical guidelines for writing a sonnet – and whether these rules have ever been broken and why and how and by whom. Finally, you can begin experimenting with your own sonnets and find someone who has expertise in the form that can revise them with you. Hopefully this will result in the kind of exchange I had with the skinniest Pacific Islander kid I ever met at Belmore Boys High School. I read out loud, 'Shall I compare thee to a summer's day?' and he responded, 'Shall I compare your pussy to my dick, bro?' Behold the Bard of Belmore.

Perhaps the most complicated literary form is also the one that most bad writers attempt to produce – the novel. Some scholars argue that the novel is a relatively new form invented by English writers some time in the eighteenth century, while others argue that it is an ancient form, starting with Lady Murasaki's *Tale of Genji*, which was written in 1010. The novel has always tended to frighten people, from prohibitions because of controversial sexual content, such as Gustav Flaubert's *Madame Bovary* (1856), to fatwas because the novel has smeared the Prophet Muhammad, such as Salman Rushdie's *The Satanic Verses* (1988). What's most intriguing about the novel to me is that it really has no parameters. A novel can be 127 pages and have no chapters, like Hemingway's *The Old Man and the Sea* (1952) or it can be 1488 pages, like Vikram Seth's *A Suitable Boy* (1993). A novel can be written as a collection of sonnets, in iambic pentameter, like another of Vikram Seth's works, *The Gold Gate* (1986), or it can be told as a collection of vignettes, like Sandra Cisneros's *The House On Mango Street* (2009). It can constantly jump first-person perspective, like William Faulkner's *As I Lay Dying* (1930), or it can be divided into three parts, such as 'heat' and 'water' and 'light' in Ellen van Neerven's *Heat and Light* (2014). A bad writer in Year Seven, who weighed 100 kilos and whose voice had not broken yet, demonstrated to me why so many young people in Australia are given the entirely wrong impression about the novel from a very young age. He said, 'I am a novelist – I've written 300 pages and it has chapters.' I told him that these were not the criteria that determine what is a novel and that it was the responsibility of his English teachers to explore with him the history and diversity of a form which has radically changed lives and shaped societies and cultures for as long as it has existed.

*

Last year I was facilitating a writers' group for Penrith City Council, which in spite of the council's attempt to attract young people drew only four participants, each of whom was old enough to be one of my grandparents. Of the four, only one had claimed to have any formal education in creative writing, but I'm certain she was lying because she came into the workshop barefoot from across the street and said that her stories were so advanced and radical that the professors at Western Sydney University had kicked her out of the course. And of the four, none of them had ever been published anywhere but in community arts anthologies, the kind that includes every participant with no edits or revisions. I spent hours listening to these seniors read what can only be described as 'roses are red' poems, filled with lines such as *I saturate my heart and soul in your love*. I also spent hours trying to offer them some helpful advice to improve their writing, to write something honest, specific, tangible, to use original metaphors and symbols that I could see in my mind's eye, and to write something that was not a rehash of what they had been conditioned to believe a poem should be. One of the participants, who was named Harry and carried a walking stick, got so agitated by the idea that some educated Lebanese boy had tips for him that he began to shout at me, 'You're just another shifty Ayrab!' Then while he swung his walking stick in my face, missing me by an inch, he said, 'Go on, if you're so clever give us a poem, go on, give us a poem!'

This essay has not been about offending bad writers, though I'm well aware that the truth is often offensive and hard to hear. This essay seeks to inspire bad writers, to encourage them to take creative writing more seriously and not to think of it as a God-given talent which just comes naturally. Creative writing is not a skill or profession bad writers can simply work out for themselves as they sit up late at night typing at their computers with dim lighting and the theme from *Titanic* playing in the background, reading back lines they wrote and telling themselves, *that's some good shit right there*. This essay demands more from bad writers, because while I am certainly critical of bad writers, I also believe that bad writers who are interested in learning can become good writers. To those who are not interested in learning, however, I'll say to you what I said to Harry: 'Roses are red. Violets are blue. I'm not a poet. And neither are you.'

A Short History of the Italian Language

Moreno Giovannoni

Morè.

Morè.

Only an Italian can say that properly and there's only one person left who calls me that. The rest are dead.

The first words I ever heard were Italian ones. The first word I ever spoke was an Italian word – *papà*. This was according to my poor mum, who stopped speaking Italian when her vocal cords froze, together with the rest of her, in a nursing home bed, a few weeks before she died. We sat with her and exchanged the occasional Italian word. We spoke Italian words to her even though we didn't know if she could understand.

For the first three years of my life my only language was Italian. In the village where I was born Italian was in the air and the language went in through your soft baby skin and one day it came out your mouth, so you had no choice but to speak Italian.

Then they took me to Australia, where I spoke English with the Australians and Italian with my mother and father. This was the same Italian that the Australians used to call Eye-talian and the people who spoke it Eye-talians (and Eye-ties for short).

I became very good at English. I was the best speller in my class, probably in the world, and the best writer in the class. I was better at English than the Australian kids were. But in prep I struggled.

One day, at the age of four and a half, I came home from school distraught because I didn't know how to spell 'cheese'. I had written c-h-e-s-s. Cheese.

Another difficult word was 'banana'. I didn't know when to stop. I wrote bana-nana-nana- ...

I asked my mother, who said it was the same as in Italian – banana – and she wrote it down for me. I thought it was a trick. How could you turn one language into another and the spelling be the same? Then I realised that what my mother had done was not just a simple trick, it was a magic trick. Italian was powerful. She had translated a word. I realised that if I could harness the power of the Italian language it could solve all my Australian word problems. On that day I became a translator. For the rest of my life I knew I would be able to say things in two languages. I knew there was more than one way of saying the same thing. The world was suddenly much bigger, richer and more complex than the Australian monolinguals realised. It gave me such confidence that 'cheese' and 'banana' were the only words I ever misspelled.

*

When my brother was born I waited for him to start speaking. Would he speak English or Italian? At first he didn't speak at all. He just cried and cried so I shoved chunks of parmesan inside his little toothless mouth, because he was obviously hungry, but this upset my mother a lot. Sadly, my brother, when he did finally start, spoke English. English was in the Australian air and it went in through your skin when you were a baby and the English came out your mouth.

Later my brother learned to speak Italian but it wasn't the same. Between us Italian wasn't our natural language, the way it was with our parents. A natural language is the one you have to speak because you have no choice. My mother and father only spoke Italian so it was natural for me to speak Italian with them. I learned that languages are either natural or unnatural.

I also spoke Italian with family friends, people who visited on Sundays and ate hard little biscuits and drank small glasses of liqueur and strong cups of coffee. They were amazed at how well

I spoke Italian and how at the age of five I could already read the Italian newspaper to my uncle Succhio who had only completed three years of primary school. When he wanted to know what was happening in the world he would hand me *Il Globo* and say: *leggi*.

At school in Australia I studied Italian and at university in Italy I studied English. The two languages were seeking some kind of equilibrium. Back in Australia at university I studied English and Italian literature.

*

When my children were born I waited to see what language they would speak and sadly they only spoke English. It was my fault and it wasn't my fault. The law of natural and unnatural language applied. I didn't know enough baby talk to communicate with them in Italian. I even asked my mother to teach me baby talk, but it was too hard and I gave up. The English language in the Australian air smothered them. It entered their little baby pores and grew there until one day they started speaking English. It was unnatural for them to speak anything else.

A language is like a mother. My biological mother was Italian but the language that raised me from the age of three was English. I would always love my biological mother and wish we could be reunited. I even wished we had never been separated.

All my life Italian has been my big dirty secret. Even now the Australians don't know I carry it around inside. I used to feel that if people knew I spoke Italian they would charge me with something: breaking some kind of law, possession of a foreign language. Because I sound very Australian it's like being undercover.

*

The natural thing for me to do was to turn my Italian into a job, so many years ago I became a translator. This meant I could read, write and speak and be paid for it.

One day I'm called to a hospital. At the patient's bedside the Australian doctor says to me in English:

Tell this man he is dying and will be dead in a few days. He has very powerful bacteria in his blood and our strongest antibiotics have been unable to kill them. In fact the bacteria have been feeding off the antibiotics. The bacteria love the antibiotics and they have been growing. He now has very healthy, large and strong bacteria in his blood and soon the blood will no longer carry oxygen but just bacteria to his brain and heart and lungs. We have told him this in English but he apparently wants to hear it from someone like you in his own language which is Italian, is that right?

I nod. I am overwhelmed at the responsibility that is being thrust on the Italian language about to come out of my mouth. I am overcome with grief but as I open my mouth and start to speak I feel that old familiarity and warmth enter the relationship that the language is gently constructing between me and the dying man. He looks at me and watches the words flow out of my mouth. He relaxes visibly when I start speaking Italian. He has no family or friends who speak Italian.

The dying man taught me something that day. When he was born, the first language he heard was Italian. Now that he was dying he wanted to be told in the same language. Dying was like a new birth. He would come out of the womb again to the sound of his death. Your own language is your mother holding your hand, caressing your forehead. You do not want to die in a foreign language. As I left I remember thinking how I hoped the last language he would hear would be Italian, but this was not likely as he would be surrounded by Australian, English-speaking palliative care nurses.

One afternoon I went to the Royal Dental Hospital. The Italian patient there was being seen by a mouth, tongue and jaw specialist.

The doctor greeted me and gestured to the patient. What the patient said almost made me laugh. I stopped myself just in time.

Mmmmlowamwololoalow.

He tried again and failed.

Mmmmlowamwololoalow

The Australian specialist said:

Tell the man this: his tongue, his mouth, his lips, have forgotten how to speak. He has lived alone for so many years and has not spoken to anyone for such a long time that he has forgotten how to form words.

The man looked at me and I repeated in Italian what the doctor had said. Then he smiled and nodded and thanked me, speaking directly to me in Italian, without a problem in the world. The Australian looked at us suspiciously. What's going on here? He decided to check whether there

had been some kind of miracle cure, and asked him in English to say his
name. The Italian man said:

Mmmmlowamwololoalow

That day I realised not only that human beings yearn to die in their own language but also that they need to speak to each other in their natural language.

But a tragedy was looming.

*

When we arrived in Australia, at first it seemed that we were surrounded by Italians speaking Italian.

As decades passed family friends got older and died or moved and disappeared off the face of the earth. After all, they were my parents' friends not mine. I lost my Italian contacts. One thing is certain: all over Australia the Italians who speak Italian naturally are now dying.

Like stars in a black night sky the lights have been going out. You don't notice at first because each star is just a tiny pinprick. But by the time most of them have gone you see a large black space, until finally all you see are the few stars that are left. My Short History of the Italian Language is coming to an end.

My mother stopped speaking and died, my in-laws and old family friends died. And now there is just one star left – my father.

Oh Morè, queste chiacchierate con te mi fanno bene, sai come mi fanno
bene? Sono una cosa favolosa.

That's my father telling me how much he enjoys our chats on the phone. With my brother, we're the only Giovannonis from San Ginese in Australia left who speak Italian.

But back to the beginning.

Morè.

Morè.

In the natural order of things my father will die soon. He's ninety years old.

He's the only person in the world now who calls me Morè.

I never thought it would matter to me to be called Morè but when I stop hearing it, it will hurt.

*

My father lives in the country and used to call me to talk in Italian about everything. One night we had people around for dinner and he rang to ask me about the life span of his goose. He had kept a pet goose for twenty years and wanted to know how much time it had left. I googled it and told him a goose can live for twenty years. *Well then*, he said, *time's almost up* (I just translated that into English for your benefit).

Another time he was in his car and he stopped by the side of the road to call me to tell me how beautiful the sunset was. My father comes from a long line of peasants. He was a tobacco grower all his life, doing hard physical work, working long hours in mud or on dry cracked earth, but part of him has always been a romantic poet. He loved reading Italian books and magazines. He loved talking.

*

In the natural order of things my father will die soon. He's ninety years old. He's the only person left in the world who calls me Morè.

My Short History of the Italian Language ends this way.

It was inevitable that it would end this way. It ends with the realisation that the worst thing for a natural speaker of Italian is the inevitable silence at the other end of the phone line.

Up a Wombat's Freckle

Barry Humphries

'I hope there won't be any colloquialisms in this fillum Barry,' said Tom Stacey breathlessly. The senior Sydney accountant had bounded across the tarmac at Kingsford-Smith aerodrome to catch us before we boarded the flight to London to start filming *The Adventures of Barry McKenzie*. The director Bruce Beresford and I were co-authors of the screenplay and Mr Stacey was charged with administering the total production budget of $250,000 advanced to us by the Australian Film Corporation. He was nervous. Naturally I reassured him: 'It's a family film, Tom,' I lied in my teeth. When the film was released on 12 October 1972 and returned its total investment to the AFC in a matter of weeks, it was, notwithstanding, excoriated by every critic, journalist and disc jockey in Australia as a vulgar calumny; a cruel misrepresentation of Australian refinement. The script was a ceaseless stream of colloquialisms – new, obsolete and invented. It was the filthiest Australian film of the year, the nadir of Australian cinema, which by then had entered its soft focus 'idyllic' phase, representing the nice Australia we all wanted to inhabit. A few short years were to pass before another film company produced a sanitised version of Barry McKenzie about a working-class fellow who chased crocodiles and always wore a hat, a hero moreover who would have delighted the Stacey family. He soon became the approved and 'iconic' Australian hero. The reader should be warned that there are one or two colloquialisms in this essay, but Australian colloquialisms are either quaint and innocent or merely filthy. However, they are always sincere. The English have twenty-five ways of saying 'sorry' and they don't mean one of them.

However, I was overjoyed to find that the term 'pillow biter' had found its way into the magnificent, second edition of the *Australian National Dictionary*, edited by Bruce Moore under the venerable imprint of the Oxford University Press. I am proud to say that I was present when my friend, the aforementioned film-maker, Bruce Beresford, coined the term, inspired in the mid-1970s by a notorious case when a leading British Liberal politician made a much-publicised response to the allegations of an importunate catamite. The blackmailer complained in a letter, read to the court, of the initial discomfort of unlawful penetration. In response, The Right Honourable gentleman exhorted his correspondent to 'bite the pillow'. This exchange, at once graphic, homophobic or obfusc, is commemorated in the term 'pillow-biter', which I managed to successfully promote, especially in Sydney where no pillow goes unbitten.

This scholarly two volume work contains a generous entry under the word 'chunder', a word unknown in my youth outside the Geelong and Ballarat grammar schools, until I relentlessly promulgated it in the comic strip of Barry Mackenzie in *Private Eye*. There the eponymous hero regularly and compulsively regurgitated. This expressive, even onomatopoeic term took off in trendy London circles and is now in universal, colloquial use.

I have in my London library, an interesting collection of Australian dictionaries from Dr Karl Lentzner's *Slang English of Australia* of 1892, Cornelius Crowe's *Slang Dictionary* of 1895 right through to the lexicons of Eric Partridge and Sydney J. Baker, and, pride of my collection, the very rare First World War publication by W.H. Downing, *Digger Dialects*. And now eclipsing them all are the twin tomes of the new *Australian National Dictionary*.

Of course this work has not confined itself to the vernacular, but there is an arresting definition on every page. I am delighted, for example, to see that the 'mallee root' merits a learned entry. In obsolete rhyming slang a 'mallee' referred to sexual congress. Mallee roots were familiar objects in my Melbourne childhood, regularly delivered by our local woodman. They were the heavy, nodular roots of various eucalypts, deracinated from the red soil of the Mallee district in Victoria which subsequently became a dustbowl. For the middle classes, they were a popular, slow-burning fuel and I often watched my father heave one onto the grate. I am reminded of an anecdote once related by the comedian, Dick Bentley. During the London Blitz there was a small and subterranean bar near Piccadilly Circus, frequented by 'sensitive' gentlemen. One evening during a heavy air-raid which jangled the crème de menthe and Kummel bottles behind the bar, an expatriate Australian ballet dancer (Robert Helpmann?), always lightly rouged, staggered down the stairs covered with dust, 'Did you hear that?' he cried. 'It blew a chip off me mallee root pendant!' A brave jest which only a Melbourne or Adelaide person would really appreciate.

Needless to say, there are innumerable expressions to describe thirst and drunkenness but there are some I have noted which have eluded the lexicographer and not hitherto found their way into any dictionary. They illustrate Australian verbal ingenuity, and in stretching the expressive possibilities of the English language, they often possess a kind of sardonic poetry. A thirsty man might therefore say, 'I'm as dry as a Pommy's bathmat', which incorporates a reference to the well-known English aversion to bathing. I've also heard an inebriated man employ what must be the most offensive rhyming slang for intoxication when he declared, 'Sorry, mate, I'm a bit Schindlers.'

Of course, the use of the word 'mate' is ubiquitous in Australia and has slowly lost its old, comradely meaning. Not seldom it can now have a hostile ring, as in 'Whadaya think you're doin', mate?' It is often used by prime ministers, especially the Honourable Tony Abbott, whom I otherwise admire, who uses the word in order to sound down-to-earth and patriotic. We have even invented a thing called 'mateship' which imputes to us qualities of fellowship, generosity and even bravery which we do not always exhibit (see under 'world-class' and 'internationally-acclaimed').

Women are not always named respectfully and are not necessarily offended when called 'horn-bags' or 'ceiling inspectors'. The female anatomy has been a perennial inspiration to the anonymous genius who enriches our language with his verbal inventions. Female breasts are 'norks' or 'fun-bags' and in days gone by, if well-developed, commemorated a famous mail-bag robbery of 1863 in the New South Wales town of Mudgee: 'She's got norks on her like a pair of Mudgee mail bags.' The shape of the female pudenda has long been compared to the map of Tasmania and the ' labia majora' has not escaped the scabrous attentions of the Australian slang-meister and, if pendulous, I once heard them compared to the accoutrement of a once popular Hollywood cowboy: 'Geez they looked like Gene Autry's saddle bags!'

The modern Australian male, like men all over the world, rarely wears a hat, but in the 1930s and 1940s he never went out bare-headed. The artist Sidney Nolan told me his uncle once mysteriously referred to the crowd at a football match as having 'heads on them like mice'. I never understood this phrase until I saw an old newsreel of a footie match (Aussies love infantile diminutives: 'footie' for football, 'chewy' for chewing gum, etc.) and seen from above I observed a multitude of grey fedoras with their pinched crowns, which resembled nothing less than a plague of mice.

The editors of the new *Australian National Dictionary* have magnificently recorded what must surely be the richest vernacular in history of human utterance, and if you don't believe me you can stick your head up a wombat's freckle.

How Not to Speak Polish

Janine Mikosza

Clipped off by infinity. Poet and essayist Joseph Brodsky is describing the ends of a bridge arching over the Canal Grande on a night trip around Venice. On my reading of Brodsky's words to Janina, she speaks of her father: she is the bridge with no ends and her father is infinity.

Two Poles walk into a cafe. One is Janina, a second-generation Australian; I am an immigrant who occasionally struggles with the peculiarities of speaking English in this country. I want to write about Janina's life, so we sit in the cafe on Acland Street in St Kilda and Janina tells me she is scared of her father. She is middle-aged – at her last birthday she turned forty-eight – but she remains scared of a man she hasn't seen for many years. The fear sticks to her guts and it is the same size as it was when she was eight, nine, ten, eleven, twelve, thirteen years old.

Here is one meaning of *fear*: when a thought of someone or something arrives unwelcomed in your mind and begins a tug of war between your heart muscle with its needy hurt and every other muscle fibre in your body, rigid with adrenaline.

To unknot this sensation, the thought requires shaking loose. To *shake loose* means its opposite here: it is to *sit still* with a thought and the emotion fed by that thought. In her hands, Janina holds a filthy folded piece of paper. She unwraps it and reveals a hand-written list of dos and don'ts for the times in the day when her heart, mind and body separate and compete for attention. *Do* sit with the discomfort, which will roll over you like a wave (but mostly like a tsunami, Janina says). *Do* name the emotion. *Don't* resist it. *Don't* chase the thought or the feeling. *Do* accept the pain, and that what you are feeling right at this moment is your hurting heart, and that it will pass. *Do* this repeatedly, for as long as it takes until the suffering ends.

Janina speaks of her father in a whisper using his given name and even this is a reluctant utterance. She was born in Australia but carries his European past in her blood, skin and muscle. For four decades Janina has not spoken about what happened to her as a child. Some mornings she is surprised to be alive, surprised that she can see out another day. She is sensitised to the intensities of daily life, and recites to me lines from a poem (by a poet whose name she cannot recall) that reminds her of this vulnerability: 'With disbelief I touch the cold marble, / with disbelief I touch my own hand.'

It is Czesław Miłosz. This, I can understand. Miłosz writes poems only in Polish, refusing to write for English speakers: 'Let them accommodate; why should I accommodate to them?' he said.

Janina says: I can only know this Polish man through translation by another.

*

Janina talks to me about a professor of literature, Elaine Scarry, whose book *The Body in Pain* explores pain as being not 'of' or 'for' something. We have a fear *of* something (terrorism, something happening to our children) and we hold a love *for* someone or something (a tiny wounded bird in our hands), but pain has no object in the external world. Pain is not *of* or *for* anything: it can only ever be itself. And pain itself has the ability to destroy a sufferer's language.

The experience of suffering great pain and watching others in pain can unmake humans in different ways, Janina says. Although the Royal Commission into Institutional Responses to Child Sexual Abuse in Australia is ongoing, and although the media is saturated with commentary on how damaging this form of abuse can be, she says the inability to understand or empathise with another's pain is why some human beings can listen to adult victims of child abuse and say: *It happened decades ago. Can't you move past it? Why didn't you speak up sooner?*

Janina knows these questions well; she regularly asks them of herself.

Vivian Gornick writes: 'the way life feels is inevitably the way life is lived'. Janina says she struggles with her shattered identity – her sense of 'I' – and now and again life feels too painful for her to continue. She says she cannot help feeling this way. She wants it to be otherwise, but she cannot find the words to make it so.

*

And what of the commissioners and county court judges exposed to accounts of institutional sexual violence against children or sexual abuse within the social institution of the family, Janina asks. Imagine the pain of hearing another's agony so intricately described and watching the faces of those reliving relentless memories from long ago.

The commissioners overseeing the royal commission have access to counselling and peer support, I say. A County Court of Victoria worker told me the court offers a similar program to help judges, associates and tipstaves with the vicarious trauma that can result from listening, hour after hour, day after day, year after year, to testimonies of sexual violence.

Does all that witnessing silence them? Janina asks.

Sometimes, I say. The county court worker said one strategy associates and tipstaves use to offer each other relief is to make inappropriate jokes and remarks that they would never say outside of the court environment. It helps lift the mood.

What's brown and sticky? Janina asks.

I laugh. A stick, I say.

It is the only joke I know, she says.

*

I cannot escape myself or my past, says Janina.

She still accepts every portion of blame for what happened to her as a child. But how can an eight-year-old be responsible for the actions of an adult? What happened to you could not possibly be your fault, I say. The moral obligation for protection lies with the adult. She says two things she does know are that the power to change the self-blame sits in her open palms, and the responsibility for staying alive is her work to do because there can be no reprieve from herself.

*

Some things only reveal themselves with time.

Janina met an Australian man a few years ago who was identical in manner to her father: infested with paranoid, vain arrogance and a pathological need for perfection and, thus, for control. With this man she replicated her father–daughter relationship. He told Janina he felt *dead inside*. Twice he told her this, once when drunk, once sober. At the time she knew anxiety and joy and living in confusion with these two emotions as well as the occasional desire to kill herself, but not the acute sensation of dying or death. After entertaining for a short time this man's past (as complicated as hers) and his determined but probably unconscious desire to destroy her, Janina recognised inside herself an empty, discarded loneliness that came close to what the man described as *dead inside*. She says it took one year of not talking, not writing, not reading, not listening to music, being visited with father flashbacks every night, four nervous breakdowns, time in a psychiatric hospital and a recovery centre before something resembling relief re-entered her life. Janina calls this year-long trudge through punishing pain and unconscious self-excoriation *survival*.

Janina says every human being on this planet has a complex personhood, and to sociologist Avery Gordon this means people 'remember and forget, are beset by contradiction, and recognize and misrecognize themselves and others'. We also suffer both 'graciously and selfishly', get stuck in our troubles, yet have the remarkable ability to transform ourselves. And to survive.

But Janina will not use the words 'victim' or 'survivor' to describe herself. She fears they will seep inside, smother her permanently, boxing her in to how she *should* be. While her days continue to contain miniature ripples of joy alongside oceans of despair, she will not carry around those words like lead. She wants a rarer and better thing: to be unlabelled. Unmarked.

After she explains to me her injurious relationship with the Australian man, I tell Janina this is what I see: she was a victim of what Freud called *repetition compulsion* – a drive to repeat an original trauma in her life in order to overcome the constant anxiety stemming from that trauma. Although she was worn down by her need to attend to the mastery of this anxiety by having an affair with identical-Father, somewhere along the way she made a conscious decision to slough away the exterior and internal threats of self-annihilation through persistence and sheer guts so she could succeed at the basics of what a life requires – that is, to survive each day.

She laughs at me. She tells me I am full of shit 'n' Freud.

*

In *Ghostly Matters*, her masterful book on the cultural experience of haunting, Avery Gordon quotes legal scholar Patricia Williams: 'that life is complicated is a fact of great analytic importance.'

Analysing the complexity of her emotions and memories is the only way Janina can understand her father.

When he calls her on the phone from the other side of Australia to ask how she is, this happens: she is suspicious, she doesn't believe him, and she doesn't trust him. Why would a man who harmed her so deeply and who remains taut-mouthed on the past want to ask after her health? Does he do it for forgiveness? Is it forgetfulness? Janina listens to him ramble and is patient when he wants to talk about his grandson, her son, who has not known one shred of vileness, and when she hangs up the phone she murders each day on her calendar with a violet pen until the next call.

Janina says some people she's met who have had stable, loving, unviolent childhoods have difficulty understanding the need to run towards something and away from it at the same time; it is beyond the exactness of personal experience. To them it is like dodging cars on a busy road, putting yourself at risk of certain harm. She says there is no point explaining that you live haunted by things that happened to you decades ago and there are pictures and sounds in your head constantly playing like an end-less looping GIF, and apart from a temporary reprieve by detach-ing from reality nothing you can do or say will make them disappear.

The best you can do is to learn how to manage your emotions and lower your immediate distress.

The ones among us who have the ability and opportunity to corral their thoughts, memories, experiences and opinions within the tidy boundaries of a story and who can disclose their trauma publicly in this way are the ones we are attuned to, the ones we want to hear. Of course they are: their voices are less messy, more *sane*, more contained than voices like Janina's. When I say to Janina I will write her story because my role is to make certain the forgettable ones are never forgotten and she displays great bravery for her survival, she says *you don't understand*.

Although I am now proficient in English, it will always remain my second-hand language, and sometimes, as the novelist Maaza Mengiste writes, 'I have fallen between its cracks trying to trudge my way toward comprehension.' But this fight to write and speak English words is also why I can face Janina and say: My struggle for *le mot juste* makes me work harder to understand what you say and mean and feel, and to know your trauma, vicariously.

*

Speak out, they say. Write what you fear and throw it out into the world, they say. It will be cathartic, they say. As a writer, Janina has met too many of these *they* people. Janina does not want to write her life story. Memoir, personal essays: she chokes on these words. The exposure of the confessional 'I'. Even though she knows the 'I' is a construction (often a confection, says Janina), it creeps through many forms of nonfiction, foregrounding the author/narrator as subject. The topic revolves around the narra-tor's perfectly flawed centre and everyone outside this self is col-lateral damage to the author's journey of discovering themselves.

(Done well, this writing contains evocative ideas and wiry mus-cle words, I say.)

(Yes, but mostly it is not well done, says Janina.)

Of course, while the narrator critiques others, they may also speak poorly of themselves ('please note my lack of education and/or lack of sophistication and/or dysfunction of some type'). Janina agrees with Maggie Nelson, who in *The Art of Cruelty* labels the principle of memoirists and personal essayists that claims *you can say anything about other people as long as you make yourself look just as bad* as a 'sham, a chicanery, one with its roots planted firmly in narcissism'.

Essayist David Rakoff wrote that he researched subjects in the hope he would find out more about himself. He called his research 'me-search'. At least he was honest, says Janina.

Maggie Nelson also wrote, 'Writing can hurt people; self-exposure or self-flagellation offers no insurance against the pain.' Janina says this is another reason why she has no desire to write memoir or personal essays, or to deliberately write auto-biography into her fiction, or to speak of what happened to her except in a general way. She has no need to injure those who hurt her. In exposing them, she harms herself: for me, this is not justice, she says.

*

Due to her aversion to writing personal narrative, but with a need to know where the roots of her family's violence took shape, Janina asks her father to write and send her his life story. She wants to know more about his childhood during the war and to find in his tale a reason or reasons for why he did what he did to her, and in the process discover more about herself (this is her 'me-search'). But she does not want to be in his presence. She uses her young son as cover (my fear is despicable, she says), and asks her father to write his life for her son so he will know where he came from.

Janina says to me: I can only know my Polish father through my son.

She asks her father to write as well as he can in English. Her son doesn't speak Polish.

I ask: Why doesn't he speak Polish?

She says: Because I don't speak it and never will, and children are given what their parents are able to give them, and nothing more.

While Janina's father hurt her body he spoke to her only in Polish. When he called her *useless, hopeless, stupid* in front of others he said it in English so she would feel the precise articulation of his words.

When he argued with Janina's grandmother, aunt and uncles he did so in Polish.

When Janina's mother called her *one of those girls on the street corner,* and when she told her husband *you spend more time with your daughter than you do with me,* she said it in English in front of Janina so her daughter would understand every word.

She shares her grandmother's name. She pronounces it with a *J* – *Jar-neena* – and I wince at its harshness. Janina with a soft *J*, like a *Y*: this is how you pronounce it, I say. But she cringes whenever it is spoken this way. My name can never be gentle, she says, and I call myself by my Australian name – Janine with a hard *J* and no ending in *a.*

Janine knows 'yes' in Polish (*tak*), but she can't remember 'no'.

Is it *net*? she asks. Or *ne*, or *nein*?

It is simple, I say. It is *nie.*

Janine says *nie*, and with her Australian accent it sounds like a 'yeah'.

*

I cannot escape myself or my past, says Janine.

But she has no need to write violent details of her childhood. As Susan Sontag once wrote, 'there's nothing wrong with standing back and thinking'. Some things can remain your own and don't have to be released to the world. If she did reveal in print the crimes against her, she could (potentially) have a sniff of temporary freedom from her suffering, and readers would congratulate her on her courage and the redemptive brutality of her self-exposure. And she could add to the literature on family violence piling up like dead bodies in bookstores. But then what? What comes afterwards? Would this revealment sustain her? Would it be effective in offering her some sense the suffering would end? She would return to the daily struggles of her life with the additional pressure of being labelled a memoirist.

There are some things broken that can never be unbroken.

Pain has the ability to destroy a sufferer's language, so Janine says: I will find other ways to describe the experience and aftermath of violence, how I feel it, taste it, hear and smell it, and write my stories not detailing explicit violence but clearly born from it. I need to write about states of uncontainment, says Janine. To make the pain *of* and *for* something.

I am not sure what this would look like, but I will not write Janine's life story. I can attend to what she says and doesn't say without locking it up into words. It is her right to argue against public disclosure, to not write of her past, and to live with ambivalence and uncertainty and contradiction. For now, we sit in this cafe and I paraphrase Brodsky's words – what makes a narrative breathe is not the story itself but what follows what. And *what follows what*, I say, is both the summation of our lives, and for each of us to decide.

Janine looks at me in my eyes, smiles and says: *Nie.* You know nothing.

Now No-One Here Is Alone

Melissa Howard

Everyone here in the waiting area of the Family Violence Court Division of the Magistrates Court is playing a game. It's called Bad Guy or Victim? Women are curled on chairs, glassy-eyed and stunned, their family and friends dozing beside them, while men pace up and down in righteous indignation, or sit texting furiously.

There are no separate floors for people who have been hurt and those who have done the hurting. I imagine that, sometimes, the lines aren't so distinct. People who have been abused often become abusive. But while compassion is human, feeling sorry for violent men doesn't get us anywhere. Many women have learned that the hard way.

Whatever our divisions, within ourselves and with each other, we're all united in this: the wait. No-one knows when they will be called to court for the magistrate to determine if a family violence order needs to be made. We are asked to set aside the whole day. There are no facilities for children and it is explicitly stated that you are not permitted to bring them. But a handful of small children crawl under the chairs or stare, slack-jawed, at iPhone screens.

There is a short sandy-haired man near the stairs with his phone. He is bristling with anger. It emanates from him – his jaw is tense and the muscles on his stocky arms bulge as he clenches and unclenches his fists. His face is crimson. He reminds me of a lover my mother had who once backed me up until my spine was pressed against the kitchen counter, his chest touching mine, his cold blue eyes locked on me, breathing heavily with unrestrained rage.

Perhaps I am projecting. Perhaps because this man looks so similar to a man I do not like I have subconsciously assigned him the same characteristics. But aggression is palpable. An angry person can change the air around them without saying a word or moving their body.

The sandy-haired man lowers the phone to his chest as a woman walks up to him, manila folders in her hands. She launches straight in. 'Do you want her to be able to contact you about the kids? What about your house? Do you want her to access the kids?'

What – hang on. I'm baffled. *He's* the protected person?

A social worker will tell me later that abusive men often claim that *they* are the victims, and will attempt to take family violence orders against their partners or former partners, clogging up an already clogged system.

Across from me, a bearded, leathered bikie with a kind, doughy face is comforting a woman with a jet-black ponytail. She is curled in agony on her chair, her face squashed against the arms like a child. I know that agony. (Watching *Heartland*, a Canadian horse TV program with my ten-year-old daughter. The grandfather, Jack, warns his granddaughter against a man she loves. 'Just because you *want* someone to change,' he said, 'doesn't mean that they *will*.')

'This time,' the bearded man tells her, '*This* time, he cannot just say sorry and come back. This time is different.'

She doesn't look so sure.

'We can help you,' he continues. 'What do you need?'

She snorts. 'A house and a job.'

'You can stay with Mum,' he says. 'She'll get on your tits – you *know* she can be annoying – but you can stay there.'

She sniffs. 'Yep.'

I catch his eye. I try to smile but that's beyond me today. He looks at me warmly. So many pockets of gentleness here. I am starved of gentle touch. The only physicality in my life is the hungry pawing of my baby son at my breast. The smallest act of love from a man to a woman – him brushing her hair back where it is getting stuck in her streaming nose – catches my breath. 'Before you know what kindness really is,' wrote Naomi Shihab Nye, 'you must lose things, feel the future dissolve in a moment like salt in a weakened broth.'

I'm not sure what I am supposed to be doing. No-one has told me. Or perhaps they did and I wasn't able to hear it. Yesterday the police told me to show up here today for the hearing for the temporary violence order. 'I'm sorry,' I said. 'It's not *real* violence.' 'Sounds like real violence to me,' said the officer.

My bones hum with anxiety. I slept in snatches last night, lying rigid with fear and anxiety. My body coursed with adrenaline. Every noise was a threat. The unpacked boxes emphasised the emptiness of the house. At three a.m. I became convinced he was on the roof. I was grateful for the distraction when my son woke for a breastfeed.

I look around the waiting area. There are perhaps eighty people, in a large circle space around the central stairs.

Is *he* here yet? My stomach is clenched. Could he do something here? Two days ago, such an idea would have been ridiculous. But the parameters of what is possible have been redefined – once again. I stand and edge up to the counter, looking around, scanning the faces of the crowd.

'I'm not sure what I'm supposed to be doing,' I confess.

The young woman behind the counter is stony-faced and uninterested. She has become hardened, already, by the daily turnover of violence and loss. She doesn't look at me. 'Sit down and the police will come and get you when they're ready,' she says in a bored voice.

I turn around and – of course – *he* is right there. I do not know who gets the bigger fright. I flinch and he flinches and I can see him calculating: how far away is he? Is he far enough? The police have placed a temporary order, meaning that he is not allowed within 200 metres of me. But the room isn't even that big and he is instructed to attend.

The vulnerability in his face makes my heart ache. My sadness sits in my throat, like I have swallowed a heavy river stone. I thought that love was stronger than demons. I was wrong. And I put all my chips down.

I believe that many women who love an angry man can see the damaged child inside him. I believe that many women see the shame in his eyes when the anger has passed and confuse it with remorse. I suspect that many women see bad behaviour as separate to the man; that it is a possession, an exception, an evil force that has nothing to do with the man they love, a force that he is also a victim of; or see him as two different people. The good one, whom they love, and the bad one. I believe many women are victims of our own malignant optimism, and of the bargains we make in our heads to allow us to continue to hope.

Later I see him across the room, and the vulnerability has gone. Once again I feel my brain trying to put these two pieces together: this is one person, not two. I turn, scurry back to my corner and I wait. I should have brought a banana. Something to calm these jitters.

An elegant woman in her forties, with long, lean legs in high black heels, smooth caramel skin and a jangle of gold jewellery around her bony wrists and ankles, is barking into the phone. 'I paid for all the furniture!' she says. 'I have the receipts to prove it!'

She has an energy younger than her face. Do love and violence make us all teenagers again? 'To suggest that domestic violence goes on between *normal* folks', writes psychologist Shari Schreiber, 'is lunacy.'

A gruff man in a beige suit approaches her and she hangs up. 'He's approached me twice!' she tells him. Who has? I look around. Which one?

'Once he said, "Paula says hi!" That's my daughter! He's insinuating he's seen my daughter. And the other time he said, "Can we say goodbye properly?" I don't want him talking to my family! He's trying to get them to get me to change my mind. Can you put it on there that he can't?'

'They'll need their own orders,' he says gruffly.

One of the other men here – a lawyer – is dressed in a way that could only be described as dapper: a blue suit, brown leather lace-up shoes, a pocket handkerchief and yellow diamond socks. His mannerisms are gentle. He radiates calm. I bet he does yoga. How is he here as a lawyer and not as a defendant?

Did his mum – we always blame the mum, don't we? – cuddle him just enough? Not too much that they are enmeshed, and not too little that they become emotionally starved. At what point do the men appear here as respondents? Ask any mother who is more sensitive – her son or her daughter – and she will nod, bemusedly, down at her son, his face buried into her tummy.

'Girls are more emotionally intelligent,' my friend Alice messaged me when I was complaining about my son's meltdowns. 'Boys are just more *emotional*.'

My breasts ache. They are filling with milk. I think of my baby son – a butterball of love and joy – and wonder at what point do these babies devolve into anger? Last month I twice took him to the gym creche. A long-haired, doe-eyed four-year-old was crying, silently, for his mum.

'That's enough, Toby,' said the plump carer, rolling her eyes. 'You're okay. Stop crying. You're okay. You're a *big boy*.' He set his little jaw and swallowed his tears. Already the world is teaching him that anger is okay, but not sadness. You're okay.

The second time, when I returned, my face red and sweaty, my baby son was sitting on a seat by the door, stifling his tears. His face collapsed with relief when he saw me. 'See?' said the carer loudly. 'You stopped crying, so Mummy came back!'

She turned to me. 'We try to get them to learn that if they cry you won't be here, but if they stop crying you'll come back.'

Jesus Christ.

'Door, Mummy, door,' said my son, frantically, pulling me towards the exit. 'Car, Mummy, car.'

*

Across from me a mousy girl in her late teens in a tracksuit is talking to her lawyer. 'My dad is sick, see? He needs me. It's just us two, see? He's been sick for years. Diabetes, emphysema, lots of other shit, and I have to be able to see him. He needs me. I need them out of the house, see.'

She is cheery. I guess, for a short time, the focus is on her, and I feel a wave of sadness for her. A sick dad – who is taking care of *you*?

The day limps on, the courts close for lunch – court hours are shorter than a working day – and I pace the streets and force myself to eat one rice-paper roll. Each mouthful is a victory.

When the court is almost closed for the day, the police lawyer comes to get me. I am relieved to be in a small room and to know that, for a few minutes, I will not need to worry about him walking past. She is calm and brisk, with shiny dark hair. She picks up some papers, scans them and adopts a stern expression. She looks me in the eye. 'Did this happen to you?'

I nod. 'Yes, it did.'

Her demeanour relaxes. 'Okay.' She scans the forms. 'Two kids?'

'Big gap, I know.'

'Oh, it's okay!' She puts down the papers and smiles warmly at me.

'I was so young,' I say. 'But sometimes I think I'd like more. Maybe one day, I think I could have more.'

'Me too!' she says. 'Mine are twenty-two and twenty-four. But I'd like to have more.'

I imagine her as a plucky twenty-year-old, bringing up her two kids while training to be a lawyer, and I feel a rush of warmth for her, for all single mothers who rise up through the fog of fatigue and the bone-aching sadness to achieve something vital.

She puts down the papers. 'He has denied everything,' she says.

My guts go hot and shaky and I think I am going to puke. After everything, he calls me a liar? (Later, a kind officer will scoff and tell me, 'Oh, they *all* do that. Mostly just to make a point.')

She explains all the terms, how far away he will need to keep from me, my new house. It's all too much, and I can't focus and my body is sore, and I start bawling.

'Do you understand it all?' she asks. 'Are you okay with it all?'

'Yeah,' I say. 'I understand it. But I'm not okay with it all. It's shit. It's so shit.'

'Yeah,' she agrees. 'It's shit.'

A knock on the door. She stands up. 'It's time to go.'

Then we are moving towards the courtroom and all that has happened and I'm so sad that I cannot bear it – after it all, it ends like this – and all the adrenaline has gone out of my body.

A year ago, my son was pulled from a slit in my belly, like a wet lamb from a sack, and I thought, I'm here now. Here is life. Here is that happy ending I knew I'd get eventually.

Two social workers from a support agency walk up to me, and the kindness in their eyes undoes me and I'm crying without any ability to hold it in. Then I am in the court – how did I get here? – and I'm sitting behind a partition and I can feel him sitting on the other side, although I cannot see him. Intimate time spent with someone gives you a hyperawareness of where they are in the world. The heart lingers long after the head has cut ties. The bonding to an unhealthy man – as many dead women could attest – is a killer.

The magistrate granted the temporary order. I do not remember walking out of the courtroom, or how I got the papers, how I got home. Did I catch the train or drive?

Brains are clever. If things are too awful they say *fuck this* and dissociate. Hearts, on the other hand, are dangerous, for they never give up hope.

A year ago, a friend lost his wife to a brain tumour. 'When life takes these turns,' he says, 'you can forget about choosing the best option. There is no best option anymore. Just shit options. Just choose the least shit one. You did that. You chose the least shit option.'

*

Months later I have to return. The process to protect women legally is a convoluted one. When I rake my fingers through my hair, wads of it come away and long blonde hairs coat all the furniture. But the order has made it possible for me to hear my phone beep or a car door slam without doubling up in anxiety, to start to envision a life.

Three times there have been odd errors made – kids assumed to be on the order, breaches not being followed up – due to information being passed around and filtered through different government and non-government agencies, different police officers from different stations. It's like an odd game of Chinese whispers, with everyone I speak to warm and apologetic and frustrated by the messy, entangled system. I am humbled by the kindness everywhere.

We queue outside to get through the metal detectors. The air is thick with cigarette smoke, and my friend Kim's sewing kit is taken by the cheery guard. 'It's probably a good thing,' she quips. 'I might want to stab him with an embroidery needle if I see him.'

We hike up the stairs. The gentle burn in my legs feels good.

'Geez, it makes you feel a bit rough, doesn't it?' says Kim as we arrive on the floor. She nods at the decor – grey and depressing and devoid of anything warm. 'I mean, a couple of plants, a picture – fuck, something.'

All the seats are taken so we find a spot around the corner and sit on the floor. This time I am a veteran, not shaking and anxious, but prepared: a friend, a bunch of bananas, a Nutella doughnut and a pen for writing. I eat the doughnut immediately and get covered in chocolatey goo.

In the loo, I wash my hands. A woman in her early fifties is waiting for a stall. She looks like the mum in *Muriel's Wedding*. I can feel the anxiety and deep grief rolling off her. Her eyes are wild, but her body tense. 'Is this your first time here?' I ask. I want to hug her.

Her face hardens. 'And the last,' she says, setting her chin with determination. I wonder how many years she invested before it was enough. How many scary, dangerous nights she put up with, hoping it would bring her one step closer to him getting better. She steps into the stall, and I into mine. We piss.

'I remember I was so anxious I felt like I might implode,' I say.

'Yes!' she says, from behind the wall. 'I need a coffee, or something.'

'This sounds weird,' I say, 'but I find that bananas really help.'

'Of course,' she says from the stall. 'The potassium.'

'Yeah. The potassium.'

I get back to the waiting area before she does. I point her out to Kim. 'Look at her. I want to cuddle her.'

'Why is no-one helping her?' asks my friend.

'It happens so fast,' I say. 'I was here eighteen hours later. Your brain hasn't caught up. I needed that time alone – without the kids! – to have a chance to process it. She may be the same. Or she might be too ashamed to tell anyone.'

'She's so old,' says my friend. 'You kind of think it'll just be young scrags.'

'Thanks.'

'You don't expect it to be someone who looks like your *mum*.'

I fish out my bananas and break one off and, feeling like an idiot, I walk over and hold it out to her. I'm so worried she's going to refuse it and I'm going to have to back away carrying my fruit, but she takes it and grips it like a safety rope. She grabs my hand with the other and her grip is vice-like. 'Thank you,' she whispers.

She peels and then eats her banana, methodically, watching me the whole time. When she finishes, she folds the skin into a wedge, walks over to the bin and puts it in and on the way back she leans down and I reach up my arms and we hug, hard, and she bursts into tears. Her face is warm and moist and snuffly next to my neck. Now no-one here is alone.

This time we are first up. A different police lawyer comes to us this time. The rooms are all full, she apologises. 'Do you mind if we talk out here?'

The lawyer is younger than us with a floral dress, wavy light brown hair and an open, trusting face. She is unblemished still. The weight of all of this hasn't affected her yet. Not yet. But it will.

This time I am prepared for the blow.

'He is still denying everything,' she tells us.

Kim snorts. 'Uh-huh. He always did. Remember that time you had to call me because …' I nod.

The lawyer explains that means despite physical evidence, it is, essentially, my word against his. New legislation rests the burden of proof more heavily on the victim. If I want the full order permanently placed we would need to come back to court. Lawyers would prepare cases, it could take a long time.

I cannot bear it. I have paced myself to make it this far. And it's near impossible to arrange childcare for the baby for a whole day. I feel that I am keeping my head above water just enough to breathe and to hold the kids' heads above water.

There is another option, she explains. 'He has stuck by the conditions of the temporary family violence order rigidly,' says the lawyer. 'So we think he's a good contender for an undertaking.'

It's a voluntary undertaking. Similar to the family violence order – the conditions are the same – but it's not enforceable by the police. If there are breaches, we must return to court. But it's practically the same thing, right?

*

Months later my son and I are in the front garden when a police car rolls to a stop, along with my heart. Oh God. Who is dead?

No-one is dead but two handsome police officers give me a pamphlet with numbers on it. 'These are people who can help you,' they say. 'People who can guide you through the court and police processes.'

My son is thrilled by their car and points at it. 'Car! Lights! Look! Car!'

'But we are all done with court now,' I say confused. 'But it would have been super helpful then. I didn't have a clue what was going on!'

Jesus, I can only imagine how hard, how *impossible* the family violence system is to navigate if English isn't your first language, or you have mental health issues.

His face crumples with embarrassed, apologetic frustration. 'It's silly, I know,' he says. 'I'm sorry. They've closed our branch and your case came into a different branch, and there is a separate branch that deals with family violence stuff and communication is ...' He trails off, shaking his head.

This same sense pervades many people I come across during this process. An apologetic frustration: I'm so sorry that this is all I can offer you. Subtext: if it were up to *me*, up to common sense, it'd be better. But the kindness, always the kindness. (But I remember with shame telling a friend who works with young Koori women and her rolling her eyes. 'Big surprise,' she scoffed. 'You're white! I've had clients beaten close to death, and the cops did nothin'. Nothin'!')

'Why did you agree to the undertaking?' asks the police officer, frowning.

'It's kinda the same thing?' I say. 'I couldn't deal with going to court again.'

He shakes his head, frustrated. 'Who told you that? It's *not* the same thing. It's *not*!'

*

But months earlier, in court, I agree and sign the undertaking. He has already signed it. 'What a moment to share,' I quip darkly. My throat closes up.

The lawyer's face crumples with sympathy. She is way too sweet for this place. 'I had a woman here last week,' she says. 'When I told her the date of the hearing she said, "That was going to be our wedding date!"'

We all sigh.

A family lawyer I know once referred to divorce as the field of broken dreams, but it's not. It's here, on this floor of the Magistrates Court. No one holds tighter to dreams than women who love damaged men. The equation goes like this: If I love him enough, he will change, and when he's fixed, we will be fixed and we will be happy. If I hang in for long enough, give enough love, if I put enough coins into the pokie machine, the machine will beep and I will get my payout, my happily ever after.

This floor is the moment you realise you've been feeding coins into a broken machine, and you can't fix anyone but yourself.

As we leave, a bunch of tall, high school students are riding the lifts, pissing everyone off. They crowd into our lift. 'People are trying to *work* here,' snaps one elegant, stern woman as she elbows through their throng and steps out of the lift. They all jeer as the doors close. The lift lurches down.

'What are you looking for?' I ask.

'The interesting cases!' says a tall Somali teenager. 'You know – murders and bank robberies and shit.'

'Try court 1,' says a woman in a trim black suit, pushing the open button and wheeling out her small suitcase. 'All the ones on this floor are just sad.'

Pluripotent

Amanda C. Niehaus

Part I

In 1911, J.F. Gudernatsch conducted an experiment on tadpoles, in which he fed them pieces of organs – including thyroid, liver, adrenal gland, pituitary gland, muscle, thymus, testicle or ovary – from horses, calves, cats, dogs, pigs or rabbits. He described the food as 'ravenously taken by the animals'. Gudernatsch found that thyroid suppressed growth in the tadpoles but caused their immediate metamorphosis. They became frogs.

Cells proliferate in my uterus, forming cerebral cortex, salivary glands, blood, nipples. She curls into herself; she twitches involuntarily. She is a germinated mung bean, pale tail pushing into my spaces, all these astonishing spaces. If only I could see her, imagine her, dream her. Could I love her any more?

Fetal skin is like tadpole skin, thin and simple. Wounds heal rapidly, may leave no traces.

A newt can regenerate a lost limb in only five months. The newt is extraordinary: most amphibians do not retain this ability after metamorphosis.

Janet Lane-Claypon (1877–1967) was one of the founders of epidemiology, the study and analysis of public health and disease. She earned a BSc and a DSc from University College in London and an MD and an MBBS from the London School of Medicine for Women and was the first woman to be awarded a research fellowship from the British Medical Society. In the first study of its kind, Lane-Claypon discovered that the risk of developing breast cancer is associated with age at menarche, age at first pregnancy, age at menopause, number of children, and duration of breastfeeding.

When she is made: my breast in his palm, nipple on tongue, rain pelts the tent so hard I can't hear his breath or his grunt or the squeak of my skin on the mat. We are enough for each other, more than, but still we need more; we need her, we want her, and after he comes, I tip my pelvis up, angle in the sperm.

Stem cells retain the ability to self-renew or to differentiate into other types of cells during development and growth or to repair tissue damage. The more cell types a stem cell can become, the greater its potency.

Potency (n.): the power to influence; also, a male's ability to achieve orgasm.

When she is real: in the clinic, I see her on a screen, all profile, seeming to look up towards my centre, and the ultrasound tech captures her, prints her out. In the rainforest, I wander too close to cassowary chicks, and their fathers – birds the size of men, with stony crests and sharp hooked claws – puff up and hiss. They are frugivorous. Peaceable. Deadly. In the lab, tadpoles transform into numbers, data, words and words and words; their bodies pile up in my thesis, in my dreams. I dissect them. I lie in bed, and the fan spins, pushing hot air around. I have never known such tiredness.

Inside, she begins to yawn.

I raise the tadpoles, each in its own sawed-off soda bottle filled with filtered water. The bottles are grouped by temperature – hot or cool or cycling between the two – and twice a day, I drop a pinch of frozen spinach into each container. It floats on the surface of the water, and the tadpole swims up, nibbles it, piece by piece, until it is gone. Vegetation becomes flesh and faeces, tadpoles become small striped frogs, and though reared apart, animals in the same treatment emerge much the same. The environment is everything.

When Lane-Claypon married in her fifties, she retired due to restrictions on the employment of married women.

Inside my breasts, multi-potent stem cells create new capacities. Ducts extend and multiply; fat pads expand with epithelial tissue; alveolar bulbs enlarge and become secretory – as in secrete, not secret. (Should not be secret.) I buy practical, rose-shaded bras with front clips for feeding.

On Friday, I must print out my thesis and carry it across campus to the Research Office, where they will stamp the time on it and prepare to send it to the reviewers. I have written the chapters, inserted the figures, formulated the conclusions; all that's left is to format, fit the words to the template.

But then she is here. Fifteen days early. On Thursday.

The day before Friday.

I want to be an academic, a scientist, a woman, a mother, her mother. But I don't know how to do this, all of it, at once. This push off from land into water, where I can't see the bottom. I have to swim; I can't swim. I'm ready, not ready.

Parity, or childbirth, is associated with cancer risk. Women having their first child at an 'advanced age' are significantly more likely to develop hormone-receptive breast cancer, which grows more rapidly in response to oestrogen or progesterone. In most studies, advanced age is defined as twenty-four years.

When she is born: I am thirty-one.

Part II
Dear Amanda, Please be aware that the last day to submit your thesis so you are not incurring any fee penalty is tomorrow. If this is not possible, then the only way to avoid paying fees is to take an interruption to your candidature. This will need to be done URGENTLY. Could you please advise whether you will submit by tomorrow? Kind regards.

Human breastmilk contains 400 different proteins and 200 different lipids; numerous factors that reduce inflammation and promote antibody production, protecting the developing infant; bacteria from the more than 200 genera that colonise the intestine; and pluripotent stem cells, which are thought to move throughout the infant's body, boosting growth and development.

When she is hungry: her face flushes, clenches; she screams and twists; she grapples for my nipple but does not latch, will not seal, cannot be filled by what I give her. She is too much and
  I am not enough.

Social psychology tells us there are four ways to respond to philosophical contradictions in the formation or maintenance of relationships: (a) select one option, and ignore or deny the other; (b) separate options into discrete contexts; (c) attempt both options but without full realisation of either; (d) construct a reality where the options are no longer perceived as contradictory.

Reality (n): the true situation as it exists, rather than how it is imagined or appears to be.

I am not going to give her a dummy, a pacifier, a silicone plastic plug. She is not that kind of child; I am not that kind of mother. But my choices are no longer mine to make, and when my skin and nerves are raw and I press the thing into her mouth, she eases.

Parity, or functional equality, remains an issue in the STEM fields – science, technology, engineering, mathematics – where women are paid less, promoted more slowly, and awarded fewer honours and leadership roles than male colleagues. Though 50 per cent of Australian undergraduates, PhD students and Level A academics in the sciences are women, only 10 to 15 per cent of Level E (professorial) academics are. Marriage and childbirth account for the greatest losses of women in academia after obtaining their PhD.

In Australia, 91.5 per cent of surgeons are male.

I used to jut into the world. Jut. Now I slump, gape, sag; my belly hangs, does not return to what it was before, could not – even if I wanted it to.

Even if I didn't.

In 1811, novelist Frances (Fanny) Burney was given a wine cordial, a stack of old mattresses to lie upon, and a mastectomy. Anaesthesia had not yet been invented. 'You must expect to suffer,' the doctor said. 'I do not want to deceive you.' He removed her breast and scraped her clean, and she survived.

Every chapter of my thesis begins the same way, with *heterogeneity, variation, change.* And yet, I am not ready when change comes.

When she is seven months old: a hard ball in my upper chest, near the armpit. I run my hand over it in the shower. I run. My hand. I pause. The physician says lactation, blocked duct, come back in a couple of weeks, have a scan in seven. Nothing to worry about.

I don't believe her.

I picture it black, bulbous, dense. I want to feel it outside my body – hold it, consider then crush it in my hands, through my fingers. But I am given a general anaesthetic. I do not see when the surgeon cuts it out and sets it on a steel tray or plops it into a specimen container to be examined by the pathologist, who will characterise it and set out my life before me, however much is left.

I wake; I gasp for words.

Gregor Samsa wakes, and he is a beetle.

I graduate in July. I have a PhD. I have a prognosis, a surgeon (male), an oncologist (female). I have a dip in my breast, a long puckered scar. I have no hair. My daughter wears pink for the photos.

When it is over: it is never over.

Pluripotent

Part III
One cell, two cells, cells in the lining of the lobule; cells transform, cells become immortal, cells become more cells, acidify adjacent cells, spread, invade, overcome; cells amass, vascularisze; cells pass into the lymph or the blood; cells move, cluster; cells colonise distal tissues; cells replicate again and again and again and again.

My cancer is confined to the breast. The right breast.
There is never a right breast.
But I survive.

In 1940, scientist and philosopher C.H. Waddington described embryonic development as an 'epigenetic landscape', later represented as a ball (cell) perched at the top of a ridged slope, ready to roll down, specialise, differentiate, slip into one gully or another, become this or that kind of tissue, nudged onto a trajectory by genes and communication among cells. To a point, each cell can be anything.

When I was a girl: I wanted to be Miss America. A detective. An otter. A writer. I ran through the yard with invisible wolves, weaving between the apple tree and the cherry, the metal swing set, the pill-shaped propane tank, under the clothesline. Sometimes, they cornered me; sometimes, I escaped. Inside the house, I pressed stories through black ink ribbons and scrawled them in notebooks with spiral bindings – stories about fairies and unicorns, ponies, children, getting lost, finding the way back.

A dead heart can be erased, washed with special detergents to remove cardiac cells, leaving behind only the structure, the matrix of proteins and fibres and vessels that held the cells in place. The heart becomes translucent.
And then it can be remade. Pluripotent stem cells, embryonic or induced, are cultured and seeded into the empty organ, and they repopulate it, grow into its scaffolding, mature. Begin to function and communicate.

No, she is the only one. The one. And only. No brothers or sisters. I will never have another child. But she is beautiful; she

is enough. She has to be enough. I couldn't want for anything more.

Could I?

When she starts school: I make carrot muffins, or zucchini, or sweet potato (no nuts), and tuck them into the steel lunchbox in the insulated bag in her too-big backpack. Her uniform is blue and white plaid, leaf-crisp. I walk her up the stairs to her class-room, and she sets her bag outside the door and says, *I love you, Mummy,* and kisses me and gives me a hug and another kiss and another hug and turns to go in. I stand and watch because I can't leave, not yet, in case she needs me.

According to the website, the objectives of the Discovery Early Career Researcher Award (DECRA) scheme are to: support excellent basic and applied research by early career researchers, advance promising early career researchers and promote enhanced opportunities for diverse career pathways, enable research and research training in high-quality and supportive environments, expand Australia's knowledge base and research capability, and enhance the scale and focus of research in the Science and Research Priorities.

I win the award, study sex and death. And I write.

The body's stem cells maintain their ability to regenerate; dif-ferentiate; accumulate mutations over time; become cancer; evade the immune system; resist chemotherapy and radiation; move through the body; persist.

I watch, on television, a tumour being taken from a woman's breast, and it shocks me: the mass is enclosed in adipose flesh, fatty meat. I cannot make out the darkness inside.

And if I only have five years left?

Evocation, according to Waddington, is '[the adoption] of one or the other of the alternative paths of development open to it.'

House of Flowers

Jennifer Rutherford

Florence and I are packing her bags when Dad calls to say my mother collapsed and has been admitted to hospital. I have been looking for a diversion, trying to hold off the moment of Florence's departure for Paris. She is sloughing off school shoes, uniform and me, running for all her life out into the dizzying world. I can see her scenting freedom on the breeze and it doesn't smell of mother, of nights chatting by the fire, of home cooking. But the packing stalls and instead we fly together to Sydney, and drive up the Pacific Highway, getting to the hospital just before closing time.

My mother has been ill for months from an infection she caught looking after Dad when he was in hospital recovering from heart surgery. Nothing stops him, not even a heart attack. Before long he was tapping out tunes with his stick as he walked the streets whistling *Ode to Joy* as jubilantly as he had all through my childhood. But the staphylococcus hooked mum and was drawing her in, cutting a channel through the soft folds of her flesh.

Dad has always been bigger than life but these days he says life is an ever-increasing diminishment and, sure enough, we find Mum diminished. The hospital room is loud with flowers. Roses and tulips boxing for attention, sunflowers slapping the day, and Mum, a solitary storm-drenched snowdrop barely able to raise her head from the pillow. They have injected her with so much cortisone that even the shower has tracked its path on her like rain falling on glass.

The next morning Florence and I are sitting in my brother's garden sipping tea – attempting to comfort each other with small pats – when B. phones to say that the chooks have been killed in the night. He has found them strewn across the garden. Floraville, lying at the doorway of the henhouse, has had her head bitten off. Not far off, Henrietta's guts are spewing out of her stomach. Lucy's red petalled crown is lying on its own, some way from what is left of her. All that is left of Milly is a trail of feathers stretching across the garden, under the fence, and into the neighbour's meadow. The fox has stopped several times to pluck out snatches of feathers, and whole clumps of them are drifting across the grass. This is what B. says, on the phone, as Florence pats me, and we sip tea, trying not to think of Mum lying in that bleak room overrun with flowers.

'Devastated' is a word Mum overuses. There are many things in her life that are devastating – hard days, heatwaves, minor injuries – but, as I drive Florence back home from the airport, I think the word has found its proper place.

*

We called them Lucy, Mildred, Henrietta Pennyworth and Floraville, each of us naming and claiming one of them as our own. I can see now that, from the beginning, I was making Floraville something beyond herself, something that belonged more to me than to herself. Call it foolish anthropomorphism, call it what you will, but from the beginning Floraville was a chook in a floral dress bound for misadventure.

Long ago I had named a French doll Floraville, although back then we named her in the language of her native tongue, Fleurville, the slight purr on the *r*, the pause between syllables – so much more evocative than the harsh conjunctive *a*. It was when my husband and I were living in Paris before Florence was born, when we hadn't yet arrived at any of the events that would tear us apart. Before the death of his parents, and before I was found guilty of a crime I have never quite been able to put my finger on. Before she died, his mother charged me with them all. I was the wrong age, the wrong nation, the wrong religion and, intractably, wrongly mannered. But my crime was all of this, and something more. Some blemish of joy rusting out the iron in him – in them. Something that got in, as he said, when he left. But long before all this, there had been Fleurville, a doll I found in pieces in a shoebox at the *puce*. Even disassembled, horsehair spilling from the tears in her cloth body, her face mired in a century's grime – I knew her as mine. Even broken she was too dear for us, but books were sold and the week's food money whittled into.

I wonder if I hadn't been so impetuous, so taken up with passing fancies, he might not have left, but who would that girl have been? Not me. Some other, more habitable person? Maybe the word I'm looking for is *decorous*, maybe I might have been more decorous.

Warm water, soap, and a needle and thread were all it took to stitch her back into life. There were small holes in her legs and arms so that her body could be stuffed into porcelain limbs and stitched back into place. I patched. I stitched. I washed. I knew she would be finely boned and beautiful, but the quizzical expression that came up out of the muddy water – a look of such perplexed intelligence – made the thrift she cost us a small penance for the joy of her sitting on the mantelpiece and being a part of our lives. She was waiting there when I brought Florence home from the hospital. Fleurville, our Sadeian heroine, ravaged by misadventure, but still bearing up. But then, the shipping company we'd entrusted with transporting all our possessions back to Australia went bust and she disappeared without a trace along with everything we owned. Perhaps she was sold off in a job lot along with our books, our china, our linen. Perhaps she ended up back in a box at the *puce*. Recomposed as she was, she might have sold for a pretty penny and started out on a new adventure. How many owners, how many mantelpieces, how many bedrooms has that glass-eyed girl seen as she moved from hand to hand for over a century? Still, I prefer to think of her in the trunk where I carefully packed her, floating down into the bottomless ocean depths, lost at sea. I often imagine her there. I can see her gently bobbing among the dishes, still puzzled, still gently questioning this new twist of fate.

Floraville the Australorp was quizzical and curious too, but far more robust in the way she leaned into life. She came into our life loudly. Chattering, vociferous, bossy, and relentlessly curious about everything human. People who know nothing about chooks imagine that there is some rightness in the fate allotted to them, as if a chook's Being is fully realised in its use value. Chooks stuff cushions, lay eggs, eat food scraps, reconstitute garden soil, fuel fast-food industries, grace tables with soups, salads, pies, dumplings and, ultimately, are fully realised stuffed with lemon and thyme, wings upturned for the roast. Clever chooks. Constantly in service at table while syllabising away at us from the sidelines. Stop. Go back. Wrong way. One is never far from a chook running amok without its head. A dumb chook, an old chook – they are the negative form of *us*. I can't imagine a woman buoyed up by the thought of becoming chook. Compliments never come in the form of a chook (chickens, yes; chooks, no), but, despite all the warnings chooks give us of how not to be, most of us, slowly, inevitably, *become* chook – ending lives of service as plucked, silenced and trussed as a chook en route to the oven.

Cheer up, I tell myself. You are not the good woman, the little red hen, doing the doing – all the way to the pot.

Nor was Floraville. *She was never going to be anyone's breakfast,* or at least that is what I had read in a fairy story about chooks and flowers – long before she lost her head. If she'd had a mind for such things, Floraville would have sided with that version of her story. Within days of her arrival in the garden she had left the caged bird behind and was running with her sisters through the dark tunnels of the garden, romancing the day with secret egg hoards and mysteries we could only guess at. Roaming with her sisters further and further afield, she crossed the creek bed and entered the thickets of briar along the fence line, and there, on the far side of a hen allowed her freedom, we would catch glimpses of her *becoming* chook. Unleashed from duty, amok with desire, perfumed with dust, she gambolled, played, discoursed, and discovered *herself*: a chook acquiring the lost art of becoming.

Chookness belongs to the undergrowth. It takes long days, long grass, hawks overhead, the neighbouring cat, rivalry, hierarchy, and the passing of seasons. There are vocabularies to learn, grammars to accomplish. These chatterers of the under-garden arrive at rhetoricity like we do, babbling first, then end-lessly repeating plosives until finally they arrive at chook song, a carolling to and fro announcing bounty, the cooings of guarded moments, the rhythmic silences, the triumphant cry of a new egg seizing the day.

Strangely, Floraville's becoming didn't preclude us. Lining up at the door every morning, she and her sisters would stand in a row peering into the kitchen, waiting for B. and I to make our first appearance of the day. Head down, tail up, eyes pinned for a sign of movement, and then the announcement: humans afoot. Floraville ran a commentary on all the goings-on of house and garden, announcing everything we did to her sisters, and then running tales to us. Bossing us along until we'd come and see, an egg dropped, food scattered.

I tell myself quietly so nobody can hear – *Floraville choreographed the day*. I would have liked to choreograph dances but my feet got in the way. I have a slight lameness that trips me up when I walk, and sends me flying when I dance. It's an awkwardness B. is rather fond of, but I guess it gets in the way of other forms of imagining. Floraville didn't have this problem. She had long, ele-gant, yellow toes, and always landed on her feet. She and her sis-ters performed the prettiest ballet when the pot of white begonias standing at the kitchen door came into flower. They could hear music, I'm sure, as they rhythmically rose and fell, as one by one each chook lifted her bottom from the ground, feet falling away below her, as she plucked a single flower from the stem, and then the elegance of that feathery plummet, a single white begonia in the beak. Always in turn, always in time, until the plant had lost all its flowers, and the dance was done.

I could tell many stories about Floraville but I doubt the world has heart enough to allow a chook much narrativisation, unless, of course, it is a chook in a children's story: then it is allowed a certain goosiness. Goosy, I think, is the right word. Even now, as I march towards sixty, I still have that same goosy look, that same goosy walk, calling out for a fox to sniff me out.

Florrie has had enough of the melodrama of the dead chooks and wants to get back to packing. *I have to be at the airport in three hours*, she says, as I fuss over what to do with the feathers. There are so many of them milling around the garden, and the neighbour's dog is sniffing out bits that B. has missed.

*

There was nothing goosy about the doll Fleurville. Finely coiffed, her floral dress trimmed with a fine lace petticoat, she was as elegant as the red and gold books that gave her her name. Hachette's *La Bibliothèque rose illustrée* with their red covers and gold lettering – how children must have loved to line *them* up on the mantelpiece.

Fleurville the doll *always* belonged in a story, *belonged to story*, for hundreds of pages have been written on the world of Fleurville and the unnamed doll that begins the Comtesse de Ségur's (1799–1874) famous and much loved trilogy. Book One of *La trilogie de Fleurville, Les malheurs de Sophie*, begins with the doll's arrival, a gift to Sophie from her father. The doll is beautiful – *la plus jolie poupée qu'elle eût jamais vue*. And, as one might expect of a doll whose beauty cries out for a smacking, she ends up in pieces in a box. Perhaps if I had given more thought to the fate of the doll in The Fleurville Trilogy (the doll starts to decompose from the moment she falls into Sophie's clutches), I might have named *my* Fleurville differently, or even left her in peace, in pieces in her box. But I'm forgetting how it was back then, my belly blossoming with Florence and salvation in reach, something I could arrive at, if only I stared down the nursery world and its demons.

On the first day of her new life in the world of Fleurville, Sophie leaves the wax doll in the sun and her sparkling blue eyes are lost inside her head. Putting things to rights, Sophie's mother decapitates the doll, plucks out the missing eyes with a long pair of tweezers, and then glues them back into the doll's head with molten wax. Then Sophie gives her a bath, scouring her so furiously that she scrubs off her face. The doll's hair is lost to a hot iron and curling wraps. Hung from a tree, her arms become disjointed and deformed, one permanently shorter than the other. Next, in yet more maternal solicitude, Sophie boils her feet off, until beauty disarmed, the doll becomes simply *ridiculous*. Only death can release her from further humiliation, and this arrives blessedly in a coup de grâce that leaves her shattered in pieces at the foot of a tree. But it's not over. The children bury her at the bottom of the garden in a box dressed in pink ribbons, watering her in along with two lilacs planted on her grave. Down in the dark soil, the broken doll in the pretty sateen box is becoming mud. *If only they had another doll to break, the children lament, then they could have another funeral.*

One can't imagine, when you read those first pages of The Fleurville Trilogy, that Sophie the doll killer will end up sharing the doll's fate. She slices up goldfish, feeds her pet chicken to a vulture, drowns a turtle, decapitates bees, bludgeons a squirrel to death, spikes a pin through a donkey's hoof and then beats it with a holly branch. Readers – they number in their millions – have adored these antics for generations.

First Sophie tortures the doll, then the stepmother tortures Sophie. First Sophie decapitates, bludgeons and perforates small animals, then she is starved, stripped, striped and humiliated by her stepmother. Ségur slips it in so you barely notice. One minute the Fleurville girls are trying to rescue a family of hedgehogs from a gamekeeper, who has shot the mother and thrown the babies into a pond; the next minute Sophie is whacking one of the hedgehogs on its head to help it die faster, only to tumble into the pond herself, and then it's her stepmother who is doing the whacking. Amid remonstrations from the good Madame de Fleurville, Sophie is beaten so furiously that the switch finally breaks, and then, with more remonstrations, she is smacked out the door. These alternations and altercations of kindness and cruelty occur with such rapidity that the reader becomes quite benumbed to them. What is at first astonishing – the slicing up of goldfish by a little girl – becomes the quite normal situation of the same girl being whipped till she bleeds.

People imagine whipping as something significant, something of such moment that there must be at least a pause after the act, but families accommodate whipping just as they do an awkward family member. Events flow. A child is opening a present, a shoe flies through the air and hits the child, the child picks herself up, and the party goes on.

Ségur's noir nursery world earned her the title of *Sade en Jupes*, although critics leapt to her defense. Some say that first the Comtesse de Ségur's mother tortured her daughter, and then her daughter created The Fleurville Trilogy as a form of witness to the brutality of her own childhood. Others counter that Ségur's fascination with the spectacle of children being smacked is repeated with such excess that Ségur was clearly enthralled by the spectacle of her own childhood beatings. The bared bottom, the raised switch, the loving hand that strikes and stripes had become a fantasy she couldn't help repeating. In one of her tales, Jacques Laurent counts nineteen cases of beating and whipping in thirty pages chosen at random. Ségur never spoke of what her mother had done to her, but she recreated the humiliation again and again, and as the good Madame de Fleurville remonstrates, she ushers Sophie and all the Fleurville girls along the path of goodness. By the end of the trilogy, Sophie is truly chastened. She has left the wild girl behind and become – as all good girls must – sized down for matrimony and maternity, but she's also left all her millions of readers with the lingering memory, as Freud wrote, of a child being beaten. Among his patients, he wrote, it was almost always the same books 'whose contents gave a new stimulus to beating fantasies: those accessible to young people such as what was known as the "Bibliothèque Rose"'.

That old fox Sade would have loved this oscillation between sermonising and smacking, and he would have known exactly what was afoot in the Chateau de Fleurville. Every little detail would have made him smirk, especially the poked-out doll's eyes that are soldered back into place with melted wax. After he'd cut up the beggar woman Rose Keller, he filled the incisions he'd made in her body with Spanish wax, and then claimed in court that it was just a balm to help her heal. Sade knew how to dress up dirty acts, but he let slip his outrage that a court would pay such heed 'to a swished tart's backside'. In *Florville et Courvalle*, Sade created his own Florville, a girl of uncommon beauty who never gets swished but is torn up just the same. Sade compares Florville's skin to a lily, her mouth to a springtime rose. This sweetness of beauty and temperament makes her ruin more delectable. She is a good girl, too, in every way, and her goodness leads her step by step into monstrosity. By the end of his tale she will have stabbed her child, slept with her brother, married her father, instigated her mother's death, and then, on learning of her crimes, shot herself in the head without, as Sade writes, *saying another word.*

Flesh was the old fox's passion, and all the things he could do to it if hatred was unhooked, but he subdued his more malevolent obsessions in *Florville et Courval* in the hope of staying out of prison. Perhaps that is why this story is more a Sadeian nursery tale than a fully fledged Sadeian bacchanal. Unlike poor Justine in *Les malheurs de la virtu*, Florville is not cut up, and she keeps her identity intact until the very end of the story, where she is shattered by the revelation that every step she has taken on the path of goodness has led her deeper into the mire. In Sade's moral universe, to be small, innocent, pretty or good is to give yourself to the strong. As Angela Carter writes of Justine, 'when she offers her innocence to others as shyly as if she were offering a bunch of flowers, it is tramped in the mud'. Sade likes to play with flowers, awarding garlands to the vicious as he crushes the petals of gentle things. Madame de Verquin, the woman whose great joy is to lead Florville into catastrophe, dies 'on a voluptuous bed whose lilac-coloured silk curtains were pleasantly set off by garlands of natural flowers. Every corner was adorned with bouquets of carnations, jasmine, tuberoses and roses.' She goes to her grave happily knowing that she will be buried in a grove of jasmine and her disintegrating body will nourish the flowers she has loved. Florville dies in the throes of despair, her body contorting in a pool of her own blood.

*

Floraville. Fleurville. Florville. That is what I'm thinking about as I stare into the devastation of my mother's skin blossoming crimson as she lies in a room overrun with flowers. Mum was born into a house of flowers. They were her father's gift to her. He was a florist. As a young girl she would accompany him to the markets to buy flowers for the shop, or work with him in the back garden tending the flowers that he would cut and sell. In the Depression she walked the streets selling posies of violets to anyone with a penny to spare. She never had many stories to tell. Story belonged to Dad, who filled the house with grand tales that

roamed from the Knights of the Round Table to the warlords of
our ancestors to the pitched battles of our people making a stand
for labour against capital. Enthralled by a story of struggle that
found its verity in the daily news, I barely noticed Mum's untold
stories as they unfolded in the garden beds that ringed the
house, in the earth she turned from clay to soil, in the azaleas
and camellias that flowered under the windowsill, in the wisteria
that crept over the front doorway, and in the embankments of
grevillea, maidenhair and bush orchid that wound down the
garden to the creek bed. Mum's photograph album was a bou-
quet of flowers. When she came to visit me in France she collected the gardens of Europe. France was geraniums spilling
over black wrought iron; England, the girl pink and boy blue of
foxgloves and delphiniums; Amsterdam, a doorstep of purple
roses in a green pot. By then, the garden of my childhood had
been replaced by a succession of gardens, each smaller than the
last, until finally my mother's house was an apartment with a
small balcony. This too she transformed into a rosary that would
have honoured Flora. When I visited her, always after a long
absence, she would bring me first to see the large vases standing
in the hallway, then the small pots on the balcony, and finally the
posies Dad gave her, which stood on her bedside table or clus-
tered on the dressers that filled the apartment. Her news was the
bouquets she had placed in the churchyard to commemorate
friends passing, or the flowers she had arranged for the Sunday
church service, or flowers friends brought, or the postcards of
flowers they had sent. But ... I am telling a story. My mother
raised five children, taught generation after generation of children to read, sewed for the poor, read for the blind. In every way,
she was a good woman. But still, the fox got in.

B. is disheartened by the task of picking up the dismembered
remnants of chook and he gives up on digging a grave in the
hard January ground. He puts Floraville and her sisters in a plastic bag in the bin, alongside the carcass of a chicken we had
eaten the night before. I fear we are all foxes, cutting up and
devouring the bodies of chooks that are kept for our pleasure –
from theirs. But sometimes, no matter how you circle an idea,
you can't seize it, not properly. I collect Floraville's feathers and
stand them up along the fence posts, and leave the last of the

eggs in the garden commemorating her secret places. They won't last long. Foxes like eggs and sniff them out. In time, I will find traces of her, turn up a scurf of feathers and remember our Sadeian heroine who became. I hope she stood her ground when the fox came for her, although headless, there was not much she could do as the fox rounded on her sisters. Maybe she ran around for a while as headless chooks do, but I suspect not. I hope that as her life leaked out of her in the dirt of the chook yard, she saw the fox dispatch her undefended sisters and knew him for what he was. A fox and a foe.

But I digress. It's time to go to the airport. Florence and I drive down the hill and wend our way through the city. I try not to let her see my devastation but I keep running out of air, my words faltering before they reach her. I don't know how I could have imagined that Flores might be allowed her freedom. But now I have to leave it to Florence to keep us on track. Turn right! she says. That's the road. No! That way. I do what I am told. At the departure gate, she turns to me and says, *it's as if you think the worst thing that's happened is the death of the chooks*. And then she leaves me – once again in the daisy chain of mothers and daughters.

Salt Blood

Michael Adams

There are no words that fit tragedy. Nothing we can say. We do not want to be told everything is all right. It is not.
—Patrick Holland, 'Silent Plains' (2014)

Its constituents are – everything.
—Victor Hugo, Toilers of the Sea (1866)

It is quiet and cool and dark blue. At this depth the pressure on my body is double what it is at the surface: my heartbeat has slowed, blood has started to withdraw from my extremities and move into the space my compressed lungs have created. I am ten metres underwater on a breath-hold dive, suspended at the point of neutral buoyancy where the weight of the water above cancels my body's natural flotation. I turn head down, straighten my body, kick gently, and begin to fall with the unimpeded gravitational pull to the heart of the earth.

Freediving, or breath-hold diving, forms a relationship at once common and unique between humans and oceans. Commonplace because we can do it from the moment we are born (having already floated in amniotic fluid for nine months), and because many native and local cultures in coastal areas around the world have long practised breath-hold diving. But also unique because 'extreme sport' competitive divers are now exceeding depths of two hundred metres on a single breath, and there are divers able to hold their breath underwater for more than eleven minutes. Freediving is both liminal and transgressive, taking place in a zone where few humans venture, and subverting norms about perceived natural boundaries. The practice of freediving mobilises what has been called the most powerful autonomic reflex known in the human body: the mammalian dive response.

While I have been a casual spearfisher for many years, I have only recently engaged with freediving in its contemporary expression. My first time freediving, I trained with divers from a centre in Bali. A small group of us spent the mornings alternating between dive theory and yoga practice, and the afternoons diving and talking. My instructors were Matt and Patrick, and my diving partner was Yvonne, young, German-born, with degrees in journalism and American studies, and working locally as a scuba instructor. She had clearly spent a lot of time in the ocean, whereas for me it was never a profession or even an intense hobby.

On the north-east coast of Bali, Jemeluk Bay is wide and peaceful, sheltered from prevailing weather patterns, and lined with small fishing villages. The volcano Gunung Agung, the most sacred mountain in Bali, rises above the bay. The bathymetric chart highlights the continuity of the volcano's slope deep into the ocean, depth falling away quickly from shore. We dive among the moored fishing boats, using a system of buoys and weights to establish guide lines into the depths. In the water, with one hand loosely on the line to keep myself oriented, I 'breathe up', building the oxygen stores in my body. Visibility is about ten metres, then light disappears into milky blue darkness as I turn and dive. The white guide rope drifts past my mask until I reach the depth plate and pause, consciously relaxing my body, emptying my mind. I watch this world, bubbles float slowly upwards, jellyfish drift past, the sun is a diffuse white ball on the surface. It is distinctly different – thicker, darker, slower, heavier, more silent, and here I do not breathe.

As I fin back up, there is a burst of flickering light as a shoal of tiny blue fish hurtle through sunbeams at the surface. Head above water, there are distant sounds of the ubiquitous Balinese cocks, faint sounds from motor scooters. Diving again, my hearing transitions from airborne sound to waterborne sound. There is an intense crackle of snapping shrimp, fading as I go deeper. Faint sounds of women singing and the thrum of an outboard motor indicate a fishing boat passing nearby. After a few dives I start to close my eyes, removing the usual visual dominance to instead just listen and feel.

Two key aspects in freediving are equalisation, adjusting the pressure inside your ears to compensate for the increased pressure outside the eardrum that the water exerts with increasing depth; and responding to the urge to breathe, your body telling you insistently that you should breathe again, very soon, followed by involuntary spasms of your diaphragm, trying to make you breathe. Yvonne and I are both good at dealing with the urge to breathe, but we are not successfully equalising, and repeatedly have to turn back at ten metres, unable to eliminate the pain in our ears. I find this incredibly frustrating, and my diving ability declines as I become more tired and tense. Equalising is psychological as well as physical – taking down the walls of protection is difficult.

After the second day, I am completely spaced out, floating, serene. I sleep lightly through the tropical nights, dreaming of the dives, the patterns of light, the flicker of fish, the still blue. And I don't really understand it: why does the mortal uncertainty of deep immersion feel nurturing, reassuring? When you are deep underwater on a breath-hold dive, the margin of safety can be very small; there is very little space between living and not: you are, both metaphorically and actually, quite close to death. I am old enough now that death is not an abstract proposition; I go to more funerals, and my near-adult children remind me of the place of death in my own childhood.

What presents itself to navigate this mortal, radical uncertainty is grace. Physical grace means ease or suppleness of movement or bearing. It is a by-product of good freediving: the equalising of pressure across your eardrums and between your lungs and the crushing ocean weight, the streamlining of the external position and shape of your body. It is achieved by aligning yourself to the enveloping, immersive environment, the context and emotion of the place and time. Grace is important. We intuitively respond positively to seeing it in others (dancers, gymnasts, athletes) because it is good for us – to gracefully align ourselves to our environment. Physical grace is coupled with spiritual grace – it regenerates and sanctifies, and gives strength to endure trials. When you stop breathing, it's good to stop thinking, too.

Uncontrolled fear when deep underwater will spike adrenaline, trigger the fight-or-flight response, and potentially kill you. You can't fight and you can't flee, you have to accept and relinquish all control, you have to trust: the crushing pressure of multiple atmospheres cocoons you in an embrace.

In practice, freediving is just holding your breath and diving underwater. It is as old as humans, and humans have long understood various aspects of how it is possible, but the knowledge is uneven. Bajau divers from the Philippines and Malaysia routinely suffer hearing loss through burst eardrums, and Greek sponge divers in the past often had significant hearing loss as well as symptoms of decompression illness. The women-only diving communities of Ama in Japan and Haenyeo in Korea appear to dive deep long into old age with no ill effects, and have done so for thousands of years. Western spearfishers tend to know about equalising, but not so much about oxygen and carbon dioxide processes in the body.

Contemporary research interprets the physiology of freediving through the concept of the mammalian diving response. This is a combination of three independent reflexes that counter the normal bodily regulation of breathing, heart rate and blood pressure, and it is described as the strongest unconscious reflex in the body. The diving response occurs in all mammals, and possibly in all vertebrates – it has been observed in every air-breathing vertebrate ever tested. It is obvious and prominent in human infants. Up to about six months, an infant immersed in water will open her eyes, hold her breath, slow her heartbeat, and begin to swim breaststroke.

It is currently assumed that there are three triggers for the diving response: facial immersion, rising carbon dioxide levels, and increasing pressure at depth. These triggers result in reduced heart rate, redistribution of blood from bodily extremities to central organs, and contraction of the spleen. All these reflexes increase access to oxygen, either by reducing the rate it is consumed, or by changing its availability in the body. Learning to understand and recruit these processes enables freedivers to routinely reach depths of twenty to fifty metres, and to set records at depths of 100 to 200 metres.

From the land or the air, the ocean surface is opaque, mobile, vast and dark. The World Ocean is animate, active, unstable, ungrounded, unfathomed. It covers 70 per cent of the planet's surface and encompasses 99 per cent of its inhabitable area. It is largely unknown. Ocean processes control the weather and continental climates. It defines the Blue Planet.

Once immersed, beneath that surface, the suck and swell of the tides feel like the planet breathing. We are surprised, sometimes anxious and then increasingly comfortable with the complexities of temperature and movement in the ocean. There are layers of warm and cold water; strong but invisible currents that can help or hinder us, be struggled against or relaxed into, rocking the body into peace. Our bodies begin to align with those rhythms: the cycle of the moon and the ebb and flow of tides, the fetch of the wind across the bay.

Mirroring our time in the tiny sea of the amniotic sac, freediving is the most profound engagement between humans and oceans: the unmediated body immersed and uncontrolled in salt water. It is simultaneously planetary and intensely intimate – the ocean is both all around us and within us. That breadth of scale can be terrifying or reassuring. It is not about discovery, it is about recovery: we can freedive expertly from the minute we are born, but slowly forget. Our cultural preoccupation with growth and exploration washes away our embodied knowledge. Aboriginal people in Australia speak of how, if the Country is there, the knowledge is always there, and remind us to draw on the whole of the evidentiary base: the world, physical sensations, dreams, emotions – not just the 'bedrock' of Western reason. Sea Country keeps its knowledge too, waiting for us to find it again.

Ten metres, thirty feet, the point of neutral buoyancy, is five fathoms in the old marine depth measure, as in Ariel's song:

Full fathom five thy father lies,
Of his bones are coral made;
Those are pearls that were his eyes;
Nothing of him that doth fade,

But doth suffer a sea-change
Into something rich and strange.

Fathom comes from the ancient word *fæthm*, meaning an arm span, 'something that embraces'. It also means 'to understand' – to get to the bottom of something. I didn't start freediving to understand mortality, but that is the direction in which it has led me. Diving is the window that, for Simone Weil, 'makes visible the possibility of death that lies locked up in each moment'. Herman Melville puts the same thought into the whaleboat: 'it is only when caught in the swift, sudden turn of death, that mortals realize the silent, subtle, ever-present perils of life'.

Although he died when I was fourteen, I saw my father's death certificate for the first time this year. Single-word entries sketched the story: at age forty-five he was living in a caravan in north Queensland, working menial jobs. He sat down alone one evening on a beach with a handful of pills and a bottle of Scotch to kill himself. He asphyxiated on his vomit and was found days later. Four brief entries on a faded government form, with a tsunami of hurt and loss behind them, and a flood of confusion and misunderstanding to come. I knew the basics of that story, but was not prepared for the shock of the typed words: 'labourer', 'caravan park', 'suffocation'.

Reading a stranger's words on my father's death certificate reminds me how little I know about him. Because of some medical training before dropping out of university, he had good knowledge of pharmaceuticals. This helped him to find work with large pharmaceutical companies and gave him access to prescription drugs from the warehouse. I remember as a boy scavenging through boxes in those warehouses and using surgical tape to construct murderous crossbows with back-to-back scalpel blades as arrowheads. We moved around a lot as he and my mother held a number of jobs. My mother left when I was eleven, and I last saw my father when I was thirteen. My brother and I had lived in ten houses in five towns by the time I finished school.

My relationship with my own son through his mid-teens was fraught. My teenage years had been marked by binge drinking, drugs and other risk-taking, but I rationalised that I was responding to a dysfunctional childhood, whereas he had two loving and supportive parents present, material security, and we lived in a beautiful place. I felt I had no road map and was just making it up as I went along. I had a stepfather in my own teens who took me into police cells and stood me in front of mangled cars with blood pooled beneath them to show me where I was going to wind up. I now wonder whether suggesting to my son that we go to a freedive school was pushing against, or mirroring, the patterns of my own past.

I have spearfished with him since he was less than ten years old, but in relatively shallow waters. One of the first times, as he stood next to me on the rocks above rolling swells, I asked him if he was ready, to which he said, 'If being totally terrified is ready, then yes I am,' – and we stepped off into the sea. He is a long way past that now and far outstrips me in his ability and comfort in the water. During our first session in Bali, I watch his grace and skill as he fins down the line and disappears into blue depth past the limit of visibility. Then a long wait until he reappears, relaxed and unhurried. He interned at the freedive school, and has now repeatedly dived thirty and forty metres. On his first attempt at that depth, he paused at the depth marker and looked back to the surface. Freedive teachers tell you not to look up or down, to keep your spine straight; five atmospheres of pressure ruptured blood vessels in his extended trachea, so by the time he was back at the surface he was coughing blood.

Divers like to underplay these injuries, so it is called a throat squeeze. You can also have an eye or mask squeeze or lung squeeze. The medical literature defines these as barotraumas, pressure-induced injuries; they can be very common in freediving. You can also 'samba' at the surface (a loss of motor control so your body does a little involuntary dance), and finally SWB, shallow water blackout: both of these are a result of hypoxia or oxygen deficiency in the brain. It is increasingly assumed that shallow water blackout is the explanation for many diving deaths generally attributed to drowning. Shallow water blackout is achieved by either consciously enduring the contractions of your diaphragm (caused by increasing carbon dioxide levels) that are trying to force you to breathe; or artificially lowering those carbon dioxide levels with particular breathing practices, so you don't get the contractions.

After my first freedive trip, I went back to riding a big motor-bike and started yoga. Freediving, yoga and motorbike riding are related practices. Yoga is not intrinsically dangerous, but yoga philosophy says 'when you hold your breath you hold your soul'. Breathing out, expiration, is a little reflection of that last gasp of death; to expire means both to breathe out and also to die. The physical movements and breathing practices of yoga take me to a place of emptiness and peace: when the breath is still, the mind is still. The BMW demands presence: it is really not good to day-dream on a motorbike. I ride nearly every day, in all weather, and statistically that will likely eventually lead to an incident. But when that happens, adrenaline and reflexes come to the rescue. Diving and yoga remove adrenaline and bring quiet and still-ness; the motorbike and diving bring presence in danger.

One winter I dived off South Bruny Island, Tasmania. Bruny was home to Tasmanian Aboriginal woman Truganini. During my school years we were told Truganini was the 'last of the Tasmanian Aboriginal people', effectively erasing the lives of the many descendants of Aboriginal people and various settler-colonist communities. I harvested from the ancestral waters of Truganini's Nuenone people: cold, deep water, rich and beauti-ful: abalone, oysters, mussels, edible seaweeds, wild spinach. The abalone industry is worth $100 million a year but excludes many Aboriginal people because of the exorbitant cost of licences, despite a 40,000-year history of sustainable harvest demonstrated by numerous shell middens. Current active divers are arguing that the stock is on the verge of collapse after only four decades of over-intensive harvest.

Walking the tidal edge on Bruny, I kept thinking about Joseph Conrad's words at the end of *Heart of Darkness* (1899): 'the tran-quil waterway leading to the uttermost ends of the earth flowed sombre under an overcast sky – seemed to lead into the heart of an immense darkness'. Tasmania is not so far from the uttermost ends of the earth, and it has a dark history, palpable in the land-scape. The idea of Tasmanian Gothic is not new, with writers Richard Flanagan, Rohan Wilson and others exploring the psy-che of the Van Diemonians. Rohan Wilson's *The Roving Party* (2011) is perhaps the most successful book I have read in pre-senting how Aboriginal people, in all their diversity, were totally compromised by the violent colonial process. There were no right decisions to be made, especially in Tasmania: all decisions had terrible consequences. (After leaving Bruny I discover, astonishingly, that the rusting hulk of the *Otago*, the only ship that Joseph Conrad commanded, lies near the shore of the Derwent River in Hobart.)

My first attempt diving at Bruny was short. It was morning, midwinter, calm, and I had just seen a trio of dolphins cruising slowly along the shore of the D'Entrecasteaux Channel. I slipped into deep water from a boat jetty and was immediately shocked by the intense cold, less than ten degrees by my dive watch. I submerged and finned west across the channel towards Satellite Island, but with visibility only two to three metres, an instant cold headache and paranoia about hypothermia, I opted out.

The second try was at Cloudy Bay, also very cold but I dived for forty-five minutes. Visibility was still limited, and big swells rolling unimpeded from Antarctica meant I could not get near to the underwater bull kelp forests, which seem to like high-energy coasts. Black cockatoos and a pair of sea eagles watched while I dressed, shaking with cold, on the rain-soaked beach.

Before Tasmania, I dive at Honaunau Bay on the Big Island of Hawai'i. Like Jemeluk Bay, this coast is dominated by a volcano, Mauna Kea – to Native Hawaiians the most sacred mountain in Hawai'i, and the tallest mountain in the world if measured from the sea floor. The first day I am just testing my gear. This is my first time diving since I scuba-dived with students on a field course. I have heard someone compare scuba diving to driving through a forest in a four-wheel drive with the windows up and the air conditioning on, and that was definitely my experience – I kept wanting to stop breathing to cut out all that noise, all those bubbles, to reject the cyborg and hybrid paraphernalia. Diving at Honaunau Bay was the opposite: serenely quiet except for the crackle of shrimp and the slap of waves.

I am diving with Daniel, an instructor from southern California who has relocated to the Big Island. Daniel is very experienced and very, very relaxed in the water. Again like Jemeluk, Honaunau Bay is unique in having great depth close to shore: the bathymetric chart here shows that within a hundred metres of shore you can be a hundred metres deep. I have never been in water that deep; on the first day I have trouble relaxing with all that blue falling away below my fins. Being relaxed is really important in freediving, but I wind up with continuous cramps in both legs.

On my third day diving we are joined by Shell, a quietly spoken instructor and international competitor. A month after we dive together, Shell will become the US women's champion in the pool discipline of dynamic no-fins, swimming 125 metres underwater without breathing in less than three minutes. Diving with Daniel and Shell is calm but rigorous, with detailed safety processes and checks. Shell is quietly experimenting with a nose clip and no mask, and Daniel is safety diver for us both as we alternate dives.

A year later, I dived in a very different way at Honaunau Bay, this time with legendary diver Carlos Eyles. All my diving so far had been within the established structures of modern freediving, with guide ropes, floats, marker plates, and lots of focus on metres of depth, minutes of breath hold, Boyle's law, and the physics and physiology of pressure. Of all the people I have dived with, two gave me stark lessons about my own attachment to this linear thinking. Rayanna, a young Brazilian woman I dived with in Indonesia, and an excellent freediver, never used a dive watch, did not measure her depth or breath hold, and helped me throw away the numbers. In Hawai'i, Carlos, who is seventy-five, did not talk about technique at all: we sat at the edge of the water and talked about philosophy for an hour before our dives together, then he taught experientially – I copied his movements. He called it 'catching the rock', demonstrating the analogy that we cannot teach through linear thinking or communication how to catch a thrown object: our brains can't compute the distances and movements and decisions, we learn it bodily. We dived for an hour or so, then swam together for about a mile, out to the northern point of Honaunau Bay and back. Next day I went back and repeated it all, but this time alone, breaking the cardinal rule of modern freediving.

The core and obvious lesson for me from Carlos was 'the ocean is not a linear system'. Nonlinear systems are typically described as counterintuitive, unpredictable or chaotic. We can think of the ocean like this, as vast, turbulent, shifting, untamed, unknowable – the dark abyss. Floating above one hundred metres of blue depth, that abyss felt very real. As Carlos says, soon sharks will start circling in your prefrontal lobes: they are just out of sight, but you are sure they are there. Carlos talked about this fear, and how you have to throw away these acculturated imaginings, these death anxieties, and focus on your body's ancient knowledge. When the fear is there, those monsters of the deep, you lose grace. Finding grace opens you to transformation. Feeling the ocean all the way through your body, seeing it in every direction you can look, experiencing sound and silence and light transformed by the depth and thickness of water – these embodied experiences unground our linear, rational, bounded structures of thought. We can let go of the anchor of imagined and irrational fears, and swim free with humility and attention. Swimming and diving alone on a quiet hot morning in Honaunau Bay, feeling strong and comfortable in my body, I was slowly unmoored, slowly floating away from risk assessments and calculations and into the warm embrace of the peaceful bay.

This ocean, these waters, are full of life and agency. Most of life lives in the sea – 50 to 80 per cent of all species live there. Their agency is palpable – their intention, attention, awareness and presence in the rock, coral, sand and salt water. So while I was alone, I was also not alone: I was surrounded by innumerable other beings, all going on with their lives and deaths in the sea about me.

In the tidal wave of current discussions about extinctions, biodiversity loss and planetary crisis, a less visible current of knowledge pulls at our attention. Everywhere, there is both abundance and loss, thriving and declining. What we term weeds, or feral species, or invasive species, or common and abundant species, are plants and animals thriving in place, and it happens everywhere. In all the world's oceans, while many apex predators are depleted, populations of cephalopods (squid, cuttlefish and octopuses) are increasing, despite continuous and heavy fishing. Cephalopods are particularly interesting, with complex intelligences described by Peter Godfrey-Smith as 'an independent experiment in the evolution of a large nervous system, the only such experiment outside the vertebrates'. In my local seas, octopuses and giant cuttlefish are quite common, often curiously investigating us as we examine them. My local rocky shores are home to the only cephalopod that can kill a human, the tiny and potently venomous blue-ringed octopus. Hundreds of human families play in that habitat daily with no fatal encounters; we peacefully share the space. Because we have forgotten this truth, that we can share, that we are all connected, planet and landscape and seascape and human and innumerable other species, we have lost perspective on change, and these become liminal experiences: looking into the large, thinking eyes of octopuses and giant cuttlefish; sinking into depth, eyes closed, past the buoyancy zone; embodying the visceral sense of release and lightness of diving on empty lungs.

Liminality is a threshold state, the border between one condition and another. It is not either of them, it is ambiguous and disorienting. In many cultures, there are three stages in the liminal transition: a metaphorical death, a test and rebirth. The liminality of freediving has multiple dimensions. It connects us to ancient stories in many cultures of mermen and mermaids: beings between human and water creature. Western cultures know them as sea nymphs, nixies, silkies, and so on. Miskito Indian divers in Central America call these beings *liwa mairin*, and in modern times attribute decompression sickness and other diving illnesses to the inimical moods of these water spirits. Diving is also in the boundary zone between earth and water, with air the defining element. It moves from light to increasing darkness with depth and back again. It moves from swimming down against the natural buoyancy of the human body to freefalling with gravity as increasing water pressure overcomes that buoyancy.

And it is liminal between life and death – at great depth, you have to be exquisitely attuned to the totality of your body if you want to keep on living. You have to understand the symptoms of oxygen depletion in the particular way that it is expressed in your own body, and confidently know how much time you have to continue swimming deeper and also make the return journey to the surface before you black out. I keep in my journal a graph illustrating this relationship, with red and blue lines showing trajectories of living and dying. Freedivers I spoke with indicated there can be a wide range of physiological indications of oxygen depletion, and they had learned quite specific cues to which they would respond. Despite this, many experienced freedivers assured me that death is seldom in their thoughts. The safety framing in recreational freedive training and diving is usually rigorous and very careful, with a number of key rules described as 'safety through redundancy', designed to keep divers well within the limits of what is safe for them individually. This is reinforced by the buddy system, so you never dive alone. Spearfishers, routinely self-taught, tend to be less particular in their approach, with hyperventilation a common practice, and many spearfishers diving alone. Lifelong surfer and diver Tim Winton embodies this, with many lyrical passages in his writing reflecting the casual acceptance of these risks.

Moving away from the regulated structures of safety and risk control lead you onto the rocks of danger and uncertainty, and danger and uncertainty, normal in most of nature, are the complements of safety and fulfilment in life. To live amid all of these you need to be present, attentive – you need to learn to fail better. Tibetan Buddhist Pema Chödrön argues that 'all kinds of things happen that break your heart, but you can hold failure and loss as part of your human experience'. You need to find again your ancient bodily wisdom, your heart's knowledge that while we are all alone, while there is always hurt and loss, your strength and beauty and intelligence and love are transmuted through your life's relationships and work to be reborn in others.

I have failed to understand my father's suicide all my life. There was no note, no message; I had not seen him for a year. Freediving has shown me a new way to understand death. In the yoga traditions, breathing in engulfs you with life. Breathing out generously gives that life back out into the world. After deep practice of yoga breath control, pranayama, the need to breathe often falls away for long, relaxed minutes. As the water closes over my head each time I dive, I let go my earthly concerns to sink into the blue embrace of an alternate world. On that dune in the tropical night, my father took a different measure on his life and cast off his quotidian moorings. One of those moorings was me, and I have to fathom the place in my life of both harbour and open sea, port and storm.

In freediving I often think about death, but it is not always 'death anxiety', as the psychologists construct it. There is real danger, as well as the imaginary circling sharks. In physiological terms, breath-hold diving is progressive asphyxiation. It is possible because of a profound suppression of metabolism: it changes the way your body functions. Surfacing after a prolonged dive, you are not the same person: your body has moved through dramatic changes, you have been to a place where few venture. If much life is lived on the surface of things, freediving lets you plunge beneath that surface. Freediving has led me to an understanding of the paradoxical joy of being close to death, the compassion and peace.

I have lived much of my life feeling marginal, feeling like an imposter in my jobs: I expect rejection, a predictable outcome of two parents sequentially leaving when I was young. Only recently have I begun to understand that there might be strengths in those places on the margin. Freediving alone, freediving actually free of all that positivist framing and safety paraphernalia and other people, brought me back to my father's death. He had become more and more marginal to what the world considers important, and eventually, alone, stepped off that edge, stepped free of all that judgement and demand. There is no possibility of answers once that boundary is crossed. Alone, immersed in the spaces of the silent water, I am maybe learning to let go of the questions.

In blue-water diving most life is not visible, for most large sea creatures live in shallower waters. In deep blue water the freediver is exposed in every direction, completely vulnerable. That vast continuous space, that absence, is an entry, an opening. Empty space is open to anyone, an invitation. Can I live without trying to fill the silences and empty spaces? Can I learn to live in these silences and spaces? In the extraordinary emptied bliss at the end of a yoga session, when my teachers cup their hands over my ears in the penultimate position of *savasana* (appropriately, the corpse pose), the muted roar of the ocean fills the silence: the tides of salt blood pulsing through my body. It feels like the hand of God.

One of my teachers in Bali urges us to swim on the shallow reef before the deep water, observing and learning local marine species and ecologies, as well as being in the sea generally: 'you need to spend time in the ocean, make it your friend'.

We become familiar with one turtle that seems always to be found in the same patch of reef, we know the batfish are curious and often come to investigate us in the deep water, we begin to understand the diurnal patterns of changing activities and species across an undersea topography that becomes familiar. And fundamentally we engage with the salt water itself: we taste it, swallow it, rinse it through our sinuses, feel it flow across our skin – it is both all around us and within us. The tears in our eyes, the sweat on our skin, the blood in our veins, arteries, organs, have the same salt concentration as ancient oceans, reflecting the time when the ocean water itself served as the fluid transport in the bodies of our biological ancestors.

Deep in the ocean's embrace, on one breath, feeling your mind and body change: freediving is a transformational encounter. Like all of life, it is a journey between two breaths, the first breath of life and the last breath before death, the last breath before immersion and the first breath of surfacing again into air. In yoga and meditation, practitioners speak of 'resting in the space between breaths'. In marine mammal physiology, researchers describe the way seals will drift underwater, not swimming, not breathing, not hunting – resting in the space between breaths. On this blue pathway, naked of technology, with just one breath, the freediver's unshielded body is open to the silent sea. The transformative encounter connects the World Ocean to the ocean within, bringing us home to the cycles of how we are born and die alone and together on this planet.

Peasant Dreaming

Sam Vincent

When we were kids, my sisters and I weren't allowed to watch TV during dinner. The risk of seeing John Howard was too much for my parents to bear. In the months after he became prime minister, Mum and Dad wore their opposition proudly, chortling of his imminent demise and slapping a 'Don't blame me I voted Labor' sticker on our dusty family van.

But as the Howard months became the Howard years, their mood turned first to frustration – Dad would refer to him no longer as 'the miserable little man' but 'the little shit' or 'the little dickhead' – and eventually to enforced censorship. Should the PM slip through their low-fi parental block, unexpectedly cropping up on the *7.30 Report* beside Kerry O'Brien, he could expect an incoming missile before having his feed cut. My mum was throwing shoes at Little Johnny long before it became fashionable on *Q&A*.

But I for one relished what televised glimpses I could manage: those bushy eyebrows, suddenly plucked to make him electorally palatable; the chunky bulletproof vest under his shirt after the Port Arthur massacre; the loud shirts at APEC summits; the louder Wallabies tracksuit on his morning power walk ... He was a strange sort of fashion icon.

My favourite item in Howard's wardrobe was his akubra hat. Reserved for visits to marginal rural electorates, it was always accompanied by a Driza-Bone coat – irrespective of the forecast – and a pair of R.M. Williams boots.

What I found most intriguing about the hat was its pristine condition. Flat-brimmed, symmetrical and impermeable, it was so different to the hats my farmer father wore in the paddocks of my youth – tatty, smelly rags of things, luridly stained bright pink with herbicide dye and full of holes to facilitate melanoma growth.

Years later, a few weeks before I turned thirty, I was at home in Canberra when my mum called. Dad was in an ambulance. He'd had an accident, and the thumb on his favoured hand was broken in several places. Farming families often need a crisis to start a conversation about succession, and this was ours. In time, my dad's thumb made a near full recovery, but since that phone call I've spent one day a week working with him as an apprentice primary producer.

In honour of this new direction, and largely in jest, a friend gave me an akubra for my thirtieth birthday. It was – I was appalled to realise when I took it out of its box and studied it – flat-brimmed, symmetrical and impermeable: Howard's hat. In becoming Dad's deputy sheriff, I resembled the Deputy Sheriff. And I felt as much of a phoney.

*

This is a companion essay to a companion edition. In 2006, *Griffith Review* published *The Next Big Thing*, dedicated to gen X writers, thinkers and activists. One of them was my eldest sister, the writer and anthropologist Eve Vincent. In her contribution, 'Confusions of an Economist's Daughter', Eve deconstructed the generational divide between her 'ratbag', World Economic Forum–blockading self (Eve was then twenty-nine) and our Keating acolyte of a father (then fifty-eight), set to the backdrop of the farm they both loved. Eve's the best writer I know.

> We lived half an hour's drive from Canberra. In the morning our dad would race into the kitchen after checking the sheep, his tie slung like a scarf around his neck. He'd leave in a hurry, his ute slipping around dusty gravel corners, the radio loud. 'Good morning, this is *A.M.*' I imagine him now, knotting his tie in the rear-vision mirror in the car park at work. My dad is a free-trade economist.

My parents bought the farm, then 200 acres of overgrazed grassland, in 1983, the year before I was born. The Hawke–Keating reform years, Eve wrote, were a good time to be in the business of offering economic advice. 'Those beautiful paddocks, scattered with rocks and flecked with scars, quickly became ours.'

'Confusions of an Economist's Daughter' caused a stir in our family. It was a brutally honest public airing of Eve's attempt to reconcile the unselfishness our father espoused with the self-interest of the economics he practised.

> My dad the economist, who worked so hard through decades of relentless change, is an unfailingly generous person, and he has poured his successes back to his family. He instilled a social conscience in us all, but he's dismayed by my interpretation of it. Most of all, I suspect the thing he wants from me is stability. He's looking for some certainty.

And now he's got it. Eve has since had children (tick), scored a plum academic posting (tick) and bought a house (gold star and koala stamp). I remain single, childless, underemployed and a renter. The farm is now 650 acres (they've bred like rabbits); our father, sixty-nine years old.

In the edition brief for *Millennials Strike Back*, there was a reference to those who came before us, the class of *The Next Big Thing*: 'In the decade since, this group has gone on to make their mark; it is now time for the next generation to take up their mantle.' And so it is I give you my own daddy issues.

*

I am a third-generation farmer, and I know how that sounds – predestined, aristocratic. But it's by default, not design. My late maternal grandfather, whom I called Papa, was a Western District grazier and longstanding president of the Royal Agricultural Society of Victoria. His was the squatter's life of horseback mustering, lawn tennis parties and gentlemen's clubs. (My dad tells a story of once answering Papa's phone and taking a message from an acquaintance, a 'Mr Fraser from Hamilton'.) But my uncles didn't want to take over Papa's farm and my mum and my aunt – who still listens to *The Country Hour* despite being a Bangalow yuppie – weren't asked. It was sold before I was born.

From there, the farming line changed sides, states and narratives.

If millennials only exist as a construct in opposition to baby boomers, that my dad was able to buy a farm and that I am now taking it on is because we are firmly placed on each side of the dichotomy.

Dad, the clever son of a clever man – my paternal grandfather, born in a bark hut in the Gippsland bush and forced to leave school at age twelve by the Depression – was never going to become anything other than a white-collar professional. But though he co-founded a successful economics consultancy and is proud of his role in helping to liberalise the Australian economy, he has always looked uncomfortable in a suit. This is a man who, when I was in kindergarten, cut off much of his left big toe with a chainsaw – and drove himself to hospital. Five years later he shot a fox *in* my sister Lucy's bedroom *while* the rest of us were eating dinner (roast chicken, which we figure attracted it inside in the first place).

Dad was raised in Melbourne but spent his school holidays 'mucking about' on a cousin's farm in the Wimmera; Mum, whom he met studying agricultural science at university, pined for a return to the land. They named their block Gollion, after a Swiss village where, while backpacking in the 1970s, they had found relations to an ancestor of Dad's, the first Vincent to arrive in Australia, in 1854.

Gollion was once part of Fernleigh, a farm established in the 1870s, but it is my parents who have most shaped its landscape since white settlement. Armed with the boomer audacity that held the postwar world as theirs to conquer, Mum and Dad built themselves a house and set about constructing their Eden. Dams were bulldozed, fences strained, and my three sisters and I enlisted to plant thousands of trees on freezing August days.

They subscribed to *Grass Roots*, the self-sufficiency bible of 1980s Australia, grew vegies, kept chooks and established orchards. Confounding the Nationals-voting 'cockies' around them, they brewed compost tea to fertilise their pastures organi-cally, restored their section of a creek to the 'chain of ponds' it would have resembled before land clearing turned it into a drain, and introduced a holistic management regime in which stock is moved regularly through many small paddocks to replicate the bunch-grazing and pasture-rest periods of wild herd and predator ecosystems. The place boomed.

But here's the thing: Dad, who 'retired' fourteen years ago, still sees Gollion as a hobby farm. Some people, he reasons, play golf when they retire; he manages 150 cows and their calves, two large orchards, a small mob of sheep and a shantytown of sheds – and, until last year, was the president of the local Landcare group. While his former colleagues cruise the South Pacific, Dad seeks adventure atop dodgy ladders or by roll-starting a rollbar-less tractor. ('Best not tell your mum I've been doing that again.')

Gollion was never meant to be a legacy project, and I was never raised to be its successor. If anything, I was raised to believe that farmers – as opposed to the 'go-getters' (a favourite expression of Dad's) of the service economy who have farms for fun – are largely 'losers' (another favourite): either lazy aristocrats who inherited the good fortune of their forebears, or uncouth bumpkins with their hands out for government assistance. Throwbacks to pre-Gough, cultural-cringe Australia. Laggards to the message that we no longer ride on the sheep's back. 'The bigger the hat,' Dad is fond of saying when Barnaby Joyce appears on the telly in his own akubra, 'the smaller the brain beneath it.'

And so, although I spent much of my childhood building hide-outs among the scribbly gums and skinny-dipping in a choice of twenty-eight dams, I only learned to link two pieces of wire with a figure-eight knot when I was thirty-one. Before 2014, I wouldn't have been able to tell you the difference between wallaby grass and kangaroo grass, what it feels like to put a rubber ring around a bull calf's testes or how to prune a quince tree.

Even now, entering the third year of my yet-to-be quantified apprenticeship, when I pepper Dad with questions and jot down his answers in a Moleskine I keep in my moleskins, I think he still hopes I'm going to wake up one day with a burning desire to be a full-time public servant who farms on the side. He seems astounded that I take an interest in continuing what *he* established, rather than leading *my* 'own life' (that is, procreating and buying a house). Dad didn't get the memo that most Australian millennials are renters, unmarried and haven't had kids yet. Nor the one that you're only able to combine full-time farming with full-time city work if you opt out of third-wave feminism. That's what happens when you spend much of your time in the back paddock with no-one for company but Suey the sheepdog.

Dad recently told me that if he had his time again he would've been an orchardist instead of an economist. And that's a shame, don't you think? That statement – and his claimed loathing of the very lifestyle he so dearly loves – betrays what I think most disturbs him about my farming future: that I wish to revert to a kind of hipster remastering of the very world his father (he of the bark hut) escaped so that Dad could become a go-getter. My father is worried that when I grow up, I want to be a peasant.

*

In June 2010, I visited Iceland on assignment for the travel pages of a newspaper. It was three weeks after the eruption of the volcano Eyjafjallajökull had grounded air traffic across Europe; when the wind blew from the south-east, a thin film of grey still settled on the windshields of Reykjavík. The tourist pap – T-shirts, tea towels, mugs – said it all:

> Don't fuck with Iceland!
> We may not have cash, but we've got ash!

Everywhere, it seemed, I encountered the hangover of the country's financial crisis: garish housing estates, half-finished, lay empty; Hummers – once longed-for trophies of success – were scorned in the street as vulgar reminders of living beyond one's means; the criminal prosecution of bankers dominated conversation. In the space of one generation, a nation of farmers and fishermen had become high financiers, and now they were asking if it was worth it. The mood mirrored southern Europe, where since 2008 thousands of young professionals, suddenly unemployed, had been moving back to ancestral plots of land. In some cases it was a question of survival: they needed something to eat.

A paradigm shift was underway, a critique of the moment when a lifestyle had been replaced with a 'career'. In a new Reykjavík bar focused on local produce, the menu captured the zeitgeist:

There is something to be said about the old days, when people worked with their hands and produced something tangible. We hope you catch a glimpse of those days as you sip your coffee or munch on some tried and true Icelandic delicacies.

Australia was spared the worst of the GFC, but not the disdain for the economic system that created it. The casualisation of the Australian workforce and the squeeze on the first-home buyers market have made emphasising saving for the future over living for the present less sacrosanct – let alone relevant – to my generation than to my parents'. Why slog away doing something you don't enjoy for a house you may never own? Better to find meaning in other facets of work than financial remuneration.

In many cases, jobs once seen as 'unskilled' are by necessity being filled by those who would have previously found work in academia, the media and the arts: just as your barista probably has a PhD in philosophy, the guy who sells figs to Canberra's best restaurants each autumn has a similarly useless degree: Bachelor of Arts (International Relations), with honours in French. (Incidentally, I actually use the French a fair bit on my rounds – you'd be surprised how many Gallic pastry chefs lurk in Australia's commercial kitchens.)

While I agree with Dad's scorn for the rising nostalgia of an insular and nativist Australia, I don't think there's anything demeaning or intellectually wasteful about pursuing the life of a small farmer. Dad's right: I *do* want to be a peasant when I grow up. Restoring lost links between consumers and producers in a broken food system is rewarding and empowering. The recent proliferation of farmers' markets and focus among home cooks and restaurant chefs on local, seasonal produce aren't merely a question of taste. They speak to a growing desire for sustainability in both the ways we produce food and the communities who produce it. I was recently called a wanker for questioning why a friend was eating an out-of-season, imported kiwifruit. I relish the title. But I also relish the title of 'writer'. For the past seven years I have worked on and off as a research assistant for a political scientist, to cover the rent and allow me to write two days a week. Initially, I approached farming the same way: when in the position to, I would use the profit from selling livestock and produce to subsidise my writing. But increasingly I don't see why the two should be compartmentalised – my 'career', such as it is, divorced from my life.

In his magisterial book *The Art of Time Travel* (2016), Tom Griffiths writes of how the late farmer-historian Eric Rolls combined his dual vocations:

> He wrote of the constant battle between words and acres, between the soil as a source of his originality and the farm as a demanding distraction. He knew that the battle to win time for writing was part of the necessary discipline.

Rolls's farm chores restricted his writing, but he recognised they also nourished it. American farmer and writer Joel Salatin calls this 'intellectual agrarianism' and sees it most purely embodied in Thomas Jefferson, who believed getting your hands dirty was crucial for deep thought; for the Romans, the notion of *otium* conveyed the prerequisite state of peace – physical and mental – for literary occupation in a rural retreat. Much has been written in recent years on the link between walking and creativity. I have found my *otium* on the farm, my mind subconsciously working on writing while I open gates and herd cattle. And among my peers it's catching on.

The average age of a farmer in Australia is fifty-eight. I'm thirty-two. A common lament of agricultural policymakers is that, with record sheep and cattle prices and emerging markets to our north, Australia could be the food bowl of Asia – but only if we can hold onto our farmers. In the most urbanised country on earth, the drain from country to city has become a torrent, leaving in its wake broken communities, farm gates locked for good.

I can only speak of my own experience, and my experience is not the type of farming Chinese consortiums have their eye on. I believe farming should be conducted within the environment, not against it. At Gollion we haven't ploughed a paddock for decades, because it destroys soil structure and releases carbon into the atmosphere. 'Weeds' are in the eye of the beholder out our way. I wouldn't be interested in growing a high-yield, herbicide- and pesticide-dependent monoculture, either: depleting soils, killing wildlife with chemicals and encouraging crop failure and disease through specialisation is part of the problem, not the solution. Is it any wonder the political party most enthusiastic about fashioning this so-called food bowl – ostensibly the farmers' party – is less enthusiastic about curbing greenhouse emissions? No farmer who cares for their country is blind to the increasingly challenging climatic conditions they face. Aside from the economic unreality of a high-wage advanced economy becoming Asia's food bowl, where still-significant mineral exports appreciate the exchange rate and high commodity prices are offset by high farm costs, it's not the lack of farmers that is frustrating this grand ideological plan so much as the land itself. But I am not alone in my friendship group in wishing to return to the land for creative, as well as moral and financial, prerogatives.

I'm currently doing a course on holistic farming near the southern New South Wales town of Braidwood. I had expected it to be full of ruddy-cheeked cattlemen in their forties and fifties; instead it is mostly people like me, tertiary-educated thirty-somethings who want to grow their own food to nourish their vocations. We are writers, a ceramicist and a filmmaker; a market gardener with a background in conservation; the manager of a local farmers' market and her partner, who feeds his chooks on maggots from roadkill kangaroos. An industrial designer by training, he recently designed and built a house for his parents from gleaned materials. It cost $60,000.

I was told about the course by one of my oldest friends, the scion of merino producers from an escarpment near the Great Dividing Range. His family are the ultimate agrarian intellectuals: they build their own unapproved dwellings and grow much of their food. This friend's dad studied law to appease his parents, only to immediately become a farmer on graduating; his middle brother, who bakes the family's bread, brews its beer and tans its hides, hasn't needed to pay tax for years.

Now that China isn't buying so much of our iron ore, our prime minister tells us, we must be more 'agile' if we are to prevent a drop in 'living standards'. But what standards are those – the wherewithal to buy more crap? Unlike most baby boomers I know, I don't think quality of life is something you'll find in the Aldi specials catalogue.

*

I like to ride my bicycle to Gollion on my weekly apprenticeship day. I prefer the way the country unfolds from the saddle rather than how it blurs by in the car. What were unpaved roads when I was a kid are now largely sealed. Only the odd stringybark has survived the march of Canberra's northern fringe over the Limestone Plains – preserved for posterity and marketing. ('The perfect place to nest', the realty billboards proclaim.)

Over the hill that marks the border between the ACT and New South Wales, the dumping starts: grass clippings and washing machines, bottles and prams. But slowly the bush asserts itself with more trees between fewer houses, cattle grazing the roadside with their heads through the fence, galahs passing overhead. Like Jehovah's Witnesses, they always work in pairs.

Hitting the dirt, my tyres turn white and I get my first glimpse of the farm – one lone old yellow box on our biggest hill – still ten minutes away. (You can see this tree from the summit of Canberra's Mount Ainslie if you know where to look.) I lock my eyes onto it to avoid concentrating on the last climb, and when I'm hurtling into our valley Gollion opens like a flower: the flood plain with its eucalypt plantations, backed by six hills (green, silver, brown or yellow depending on the season), themselves backed by the distant smudge of the Brindabellas (always blue).

I don't know when I will be handed the reins of Gollion. That will be the true test. Sometimes I doubt whether I am responsible enough to manage it: I can be as reckless with my money as the next young cafe-breakfast enthusiast. I recognise how privileged I am to be in this position, but it also scares me.

Nor have I yet decided what I will farm. I enjoy working with cattle and would like to keep them, but I think I like growing fruit the best. With Dad's help, and on the back of feedback from chefs I already sell to, I am establishing an organic orchard of eighty black genoa fig trees; in the future, I want to explore growing pomegranates and maybe pistachios. I like the long game of seeing plants grow: if it's true that millennials suffer from the need for instant gratification, this has been a good antidote.

But for now, I'm still in training. The days I spend with my dad on the farm are ones of quiet, wholesome routine. Straining up fences. Marking calves. Shovelling compost. Planting trees.

There are rituals to observe: morning tea with Michael Cathcart; lunch with Eleanor Hall; afternoon tea with Phillip Adams. Opening the ute door for Suey the sheepdog; swearing at Suey the sheepdog when she refuses to hop in next to us. Dad and I don't say much to each other while we work, but I'm sure I'll look back on these days as among the richest I've spent with him. There is a silent transaction underway. Skills are being taught. Knowledge shared.

Bearing witness to it all, in sun and rain, is my akubra. I call it J.H. In the two and a half years since I turned thirty, J.H. has slowly come to fit my head – and my nascent identity as a primary producer. After hundreds of hours of being sat on, blown off and retrieved, it is now, thankfully, a sweat-stained, smelly and misshapen piece of rabbit felt.

I've come to rely on J.H. Maybe a little too much. I recently accompanied my parents to a cattle sale in Victoria's Western District. Naturally, I wore my akubra. Among this crowd of beetroot-faced, overweight cattle prospectors, J.H. was among the dirtiest, biggest hats. I looked the part – much to Dad's chagrin. Worse than John Howard, he remarked as we got in the car to leave, now I looked like a member of the Young Nationals.

The Bystander

Lech Blaine

There were seven of us. Five in the car, two in the boot. We were driving to a party no-one knew for sure was happening. This is how our nights played out. We followed hints and whisper trails of action, motivated by the thrill of the chase, or maybe just the fear of staying still and missing out and remaining unseen by the enormous crowd of people that populated our imaginations.

Except now, with smartphones and social media, we were one step closer and three steps further away from the crowd. We didn't need to be creative. We could see with our own eyes, in real time, exactly what we were missing out on and who we weren't being seen by. So we climbed in cars and drove in the general direction of attention.

The trip began on a semirural street. Narrow road. Trees climbed higher than my line of sight. Before we left, I snuck outside and jumped in the front passenger seat. I was short and chubby with dark hair that ran a mess beneath my ears.

Tim sat in the middle of the back. Tall and square-jawed. He'd been my best mate since Year Eight. We went to St Mary's, an all-boys Catholic school near the centre of Toowoomba.

Everyone else went to Downlands, a more elite private school on the richer side of the city. Henry was back left. Soft features and bottom lip permanently split. Will was back right. Large and laid-back. Dom was the designated driver. He was excitable, with a hint of an American accent.

The final two were out of view. They'd drawn the short straw of the boot. Hamish had pale and lanky limbs. He was quiet with a sly grin. Nick was short with thick arms and legs, a wild and prodigiously gifted rugby league player.

Eighteen months earlier Nick had switched to Downlands on a rugby union scholarship, drawing Tim and me into a different social orbit altogether. My dad was a country publican. Tim's dad was a meat worker. We'd been accepted into a sphere of old money and new homes built on sprawling acreages. It was our final year of high school. Everything was ahead of us.

Up front there was nothing between the road and me except the windscreen. The speakers blasted 'Wonderwall' by Oasis, an elegy hidden inside a singalong. My memory is a blinking mixture of lyrics screamed out incoherently and the stink of beer and sweat and cigarette smoke. A million things and nothing in particular.

The trees disappeared abruptly, razed for the New England Highway. We waited at a freshly erected set of traffic lights. To our right was Highfields, a planned community fifteen minutes north of Toowoomba.

When the bottom circle of the lights blazed green, we turned left towards the city. No other traffic to clash with. The singing petered out. We concentrated on our phones or on the windscreen. The car accelerated. *Sixty, seventy, eighty, ninety.* I kept my eyes straight and my breath bated. Billboards flicked white streaks behind me. I felt light in the head and heavy in the feet. The road, half-lit and disappearing, burnt a blur into my brain.

My iPhone began to vibrate. I'd been texting a girl about a rendezvous planned for later that night. Sex was at the centre of my attention. I looked down to read the message. It was littered with emoticons. I typed a one-word response with two exclamation marks, but I never got around to pressing send.

There was a glitch in our direction. My gaze shifted quickly between the two competing sheets of glass. We'd drifted onto the left-hand shoulder of the highway. The back tyre left the road for a fraction of a second, spinning out in the mouth of a gravel driveway.

Dom reefed on the steering wheel, a knee-jerk attempt to regain control. He overcorrected the overcorrection. We zigzagged across the highway – right towards the median strip, left towards the shoulder, and right towards the median strip again.

My first instinct was exhilaration. It looked like we were driving into farmland. Nothing serious enough to scream about. But my geometry was bad. Blame it on velocity. At ninety-five kilometres per hour, the car moved twenty-five metres every second. It took us approximately three seconds to travel from the gravel of the hard shoulder to the trees on the median strip.

The car ploughed front-first into the vegetation. The windscreen filled with greenery. As we flew through the branches, the front of the car scraped the stump of a tree, spinning us another ninety degrees.

The median strip led to the other side of the highway. We emerged boot-first into a flood of oncoming headlights. Screams howled from the back seat. I'm dead, I thought. Then it hit. Another car, speed meeting speed, like two protons colliding.

*

I didn't get the luxury of a concussion. I stayed awake the whole way through. There was a glimpse of black, a few seconds max, when my head reeled from the soft impact against the dashboard. White pinwheels spun on the inside of my eyelids. Blood flooded back into my feet and fingers.

After that everything went berserk. Liquids pissed from unseen engines. Radiators hissed with steam. The windscreen was missing. The wipers whipped against thin air.

I sat there for a long time, dazed and amazed to be alive, staring blankly at the bonnet, which faced back towards the missing windscreen. I couldn't see what we'd hit or been hit by. A sticky fluid broke waves against my ankles.

I've pissed myself, I thought.

I looked down with mixed relief. Half a carton of wasted beers. I pulled my feet back towards the seat. My thongs floated in the foam. I unclicked the belt. My hand was like the claw inside a toy machine. I made it move without feeling anything. I wiped blood that wasn't mine onto the sleeve of my jumper. I flicked shards of glass from my clothes with numb fingers.

My iPhone was missing. I searched frantically and found it down beside the seat adjuster. The screen resembled the windscreen, completely shattered, but that damage was pre-existing. It was 9.53 p.m. I looked beside me. Dom lay facedown on the steering wheel. I looked behind me. A mess of heads and limbs leaned forward. Will and Tim and Henry. Necks bent at unnatural angles. Sick sounds issuing from their lips.

I reached out and shook each of them by the arm, gently and then more urgently, to absolutely no avail.

'Oi,' I yelled. 'Hey!'

This was the loneliest moment of my life. It was like waking up in a nuclear bunker where everyone else had been gassed.

So I waited. At no stage did it occur to me that they may not wake up. I underestimated death, the ease and speed with which it can sneak under your guard. My only visits from the grim reaper came in the dim minutes every morning and night via radio and TV. Earthquakes and tidal waves. Hijacked planes and celebrity suicides.

Death had less credibility to me than a reality TV show.

*

A shadow streaked across the headlights. This came as a revelation to me. I could leave any time I liked. The shadow came to the driver's side window. It belonged to a heavy guy with terrified eyes.

'Shit!' he screamed. 'What happened?'

'I don't know,' I said.

'Shit! Shit! Can you turn the car off?'

I hadn't noticed it was still going. The engine revved and dropped again, lead foot on the accelerator. I reached for the keys. The ignition was missing. It was hidden in a mess of plastic.

'I can't find them,' I said.

The man stuck his hand into the plastic and made the motor stop. Everything he said confirmed the dire straits we were stranded in.

'HEY, CHAMP! Relax. Everything's gonna be fine!'

I reached for the door handle. It had been obliterated on impact. The window winder was gone. Mine was the only window still intact. I was trapped in a fast-moving disaster. Each new fact was more startling than the last.

Meanwhile, a team of swift Samaritans was assembling beside the car. They divvied up the serious injuries between them. A blonde woman joined the man at the window. She was fearless. Later I found out she was a nurse on her way home from patching up other people's broken body pieces.

'Get me out!' I screamed. At this stage in the proceedings, the police reports describe me as being *hysterical*. The reports have only a passing resemblance to my memory.

'Sweetie,' said the woman, 'I'm going to need you to be brave. To sit still for a little bit. Is that something you can do for me?'

I nodded dishonestly. I had no intention of staying in the wreck a second longer. My eyes scanned for an exit route. I found one through the driver's side window. The woman's eyes went wide.

'No! Don't!'

I climbed over the top of Dom, hands pitched into the void, leaving the first responders with no choice. Cowardice is easy to commit and difficult to live with. They helped yank me to safety. My feet hit the bitumen with relief. I started running to the rear of the vehicle.

'Wait!' said the man, or the woman, or maybe it was neither of them. Fresh responders were arriving every second.

The boot was ripped open like a tin of tuna. Hamish reclined against the bumper. One hand reached back inside the boot. I used my iPhone to light up his face. Eyelids shut and unblinking. Blood dripped behind his ear.

The rest of the boot was crushed into a crawl space. I searched frantically below and beside the car. Nick was nowhere to be seen. I wondered if he'd ever been in the boot to begin with. I hadn't seen him climb in. I just *knew* – that sudden certainty produced by a stray sound or throwaway phrase.

A woman rubbed my shoulder. The situation permitted these strangers to lay their fingers all over me.

'He'll be okay!' she said.

I broke free and searched further afield from the car. Twenty metres away, I located a silhouette on the highway. I sprinted over to the shadow, using my iPhone as a searchlight.

Nick lay parallel to the fog line, eyes facing his brain. The glow from my iPhone illuminated the white shock of his skull. He'd been ejected headlong from the boot. A crooked *Z* was carved from his hairline to his eyebrow, deep and gushing with blood.

I noticed bystanders behind me. Half-a-dozen of them. Where did they keep coming from? A shadow pulled me aside, no gender in the lunar gloom.

'Leave him be,' the stranger announced to me. 'He's *fucked*.'

'Ambulances are on their way,' said another.

They were right. I heard the faint suggestion of sirens. The bystanders seemed down-beat, afraid of losing their proximity to the action. I clapped my hands enthusiastically.

'Hang in there, buddy!' I yelled. 'You'll be right!'

The bystanders looked my way admiringly. I just stood there, grimacing, wishing I were somewhere else.

*

Soon the dead end of the highway was alive. Sirens screamed in the south-easterly wind. Cones of red and blue spun on the road like strobe lights. Fire engines. Police vehicles. Ambulances. Utes and four-wheel drives of indeterminate authority. It was a night-club for lifesavers. An endless stream of high-visibility men and women, pirouetting between each other seamlessly.

The emergency workers didn't need to learn the narrative. This was bread-and-butter stuff. Saturday night. The high-speed ambition for mischief and risk. Young men bored literally to death. It was the same operation every weekend since they'd become accredited. They relieved the first responders of their responsibilities. They herded bystanders to cheaper seats further away from the main stage. And then they tried to save lives.

This would be a fine opportunity to describe what it's like to watch your best friends dying and being revived across a highway, or the shocking split between stopwatch youth and clockwork eternity, but from this point onwards I don't really remember anything about my friends. I seem to remember everything *except* their bodies and the medical attention they were getting.

Life is easy to see. Death is left to guesswork.

I drifted barefoot across the blacktop, careful not to land on broken glass, mostly unfazed by the mayhem. My main impulse was to put some distance between my body and the metal wreckage.

There was a grass clearing adjacent to the highway. I slipped into a spontaneous mob of onlookers. People swarmed from parked cars and nearby properties. They were drawn like mosquitos to the LEDs erected at opposite ends of the crash site, a plague of strangers in a nightscape exploding with light. I became a blank face in a contamination of curiosity. Nobody suspected my connection to the event.

Beside me was a man wearing boxer shorts and thongs. He gripped his jaw like it might fall apart if he let go for just a second.

'Well fuck me dead,' he said.

I shook my head indecisively. The sirens went quiet. The spotlights shone like twin midnight suns. I heard the same ringtone sing from different phones. Someone offered me a cigarette. I declined. Ambulances left. The sirens started again. More bystanders arrived. They tried to appear only mildly interested in the wreckage. Bodies faced away from the road, necks craned back towards the spectacle. This is where everything met. Death, energy, attention. The saving graces of a mundane life.

'So what do you reckon happened?' he asked.

I stared hard at the cars. The roof of our 1989 Ford Fairlane was pitched into a tent. The doors were bent off their hinges. Blood covered what was left of the rear windscreen. I ran one hand through my hair and the other across my chest.

How could I possibly associate my racing thoughts and beating heart with this bloody artifice of body bags and CPR kits?

'No idea,' I said eventually.

An eavesdropper strode over like she'd just checked on the progress of her tomatoes in the front garden.

'I got right up close,' she said. 'Beers everywhere. Kids no older than fifteen, I reckon. *Drunk*. Probably on *drugs*! I just feel sorry for the other poor bastard. Brand-new friggin' car as well ...'

I nodded with municipal vigour in my chin. Only now did I really see the other vehicle. It was a dark blue Holden Viva. The driver of the other car was an old guy with no hair sitting on the bitumen. He was alive. Face cut up and bathed in blood.

Do I remember these details, or were they gleaned from the newspaper articles that came later?

The depiction renovates the event.

The narrative bleeds into reality.

In my memory, the driver leaned against the side of his destroyed pride and joy, same pissed-off face as in the paper, resistant to the paramedics, like he was trying to squeeze in private time with a dying loved one.

You can't keep secrets in a catastrophe. News crews beat most of the emergency workers to the scene. They were bystanders for hire, capturing proof of the crash before it vanished entirely.

The presence of cameramen and -women gave licence to the amateur bystanders beside me. They spat clipped phrases into their phones – 'THERE'S BEEN A CRASH!' – the TV script of an emergency, making apologies for running late that were fake, of course, otherwise they would've climbed back in their cars and tried to leave. The truth is there's nowhere in the world they would've rather been than *here*, observing the event in the first person.

I looked into their eyes for a guide to what I should be seeing.

No fear, only awe.

Pretty soon they were on their third and fourth and fifth phone calls. 'It's pretty bad,' they whispered.

Already, the priority of the bystander had skipped from witnessing to describing the event, which is why they missed most of what they were seeing, filling in the gaps later with lies and speculation.

The more candid bystanders cut out the middleman of memory. One guy aimed his smart phone in the direction of the cars. A flash exploded from the roadside. Digital devices cave in quickly to our most primitive desires. Some of the witnesses held up phones without committing to the pictures, leaving their memories unverified, as if they only needed the screen to *see*.

I didn't begrudge them souvenirs. I considered myself one of them. But I'd stood by long enough. I wandered in the general direction of the city. Nobody tried to stop me.

Traffic was backed up behind the horizon. Two columns of red and yellow pixels divided by a black strip. Police diverted a trickle of pissed-off motorists to the other side of the highway. Car horns blew so far and wide that it sounded like a cathedral organ.

How had I not heard that shrill sound until now?

I felt sick. Forget about death and grievous bodily harm. My biggest fear was recognition. The vista was a Milky Way of witnesses. Blank gazes framed by glass windscreens. Cars flanked by complete darkness. No stars in a slightly silver sky. My bones glowed with guilt. I started fading out, head light and body leaden, one step behind myself, hiding on the sidelines of my own life.

*

'We've been looking for you.'

The statement came from behind me. I turned around and came face to face with one of the police officers I'd been eagerly evading.

'You were in the crash?'

The question sounded rhetorical. My legs trembled. A dry heat engulfed my throat. But I was ready to accept whatever plot twist was next suggested to me.

'Yep,' I said.

The policeman looked back towards the crash scene.

'Come with me,' he said.

We walked back towards the glowing dome. I hadn't even *left*, I realised, having made it only twenty metres or so from where the multitude of witnesses began to thicken until containment by police tape.

Where did all the time go? Nowhere. I've just spent so many years remembering the intervening period between escape and discovery that those vivid few minutes have proliferated into hours.

The policeman veered unexpectedly away from the crowd. He turned right onto a driveway and right again onto the highway. We emerged into the darkness created by a shield of emergency vehicles. A policewoman was waiting beside a fire engine. They didn't need to undo me through routine. The story was formed and pouring out of me in breathless declarations of innocence.

'I was sitting up the front and saw the trees and next thing you know we skidded and got hit and I don't know who hit who or which way we were going or where we were going or whose fault it was *IT ALL HAPPENED SO QUICK* you know what I mean? Like a bolt from the blue and Dom wasn't even drinking or speeding we were just driving back into town it was so random ...'

'We know you're still in shock,' said the policewoman, 'but later we're going to need you to be clearer with us.'

That was it. No nice sentiments about keeping my chin up. They left me adrift in a wilderness of unlit bitumen. The roadside was a garbage tip. Broken glass sparkled in the dark. Shopping bags flapped along the fence like jellyfish trapped in a shark net.

I sat cross-legged on the blacktop, leaning against the bright red metal of a fire engine, wading through the meditative blamelessness of nobody knowing what I'd seen or been involved in.

After an extended delay, the same cops returned with bottled water and the news that I didn't need to be there any longer.

'You're free to leave,' said the man.

'What do you mean?'

'Unless you have more information,' he said, 'go home and get some rest. You've got a long road ahead of you.'

I had no intention of getting on that *long road* any sooner than I needed to. They were insistent. I gave them my sister's mobile number. They called her and handed me the phone. Hannah was asleep twenty minutes away.

'I've been in a car crash,' I said.

Nothing about my tone suggested anything more serious than a minor traffic matter, but already Hannah was crying on the other end of the line, swiping through the mind archive of images that opens whenever you hear the phrase *car crash*.

'I'm fine,' I said.

The police gave her directions. I followed them around to the other side of the remaining fire engine. A few latecomers loitered miserably behind the police tape, ruing whatever they'd been doing at the expense of the event.

The only piece of trivia still at the scene was hidden in the back seat of a police car, wrapped in a tinfoil cape like a lunatic. It came in plastic packaging that said 'Survival Blanket' on the front and 'Made in China' beneath the barcode on the underside. Asian labour for Australian mass emergency. I slumped to the side, eyes tightly shut, not because I was tired, but so I didn't have to see my insane reflection without filter or special effect.

*

Suddenly my sister was tapping her knuckles on the window of the police car and then she was hugging me for dear life on the highway and after that I was sitting in the back seat of her boyfriend's white Toyota Camry as he sped over the ridge that made a colosseum of the crash site, no sound inside the car except for the whisper of the demister, a few lonely cones of red and blue blinking behind me like Christmas lights on Boxing Day. I was starving and needed to piss but there didn't seem to be any sensitive way to say this.

'The police told me you should go up to the hospital to get checked out,' said my sister. 'They told me there's complications that can come up even if you feel completely fine. Brain bleeds. Blood clots. They said it's not looking good for some of your friends. They might *die*, Lech. What the hell even happened?'

She knew more about the evolving storyline than me. 'The car came out of nowhere,' I said. 'Like a shooting star.'

Hannah stared at me in the rear-view, irritated then amazed. She saw a person where a ghost was supposed to be.

'This isn't poetry, Lech,' she said. 'This is real life!'

'They'll be fine,' I said, falsely confident, and this seemed to settle the matter for the time being, windows demisted and the car interior regressing into a silence that seemed prehistoric.

We climbed over Blue Mountain Heights and began our descent into the outer limits of Toowoomba. The classroom myth I believed when I was a little kid is that my hometown was built in the crater of an extinct volcano, and that's how it appeared to me now: low and half-lit suburbs spilling down slopes into a beaming CBD.

The descent evened out. The windscreen panned to street level. We idled at a red light. The light turned green. Within 500 metres the heavy industry was replaced by trees. No-one spoke. I realised we were driving in the wrong direction.

'Where are we going?'

'To the hospital,' said Hannah. 'Mum and Dad are meeting us there.'

I felt anxious and angry simultaneously.

'Why,' I said, 'would you tell them?'

Hannah gave me a filthy look.

'Because they're our parents, Lech.'

We arrived at the hospital, a precinct of rectangular prisms that became a leviathan at night, shadows filling the gaps between right angles. I thanked my sister and her boyfriend without any real sense of gratitude. They lingered in the loading zone a minute, waving ridiculously in my direction, before driving quickly away.

*

Nothing prepared me for the vision I saw irradiated below the red glow of 'Emergency'. My parents stood in quiet conversation, smiling tenderly at each other. They'd separated two years earlier. To the best of my knowledge they hadn't been on speaking terms for three months.

'Hey,' I said.

Mum hugged me. 'Baby!'

Dad shook my hand with too much firmness, nervously, like he'd been caught philandering but in reverse.

'G'day, mate!'

Only seeing them together in the flesh did it occur to me how outrageously old and worn down they were.

Mum was a textbook androgynous housewife. Liquor and cigarettes had exhausted her at a quicker than normal clip. Short grey hair and husky voice. Skinny limbs and swelling pot belly. I had no idea she didn't fit the bill of femininity until it was suggested to me, repeatedly, by high school friends and enemies alike, who told me she looked like a man or, less insultingly, a lesbian.

Dad was an exaggeration of his own gender. He reeked of barroom charisma. Face red with high cholesterol. Beer gut bloomed into obesity. His menace was like good real estate, appreciating with age. Fists the size of bricks dead-ending arms thicker than fire extinguishers. Legs dark and carved with muscle.

Both of them were burning with questions. They wanted to know every gritty particular of the crash.

'It came out of nowhere,' I said again and again and again.

'Oh, Lech,' said Mum, 'those *poor* other parents. We're so lucky. You wouldn't have gotten in the boot, would you?'

'I don't know. Probably.'

Dad nearly spat his fake teeth onto the footpath. 'Christ! Get off your high horse, Lenore. We used to drive around with half the town hanging out the car. We've put our own kids in the boot!'

Mum put her rough fingers where blood was flecked on the sleeve of my cashmere sweater. 'Remind me to get this soaking as soon as we get home,' she whispered sombrely.

We stepped inside the sliding doors. The waiting room was a patchwork of late-night mishap. Babies wailed due to inscrutable ailments. Their parents wished they were dead or at the very least asleep. Everyone avoided making eye contact with each other except for the unashamedly insane.

A speed freak with dreadlocks and no shirt kept publicising a graze bleeding from his shoulderblade to the unwavering uninterest of the female administrator behind the plexiglas.

'I'm gonna lose my fucking arm!' he screamed.

'Please remain patient until you arrive at the front of the line,' she said into a table-mounted megaphone, dull tone and dead eyes.

I told my parents to sit down while I waited in line but they insisted on staying posted at my hip.

'We're here for *you*, baby,' said Mum.

Dad sighed for five minutes, eyeballing anyone who breathed in our direction, before pulling me forward by the elbow without warning.

'My son was in the car crash at Highfields!' he declared to a line brimming with legitimately sick and injured citizens.

He had a strong presentiment of the currency of tragic events. Every eyeball in the line zoomed in my direction. A pregnant woman held her breath. An elderly man with a purple island floating over his cheek stepped from the front of the queue and ushered me forward.

'Lucky bugger,' he said. 'Lucky lucky lucky.'

The previously sedate receptionist was wide awake.

'Hi,' she said. 'They told me you might be coming. I'll let the doctors know you're here. Step right in.'

How on earth did they know who I was?

The pressurised doors hissed and swung inward. The next hour was a whirlwind of medical professionals indemnifying themselves and pretending there might be something wrong with me.

The radiologist leaked tear streaks on my sweater before taking X-rays of my internal organs.

'When I heard,' she said, 'all I could think about was my son. Bradley. Same age as you. You kids think you're bulletproof ...'

I was led back to a doctor's office where Mum and Dad sat holding hands. For a horrifying second I thought they'd been about to kiss. The only time I'd ever seen them press their lips together was on their twenty-fifth wedding anniversary. He opened his mouth over hers under intense pressure from Hannah and me.

After that were years of sighs and shouts followed by the tears and then silence of their separation.

Now they had something to celebrate again.

'How'd ya go?' asked Dad.

'Great,' I said.

The doctor was a tall man with a weak smile. He asked me the most mind-numbingly dumb questions: my full name, what day and month it was, who was the current prime minister of Australia.

'Is all of this really necessary?' I asked. 'I feel fine.'

'This is all just a precaution,' he said. 'We need to be extra careful with car crashes. Especially when there's been a casualty.'

The room went silent.

Casualty.

What did he mean?

I knew what he meant, but I needed it spelt out for me.

'Someone died?'

The doctor was stricken.

'Um,' he said.

'Who?'

'Ah,' he said.

The doctor looked at my parents to save him, but they were even hungrier for an answer than me, so he reviewed the crash statistics on the clipboard in his glove-covered hands.

'William,' said the doctor. 'He passed away on impact.'

Passed away.

I scrutinised the phrase for longer than I needed to, trying to find a loophole from the bleeding obvious.

'He's dead,' I said.

'Yes. I'm sorry. I thought you knew.'

The air sucked out of me. Silence drew attention to hospital clatter. Nothing mattered or made sense. I didn't question how a person could be dead a metre away without me noticing. I wondered what was making the whirring sound down the hallway, fingers clicking like crickets, jingle of car keys and shrapnel in the pockets of passing patrons. My brain felt scraped out and put back in the wrong place. Everything so close and far away. The sensation of listening to voices underwater, in a different dialect, a distant century and tense. No line of thinking I could link with a distinct feeling.

*

I have the weakest recollection before leaving the hospital of hovering inside an emergency theatre leaking with light where Nick and Tim and Henry lay beside each other on metal beds, brains swelling against their skulls, breathing devices exploding from their throats, begged by their devastated parents to stay alive at least for the helicopter rides to Brisbane and the Gold Coast.

Will was dead. Hamish lay in a separate operating theatre. He passed away that morning. Henry died five days later in Brisbane. Nick came out of his induced coma within the next week, but he was never really the same. Tim stayed in a coma for months. He lost the ability to walk or talk without assistance. Dom spent the next two years in a state of legal and existential limbo. His legal team told him to hope for the best while expecting the worst: potentially five years in a prison cell. The jury found him not guilty.

I remained the same bystander from the beginning until the end, estranged from reality, present and completely apart, no physical or legal scars to verify my participation.

The bereaved families were amazingly gracious. They remained so throughout the tragedy, saying how glad they were I was okay, even if it came at the expense of their own flesh and blood.

What could I possibly say? I was a contortion of remorse. A mannequin reading from a script of bad clichés.

From that first night at the hospital, the least important details stick out in my memory. Ambulances at the end of the loading bay. The three a.m. shadow of agony around the eyes of the mums and dads.

For the life of me I can't remember the faces of my friends or any final sentences I might've said to them.

This is trauma. It's an antivirus program that deletes the most malicious content from your memory. The problem for some people is that the data resurfaces when they least expect it. My spyware was incredibly efficient. Trauma wiped my brain clean. The crash is a black hole expanding in the headlights, a fresh centre of gravity for the rest of my life to hang around indefinitely. There's just blank space where my friends used to be. That doesn't mean I'll ever stop trying to see them. Missing content might be the lesser of two evils, but living with experiences you can't remember is no easy fix.

Why She Broke

Helen Garner

It happened in broad daylight, one April afternoon in 2015, while the citizens of an outer-western Melbourne suburb called Wyndham Vale were peaceably going about their business.

A chef, on her way to get a tattoo, was driving past Lake Gladman, a reedy, rock-edged suburban wetland, when the blue Toyota SUV in front of her suddenly pulled off the bitumen and stopped on the gravel. As the chef drove by, she caught a glimpse of an African woman sitting huddled over the steering wheel with her face in her hands. Kids behind her were rioting: a little one was thrashing in his booster, a bigger one dangling off the back of the driver's seat. Minutes later a passing teacher saw the Toyota 'drive full bolt, straight into the water'. A man who lived opposite saw it hit the water; he heard splashing and wheels spinning as the vehicle moved further into the lake. A young boy raced home on his bike: 'Mum! There's people in the water!' Someone was screaming – a long, wordless wail.

A sales manager ran out of his house and waded into the lake. The water wasn't deep enough to engulf the car. Its roof was still above the surface, but it was filling fast. The driver must have scrambled out through her window: she was standing beside it in the water. The frantic salesman tried to break one of the rear passenger windows with his fist and his elbow. It wouldn't shatter. He yelled for a rock. A courier on the bank tore off his steel-toed boot and chucked it to him. He smashed the window and fought one child free of his harness. The hysterical teacher on the bank, crying out to triple-0, saw another kid on his back in the water, trying to keep his head above the surface, but sinking. Rescuers were shouting to the mother: Were there more children? How many were there? She stood silent beside the driver's door, gazing straight ahead.

Her name was Akon Guode. She was a thirty-five-year-old South Sudanese refugee, a widow with seven children. Three of them drowned that afternoon: four-year-old twins Hanger and Madit, and their sixteen-month-old brother, Bol. Their five-year-old sister, Alual, escaped the car and survived.

What Guode said, when the police questioned her, was so vague, so random that the word 'lie' seemed hardly to apply. She denied everything. No, she had not been to the lake. She didn't even know where the lake was. She was going to Coles to buy some milk. On the way to the supermarket she took the children to a park, to play. She meant to drive home, but she became dizzy. She missed the turn and went straight ahead. She didn't know how she ended up in the water.

'Dizzy'? Such a feeble word, so imprecise, so unconvincing. Her teenage daughter said it. The father of the dead children said it. People turned from their screens and looked at each other with round eyes. Hadn't we heard this before? Was it a copycat thing? I asked a police investigator who worked on the long and gruelling murder trials of Robert Farquharson, the father of three boys drowned in a dam in 2005, whether he had been having flashbacks. 'No flashbacks,' said the detective calmly. 'But a very strong sense of déjà vu at the scene.'

It would be hard to imagine anything that looked less like an accident. Not only were there eyewitnesses to the deed, but six houses along the shore of Lake Gladman are fitted with CCTV cameras. The police had been able to put together, with a few small gaps, a video recording of the fact that the mother had driven along the lake five times that day before she planted her foot and went into the water. But Guode pleaded not guilty to all four charges: one of attempted murder for the girl who survived, and three of murder for the twins and for the boy who was not yet two years old.

Like several of my women friends, I flinched from the story yet
followed the media reports out of the corner of my eye. We emailed
each other, we texted, about women we had known (or had
been) – single mothers who slammed the door and ran away, or
threw a screaming baby across a room, or crouched howling with
one hand on the phone, too ashamed to call for help. The flash-
point was the glimpse that the chef had caught as she drove past
the clumsily parked Toyota: the frantic mother hunched over the
steering wheel, going off her head while in the back her children
went berserk. 'How many times have I been there?' whispered my
neighbour, a grandmother. 'I have to know why she broke.'

I heard that at the committal hearing, in June 2016, Guode
collapsed wailing in the dock. Her counsel had to get down on
the floor with her to comfort her. The magistrate found the evidence against her sufficient to commit her to a trial by jury.

Then, at the turn of the year, I heard that the Crown had
agreed to change the third murder charge, of the toddler, to one
of infanticide. Once she was arraigned on this new charge,
Guode pleaded guilty to all four counts. This meant that there
would be no jury trial, but just a two-day plea hearing in the
Supreme Court before Justice Lex Lasry, who in 2010 had heard
Robert Farquharson's excruciating second trial and given him
three life sentences, with thirty-three years on the bottom.

*

The court documents tell Akon Guode's story in broad strokes.
She married in South Sudan as a teenager. By the time her husband, a soldier in the rebel army of South Sudan, was killed in
the civil war she had two children. As a widow in a country where
Christian and African traditional customs often blend, she could
never remarry. She would remain a member – or perhaps one
could say a possession – of her late husband's family: she was
given to one of his brothers. 'This is customary once the husband dies,' explained an 'aunty' of Guode's at the committal,
through an interpreter. 'You don't go out. You don't go anywhere
else. You stay with the same tribe because you got married for
cows. As a dowry.' Guode's third child was fathered by a man we
would think of as her brother-in-law.

With the three children in tow, she walked to Uganda in eighteen days, foraging for food along the way. When they got there, another of her late husband's brothers, already living in Australia, offered to sponsor her and the children: she was granted a global special humanitarian visa. They arrived in Sydney in 2006 and stayed with the brother-in-law until 2008, then moved to Melbourne, where the cost of living was more manageable, and were given temporary shelter by her late husband's cousin Joseph Manyang, his wife and their three children.

Manyang helped Guode settle in to a rented house of her own. Soon she and Manyang, unknown to his wife, began a relationship. In 2009 Guode gave birth to a girl, Alual – the only child who, five years later, would emerge alive from the car in the lake. The family name on the baby's birth certificate was Chabiet, that of Guode's late husband.

'You had no idea you were the father,' Joseph Manyang was asked at the committal, 'until the child was one year old?'

'I asked her about the father of the child,' said Manyang. 'She told me, "I can't tell you."'

It was confirmed by a DNA test, after the day of the lake, that the child was his.

The relationship continued. In 2010 Guode had twins, a boy and a girl. By now Manyang's wife was no longer in ignorance. She felt it sorely; she raged. Later, in court, she would deny that she came to Guode's house and beat on the door, shouting insults and threats while the family lay low inside. There was an unpleasant confrontation at a shopping centre. Manyang moved out of the marital home and set up on his own. He visited each woman and her set of his children once or twice a week. The community hummed with rumours. Guode's link with Manyang, though it had been so fruitful of offspring, could never be officially recognised: she was obliged to remain forever a widow. Could she have gone on hoping that the relationship had meaning, and a future?

Guode was running her household on Centrelink payments and on Manyang's sporadic contributions. In 2012 she worked for twelve months at a family day care centre. Like most refugees she was regularly sending back as much money as she could spare to her parents and her extended family in Africa. Then, in

2013, she became pregnant again. Shortly before the child was born, Centrelink, in a contretemps about an overpayment, suspended her benefits. A repayment scheme was eventually put in place, but she was barely squeaking by from week to week.

Meanwhile, somehow, her six children were well cared for. Their education mattered to her: they went to school, they did their homework. Akoi Chabiet, her eldest child by the husband who had been killed in the war, was an assiduous helper in the house and a keen high school student. The girl had plans for a life. She wanted to go to university, and was prepared to work for it.

Guode went into labour on 21 December 2013. Because she already had more than five children, she was what is known in midwifery as a grand multi. The birth of a child that follows caesarean twins, as hers had been, is always high-risk, and the hospital was ready for it. But things did not go smoothly. After she had given birth she kept bleeding, and they could not stop it. A consent form for whatever life-saving treatment might be needed was brought to her. She signed it. By the time they got her to the holding bay outside theatre, where the doctors were waiting for her, her haemorrhage had reached emergency proportions. 'I remember the linen underneath her,' said the midwife at the committal, 'being quite soaked with blood, and I remember her looking down and being aware of the blood loss herself.'

But in the holding bay she said no. She flatly refused to go through the door. They couldn't understand it. Three doctors tried to explain to her what they might need to do. She would not give eye contact. She kept holding up her hand and turning her head away, saying, 'No. No.' She wouldn't let them phone the man she referred to as her husband. Staff rang every number they could find. Many of them were incorrect or disconnected, or the calls were picked up by young children. They got through to a sister-in-law, who backed Guode in her refusal. Then, for some reason, Guode ran out of fight. She surrendered. They wheeled her in. She had lost half the blood in her body. As part of the full resuscitation they had to give her, to prevent her from going into shock, they inserted an intravenous cannula into the internal jugular vein in her neck. They managed to save her without surgical intervention.

Around Christmas 2013, Guode made it home with her new baby, a boy called Bol. Postnatal checks of mother and baby raised no concerns, either physical or psychological. None of her other children's births had brought on postnatal depression, but plainly Bol's birth and its aftermath had knocked her around emotionally and psychologically. She thought her debility was due to the cannula that had been put into her neck. She complained occasionally of headaches and dizziness. Often she could not get out of bed. She slept all day and was unable to do the work of a mother and a housekeeper. She became distant from her children. She stopped going to social events. Her community, she felt, was turning its back on her. Rare visits from other Sudanese women she experienced as meddling rather than assistance. Gossip intensified. When Bol was six months old Guode had to ask Manyang to undergo a paternity test, to put paid to rumours that he was not Bol's father. The test showed that he was.

Manyang's visits, according to Guode's daughter Akoi, had tapered off during the pregnancy. By now, Akoi said, he was offering little help with household matters or child care. He was busy with his own concerns: he had two jobs, and would occasionally call Guode from work. He seems to have lost interest in the sad, overburdened woman. The one who picked up the slack was Akoi.

Akoi's teachers, sympathetic women, began to notice that the girl was distracted, even disengaged. Her schoolwork was falling away. She began to turn up late. When they investigated they found that as well as studying for her Year Twelve exams she was running the entire household, shopping, cooking, cleaning and washing, as well as managing the diabetes of her little sister Alual.

Akoi described her mother as 'ill'. Her teacher suggested 'depressed' as a more accurate term; she tried and failed to find a support group in the area for Guode. She thought there might be a stigma against mental illness among Guode's people. Indeed, a leader of the South Sudanese community, a respected lawyer who is held in equally high esteem in the world outside it, told the committal hearing that Sudanese people 'are highly unlikely to suffer ... mental illnesses, due to a chain and a web of support that surrounds us individually and as a community. So when someone ... is in trouble, whether they have seek or not seek, and people notice, people will go out and support that person, and they will go above and beyond.'

Joseph Manyang told the committal that he had had no idea Guode was in financial trouble. He said that if she had asked he would have given her money. But by March 2015 the debt collectors were after Guode for unpaid phone bills to the tune of hundreds of dollars, and for gas and power bills that topped $3000. To Centrelink she owed $12,000. Between 2008 and the day of the lake she had managed to send tens of thousands of dollars back to her family in South Sudan, and her obligation to provide money was ongoing. At the committal, the community leader, loyal to his people, disputed this point: 'It is not an obligation. I would call it a moral duty.' Under the circumstances, this seems a very fine distinction.

Call it what you will, this woman had been reduced to little more than a conduit for babies and for money. Is it any wonder that she laid her burden down and turned her face to the wall?

Down in Gippsland, where many Sudanese families have settled, Guode had a friend who was fond of her, an 'aunty' from her mother's side called Abook Kon. She worked as a school crossing supervisor for the Latrobe City Council. A woman of resolute address, Kon spoke briskly to the committal about Guode's pain at Joseph Manyang's neglect. 'She had no right to be upset, because here she's not married to him. He's married to another lady. She had no right to be upset ... He can father her kids, but she can't be upset because he's not spending time with her ... The other lady has the right to be upset – Joseph's wife.'

But Kon had seen how unhappy and lonely Guode was in Melbourne, and suggested she move with the children to Morwell, in Gippsland's Latrobe Valley, where there was plenty of government housing. Guode had said she would wait till Akoi finished Year Twelve, and then make the move. Over many months she put it to Manyang. He would not have a bar of it. He would have to make a two-hour drive to see his children: it was too far. But Aunty Abook worked on him, and in the end he agreed that they could go.

This plan gives off a strange static of unreality. Nobody mentioned it in the aftermath of the drownings. Even Homicide didn't learn of it until many weeks into their investigation. They found that Guode had given notice to her landlord, but had not told the school that her children would be leaving. Perhaps it was only a fantasy of rescue, a dream? She was in no state to handle the logistics of a wholesale domestic uprooting. She had seven children, the youngest only a toddler. She had no husband beside her, and no right ever to seek one. She was exhausted, isolated, mentally ill – poleaxed by postnatal depression. She was losing her grip.

*

A faint clink of cuffs at the door from the cells, and in she came. In the shots taken at her children's memorial – her head bound in black cloth, her skin gleaming in candlelight, her eyes distant and dull, her mouth half open as if to gasp or groan – she had been a figure from ancient myth, massive and block-like. Now, ushered past us to the dock for her plea hearing, she was a prisoner in a modern story: bareheaded, her hair cropped, in a charcoal top and jeans too short for her long legs. Her skin had lost its lustre: it was matte, reflecting no light. Between the interpreter and the glaring-blond, gum-chewing security guard, Guode took her seat and was swallowed up in the court's dark timber.

The prosecutor, Kerri Judd QC, laid out the Crown case. On a smartscreen she drew with one finger a wobbly blue worm that traced the wandering path of Guode's blue Toyota on the afternoon of 8 April 2015. At one p.m. Guode loaded the four youngest children into the car and set out, telling Akoi they were going 'to visit Grandma' and to take Alual to a medical appointment for her diabetes. But they went instead to Manor Lakes Boulevard in Wyndham Vale. She drove in several slow, random passes along the lake and back and along again. At 2.18 she called Joseph Manyang. He did not answer. At 2.45 her mother called her from Sudan and they spoke for several minutes. She paused at a park and briefly let the stir-crazy children out to play, then drove on. Just after three, Akoi called her twice. Guode said she would be home soon. At 3.40 the passing strangers saw the car airborne and heard it hit the water.

Judd, a straight-backed woman with an elegantly boyish hair-cut, ran through these facts with a crisp clarity. After each demonstration of the gap between the evidence and the account Guode had given the police, she would raise her head from her notes and look directly at the judge. When she reached the account of the man who smashed the window and hauled out Bol, already frothing at the mouth, a soft, low sound flowed through the court. It was Guode, keening: she leaned forward on her elbows and wrapped her arms around her head. People did not know where to look. They covered their eyes and turned away.

The thrust of the Crown's opening was that Guode's crime against four vulnerable and helpless children – this 'gross breach of trust' – was 'not a quick, spontaneous act'. She had driven back and forth along the lake several times and chosen the only possible entry point. Once in the water she accelerated. She did nothing to save her children or to help strangers who rushed to the scene, but got out through the window, leaving the children inside. She lied to rescuers about the number of children in the car, and she lied to the police investigators. She had shown little or no remorse.

Guode's counsel was Marcus Dempsey, a light-voiced, tensely composed man with a face as pale as a teacup. His task was to set her actions, or failures to act, into the deepest possible context.

First he named the elephant in the room – 'the inevitable comparison with Farquharson'. He dealt with it by quoting a blunt general statement made to a 2004 Victorian Law Reform Commission review of defences to homicide: 'While men kill to control or punish their children or partner, women kill children because they cannot cope with the extreme difficulties that they encounter in trying to care for their children.'

In 2004, he said, the law had been changed to recognise that the devastating effects of postnatal depression on some women's mental health can persist much longer after childbirth than was previously understood. The period of time during which a moth-er's killing of a child could be regarded as infanticide had been extended from one year to two. Infanticide carries a maximum penalty of five years' imprisonment. But no Victorian mother has ever been sent to prison for infanticide. The usual penalty is a community-based corrections order with psychiatric supervision and treatment.

Anyone who has read the sentencing remarks of judges in these rare and dreadful cases would understand their urge to have mercy. But only one of Guode's children fell into the age bracket for infanticide – poor little Bol, in his booster seat, only the top of his curly head visible to the man smashing the car window with a steel-capped boot. The twins who drowned were four. The girl who survived was five.

So Dempsey outlined a further recommendation by the commission that had not been taken up: that a mother who kills a child under two, but who, at the same time and *while suffering from the same mental disorder*, kills another of her children who is older than two, should not face both infanticide and murder charges. The line drawn between the two charges in a case like Guode's, said Dempsey, was arbitrary and artificial. It did not make sense. There was no legal or moral reason to draw it.

'We're asking Your Honour,' he said, 'to view Akon Guode's conduct through the prism of infanticide, rather than as a murder first with an infanticide tacked on the end.' Infanticide was 'at the heart of all her conduct'. Otherwise, he said, what she had done was 'inexplicable and unfathomable'.

*

Dempsey's account of his client's life had a stride to it, and more nuance than the committal transcript offered. Her father had six children with one woman and five with another; the families lived in separate compounds. Guode's was a love marriage. Dempsey sketched the disruption of their lives by the civil war, her move to Eritrea with the children while her husband fought, his death. He described the conditions of the walk to Uganda with her children, in the endless column of refugees: the violence of the soldiers, the ubiquity of rape, these historically documented facts.

The permanent visa Guode has is granted only on grounds of 'substantial discrimination amounting to a gross violation of your human rights in your home country' – the kinds of things that qualify as crimes of war. But now, charged with four crimes of her own, Guode had declined to draw on her experiences in the war zone to allow a diagnosis of post-traumatic stress disorder to be made. She simply would not go there. 'Typically,' said Dempsey, 'she withholds that information when cynically she could volunteer it to extract sympathy or pity.' In short, her lawyers had come up against a roadblock: her character.

At a very young age, it seems, she had learned from brute reality the pointlessness of protest. She had been obliged to develop what the defence's forensic psychiatric witness, Dr Danny Sullivan, called 'a personality style of extraordinary resilience and stoicism'. And in the face of her many displacements and disappointments she maintained this stoical carapace, said Dempsey, all the way to 2015, by which time she was 'utterly broken'.

A guilty plea raises certain crucial questions. Does the person acknowledge responsibility for her actions? Does she feel remorse for what she did? Guode's impenetrable stoicism made the extent of her remorse almost impossible for the court to determine. And there was a contradiction in her position: although she had pleaded guilty, she continued to insist, in her interviews with Dr Sullivan, that she had never meant to kill her children. 'She acknowledges her responsibility,' said Dempsey, 'to the extent that her personality permits her to, and still live.'

Justice Lasry pressed Dr Sullivan to point to some specific event that might have pushed Guode over the edge from her 'major depressive disorder' – a malaise that everyone agreed strikes much deeper than 'normal human misery', and from which there was no doubt that she profoundly suffered – into a state in which she was capable of killing her own children.

'There must have been something, mustn't there?' said the judge. 'Does it not follow from what she did that there must have been something dramatic which accentuated her condition?'

'In many cases,' said the psychiatrist helplessly, 'it can just be the ebb and flow of human suffering, and the person reaching the threshold at which they can ... no longer go on.'

No-one in a court speaks the language of psychoanalysis, I know, but listening to this description of an ironclad endurance forged in extreme adversity, I remembered a remark by the

British analyst Wilfred Bion that had always mystified me but now made sense: 'People exist ... in whom pain ... is so intolerable that they feel the pain but will not suffer it and so cannot be said to discover it.' A woman psychiatrist in Melbourne who has worked with many refugees from the Sudanese conflict had described Guode's experiences to me as '*unprocessed* – repressed'. Guode was lost in her own numbness. How could she ask for help, or admit – even to herself – how far down she had slid? A woman with seven children to raise, but with no adult companion to love her and help her and hold her together, is not free to let herself go into grieving for her losses.

And perhaps the trigger event that the judge was seeking was not proximate to the crime, but went back to the existential battering she had suffered a year and a half earlier, at the bloody birth of her seventh child. A moment that still haunts me was Guode in the holding bay, refusing to go into the operating theatre – face turned from the fast-talking doctors, eyes closed, hand up: no, no.

At my first reading of the committal transcript, skimming for drama instead of sifting for fact, I had without hesitation interpreted her refusal as a suicidal dropping of her bundle: *I can't take any more. Let me be, leave me alone and let me go.* But the psychiatrist Dr Sullivan had not been able to establish any 'suicidal ideation', past or present, in his interviews with Guode. When court rose that day I went back to the transcript. What I found there rocked me. How could I, as a woman, have failed to grasp the nature of the last-ditch 'life-saving treatment' for which they were insisting on her permission? Appalled by the terrible flow of blood, I had thought only of transfusion. But there it was, in prosecutor Michele Williams's re-examination of the midwife:

'And the ... hysterectomy that would be performed if other methods failed ... That's what she was refusing?'

'Yes.'

Could it be that this woman, widowed, passed from hand to hand and abandoned, overwhelmed by her own fertility, estranged from her community and up to her neck in debt, was prepared to risk bleeding to death on a hospital gurney rather than consent to the surgical removal of the sole symbol of her worth, the site of her only dignity and power: her womb?

Surely, a woman whose life had lost all meaning apart from her motherhood would kill her children only in a fit of madness.

*

If a full-bore jury trial is a symphony, a plea hearing is a string quartet. Its purpose seems to be to clear a space in which the quality of mercy might at least be contemplated. There is something moving in its quiet thoughtfulness, the intensity of its focus, the murmuring voices of judge and counsel, the absence of melodrama or posturing. It's the law in action, working to fit the dry, clean planes of reason to the jagged edges of human wildness and suffering.

Justice Lasry had made it clear, in his uneasy questioning of the defence's psychiatrist, that he was not considering imposing a life sentence. Nor, said the prosecutor, would the Crown be seeking one. Now the judge told the court that he had to leave town next morning to hear a murder trial in Bendigo. It would take at least three weeks. He would not be able to turn his attention to Guode's sentence until well after that matter. He adjourned the hearing early in the afternoon of its second day, and everyone but the prisoner got up and went back to their ordinary lives, to wait for the call.

I have never much envied judges, but for Justice Lasry in this case I felt no envy at all.

What would follow if he were persuaded by Dempsey's eloquent plea to consider all Guode's actions under the merciful shelter of infanticide? Imagine the screaming of the tabloids. Weak judges! Soft on crime! These refugees – they come here and think they can get away with anything!

If Akon Guode did go to prison, she would almost certainly have her visa cancelled once she had served her sentence, and would be deported. If the government paid attention to the country reports issued by its own Department of Foreign Affairs and Trade, it could hardly send her back to Sudan, a land racked by civil upheaval and famine, where rape as a tactic in areas of conflict is common and accepted, and women have no protection. The only avenue open to her here would be to apply for a protection visa, and that would be a long shot. Where else could she be sent? Most likely to a detention centre, where she might languish for years, a stateless pariah.

*

On the train one morning I struck up a conversation with a thoughtful-looking VCE student who was carrying a copy of Euripides' *Medea*. I asked her what she made of the famous play. She reeled off the things that students are taught to say about it. I wanted to know if she shared my anxiety. I said, 'She did a terrible, terrible thing. But she was very badly treated. She was betrayed. She was –'

The girl flushed and leaned forward. She put out both hands to me, palms up, and whispered, 'But she was – *a mother.*'

I had no reply.

I was troubled, and I still am, by the finality of the word 'mother', this great thundering archetype with the power to stop the intellect in its tracks.

'The herculean task of being a mother,' said Marcus Dempsey in his final submission, 'has now fallen to Akoi.'

In the shadow of this ancient duty, so implacable and profound, can mercy hold up its head?

Helen Garner's Savage Self-Scrutiny

James Wood

In the early 1960s, when the Australian writer Helen Garner was
a student at the University of Melbourne, she had a brief relationship with a twenty-four-year-old man who was her tutor. With
characteristic briskness, she tells us that she learned two things
from him: 'Firstly, to start an essay without bullshit preamble,
and secondly, that betrayal is part of life.' She continues, 'I value
it as part of my store of experience – part of what I am and how
I have learnt to understand the world.' A writing lesson and a life
lesson: Garner's work as a journalist and a novelist constantly
insists on the connection between writing about life and compre-
hending it; to try to do both responsibly and honestly – without
bullshit preamble, or, for that matter, bullshit amble – is what it
means to be alive.

'Honesty' is a word that, when thrown at journalism, unhelp-
fully describes both a baseline and a vaguer horizon, a legal
minimum and an ethical summum. Too often, we precisely
monitor the former and profligately praise the latter. In Helen
Garner's case, we should give due thanks for the former and precisely praise the latter. As a writer of nonfiction, Garner is scru-
pulous, painstaking and detailed, with sharp eyes and ears. She
is everywhere at once, watching and listening, a recording angel
at life's secular apocalypses – 'a small grim figure with a notebook and a cold,' as she memorably describes herself. She has
written with lucid anger about murder cases, about incidents of

sexual harassment, about the experience of caring for a friend dying of cancer.

But Garner is, above all, a savage self-scrutineer: her honesty has less to do with what she sees in the world than with what she refuses to turn away from in herself. In *The Spare Room* (2008), her exacting autobiographical novel about looking after that dying friend, she describes not only the expected indignities of caring for a patient – the soaked bedsheets, the broken nights – but her own impatience, her own rage: 'I had always thought that sorrow was the most exhausting of the emotions. Now I knew that it was anger.'

There seems to be almost no episode from her own life that she has not analysed. It is characteristic that her reference to her affair with her tutor appears in *The First Stone* (1995), her account of a 1991 sexual harassment case, in which two female students at the University of Melbourne accused the master of one of the university colleges of making inappropriate advances: that book is both a report and a deep self-reckoning. Garner's readers are familiar with Mrs Dunkley, her fifth-grade teacher; the failure of Garner's three marriages; her two abortions; her dismissal from a teaching job at a Melbourne school (for daring to talk to her thirteen-year-old pupils about sex); her struggles with depression; her feelings about turning fifty; and the complex stitch of fury and liberation at being, now, in her seventies.

Her book *Everywhere I Look* (Text Publishing), selects essays and shorter journalistic pieces from the past fifteen years. The no-bullshit-preamble rule is sparklingly employed. 'At the turn of the millennium I reached the end of my masochism, and came home from Sydney with my tail between my legs. Single again.' So begins a gentle reflection on learning, once more, how to live alone. 'My First Baby' opens thus:

> This isn't really a story. I'm just telling you what happened one summer when I was young. It was 1961, my first year away from home. I lived at Melbourne University, in a women's college on a beautiful elm-lined boulevard. I was free and happy. Everyone was clever and so was I.

There are tender, funny sketches of literary friends (the novelists Elizabeth Jolley and Tim Winton), portraits of her grandchildren, reminiscences of childhood, and, as ever in her work, lovely, loitering descriptions of Melbourne, the city she knows best.

Garner is a natural storyteller: her unillusioned eye makes her clarity compulsive. In one of the longer pieces in this book, 'Dreams of Her Real Self', she recalls her late mother and illuminates with relentless candour her mother's shadowy presence. Her father, she tells us, is easy to write about; he was vivid, domineering, scornful, and babyishly quick to anger. One of Garner's husbands, having been subjected to a paternal inquisition, described him as a 'peasant'. He was 'an endurance test that united his children in opposition to him'. But she finds it difficult to write about her mother, in part because her father 'blocked my view of her', and in part, we learn, because she was willing to be blocked.

So Garner's reminiscence breaks into short, discontinuous sections, as she appraises, from different angles, the unassertive enigma that was her mother. She did not easily show affection, she was patient, timid, unconfident, law-abiding – and, probably, Garner decides, 'she was afraid of me'.

> She did not sense the right moment to speak. She did not know how to gain and hold attention. When she told a story, she felt a need to establish enormous quantities of irrelevant background information. She took so long to get to the point that her listeners would tune out and start talking about something else. Family shorthand for this, behind her back, was 'and then I breathed'.

What gives the memoir its power, as so often in Garner's writing, is that she is unsparing, in equal measure, of her subject and of herself, and that she so relishes complicated feelings. She chastises herself for not being more responsive while her mother was alive; posthumous connection is, after all, too easy. She longs for her to return, but has difficulty regarding the woman's life with anything but horror. She was about twelve, she recalls, when she realised that her mother's existence was divided into compartments:

None of them was any longer than the number of hours between one meal and the next. She was on a short leash. I don't recall thinking that this would be my fate, or resolving to avoid it. All I remember is the picture of her life, and the speechless desolation that filled me.

In some ways, it is a familiar portrait: an educated and liberated intellectual, the beneficiary of higher education and modern feminism, measures, with gratitude and shame, the distance between her mother's opportunities and her own. But it is made singular by Garner's almost reckless honesty, and brought alive by her mortal details: 'She used to wear hats that pained me. Shy little round beige felt hats with narrow brims. Perhaps one was green. And she stood with her feet close together, in sensible shoes.'

'Dreams of Her Real Self' is ultimately an essay about gender and class, categories that have absorbed Garner for much of her work – precisely, it would seem, because gender and class are not categories so much as structures of feeling, variously argued over, enjoyed, endured and escaped. Her first book, *Monkey Grip* (1977), is an intelligent, tautly written novel that chronicles some of Garner's own experiences from the 1970s, in particular her life in what she has called 'the big hippie households' of that era, 'when group dynamics were shaky and we were always having to split and start anew'.

But she established her reputation as a nonfiction writer, and established the characteristic Garner tone, with *The First Stone*. A twenty-one-year-old law student, whom Garner renames Elizabeth Rosen, levelled charges of sexual assault against the middle-aged master – 'Dr Colin Shepherd', in Garner's telling – of Ormond College, the largest and most prestigious residential college of the University of Melbourne. She alleged that during a private, late-night talk in his office Dr Shepherd told her he fantasised about her, and that he put his hand on her breasts. Rosen and another student testified that, later in the evening, at a college dance, Dr Shepherd groped them while dancing with them. Shepherd forcefully denied all the allegations. He was convicted of a single charge of sexual assault, which was overturned on appeal; he resigned anyway, in May 1993.

Garner first read about the case one morning in August 1992, in the Melbourne *Age*. Her early reactions were instinctive. She was puzzled by the young women's recourse to the law. Why didn't the students just sort it out locally, immediately, or get their mothers, or friends, to mediate? Garner's own friends, she tells us, 'feminists pushing fifty', were in agreement. Seasoned victims of such fumbled advances (or of far worse), they didn't doubt the veracity of the allegations, but 'if every bastard who's ever laid a hand on *us* were dragged into court, the judicial system of the state would be clogged for years'. Garner wrote to Dr Shepherd, sympathising with his treatment at the hands of 'this ghastly punitiveness'.

The First Stone is subtitled *Some Questions about Sex and Power*, and, in ways both conscious and unconscious, it obsessively pursues the questions raised by Garner's reflexive response to the case. She defends that initial reaction, but spends the entire book worrying away at it. *The First Stone* attacks and retreats like a baited animal. Garner persists in faulting the students for not acting pragmatically; these were not 'earth-shattering' offences, so why not deal with them swiftly, then and there? A repeated line of attack is that the students and their defenders use the word 'violence' where, she believes, 'it simply does not belong'. To insist on abuses of institutional power, Garner suggests, nullifies the fact that all relationships contain asymmetries of power, and that there are 'gradations of offence'. And power is always complex. She seems irritated by Rosen's testimony that Dr Shepherd's advances left her feeling 'humiliated and powerless to control what was happening to her'. Why so powerless? When Dr Shepherd got down on his knees and grasped Rosen's hand, as she alleged, 'which of them does the word *humiliated* apply to, here?'

But at other moments, in retreat, she worries that she herself has changed. An ageing but committed feminist, a child of the 1960s and '70s, she's perturbed that she finds it so easy to side with the man and so hard to sympathise with the women. Perhaps she's punishing the students 'for not having *taken it like a woman* – for being wimps who ran to the law to whinge about a minor unpleasantness, instead of standing up and fighting back with their own weapons of youth and quick wits.' She enriches this rhetorical back-and-forth in other ways. She tells us about her short affair with her tutor, and about an incident in the early 1980s when a masseur, in the middle of a private session, bent down and kissed her on the mouth. Looking back, Garner is clearly astounded that she said nothing to the man. Above all, she was merely embarrassed. And, when the massage was over, she said goodbye, went to the reception desk – '*and I paid*'.

She usefully explains that Ormond College was for decades a bulwark of male institutional power: women, admitted only in 1973, were not always made to feel welcome. She conducts revealing interviews with some of Ormond's most entitled male graduates, who talk casually about their bad behaviour – food fights, public drunkenness, running around naked. After a particularly squalid battle in the dining hall, the master upbraided the young diners with these telling words: 'The Hall's been raped – you promised me this wouldn't happen.' Garner lets that verb hang, or hang itself.

The First Stone quickly became controversial enough that the author felt compelled to write a formal reply to her critics. The two victims refused to speak to her, a decision hardened by the revelation of Garner's letter to Shepherd. It is a refusal that Garner returns to with mounting frustration; her book takes on a curiously blocked, repetitive, almost *victimised* quality, as if she were herself responding to a violation. She attacks modern feminism ('priggish, disingenuous, unforgiving') as if it had put her on trial. Which, in a sense, it had: the victims' allies and defenders soon made up their minds. Garner was on the wrong side; it was understood that she was writing 'the pro-Shepherd version'. Some feminists boycotted the book when it came out. University professors reportedly told their constituencies to avoid it.

The First Stone is, certainly, a very parental book: a woman old enough to be the mother of the two students looks on bemusedly, with the advantages of experience and hardened wisdom, and finds herself disappointed that the youngsters just aren't a bit tougher. And, even as she writes about the complexities and hidden potencies of gender, Garner comes to the scene – again, like a certain kind of parent – with rather stubborn ideas about male and female rôles. She upbraids the victims for avoiding conciliation, a 'feminine – almost a motherly – way of settling a dispute', and instead accuses them of charging past conciliation into 'the traditional masculine style of problem-solving: call in the cops ... hire a cowboy to slug it out for you in the main street at noon, with all the citizenry watching.' Of course, the gun smoke of essentialism reactivates the very warfare that Garner seeks to heal. When she rhetorically asks that question about who is truly humiliated, the man on his knees in supplication or the woman somewhat distressed in the chair, couldn't the reply be – both?

Yet, more than twenty years after its publication, *The First Stone* also seems a brilliantly prescient book – in its complexity, in the tense torque of its self-argument, and in its very vulnerability and stunned intolerance. Feminism had indeed changed between the 1970s and the 1990s, and Garner's narrative registers, with often uncomfortable honesty, a generational shift. Sexual harassment was coming to be seen as, invariably, a matter of institutional power. There was no narrative space left for Garner's blithe admission of her youthful affair with an older tutor, and certainly not for her appreciation of its educative richness.

In similar ways, Garner's most recent full-length work of nonfiction, *This House of Grief* (2014), makes its complexity out of an honest vulnerability. It recounts the two murder trials of Robert Farquharson, who was charged with murdering his three small children in 2005. On the way to return the kids to his ex-wife after a Father's Day visit, he swerved off the road into a deep pond. The children drowned but Farquharson escaped, abandoning the car in the icy water and hitching a ride to his ex-wife's house. Farquharson was convicted of murder in 2007, won a retrial in 2009, and was convicted again in 2010. He was given a life sentence.

Garner's book is superbly alive to the narrative dynamics of the case; she tells a grim story of unhappy marriage, limited social opportunity, bitter divorce and spousal grievance. Again, as in *The First Stone*, what consumes her are the difficult questions that seem to lie beyond the reach of formal narration: the deepest assumptions of class and gender and power; the problem of how well we ever understand someone else's motives. In her reply to the critics of *The First Stone*, she describes 'eros' as 'the quick spirit that moves between people – *quick* as in the distinction between "the quick and the dead". It's the moving force that won't be subdued by habit or law.'

That quick spirit is the free devil, the human surplus that she tries to capture in all her best work. The law's fine calibrations are coarsely related to this kind of narrative work: the evidence that helps us make sense of a catastrophic or a complicated incident is often not the same evidence that helps the law make *its* sense. Paradoxically, the legal process tempts writers (notably Janet Malcolm, Garner's admired model) because trial machinery appears to operate like the machinery of narrative, pumping out its near-simulacra for the benefit of reporters, TV journalists, voyeurs and jurors. Garner quotes Malcolm: 'Jurors sit there presumably weighing evidence but in actuality they are studying character.'

At the heart of the Robert Farquharson case is a large narrative question that frequently abuts but finally diverges from the smaller legal question before the jury: Why? Attracted and repelled, Garner circles around the unspeakable, abysmal horror. Can any story 'explain' why a man might murder his children? She doesn't pretend to possess the explosive answer, and frequently confesses appalled stupefaction, but her book walks us along an engrossing and plausible narrative fuse. Robert Farquharson emerges from Garner's account as limited in intelligence, expression and will. He lived in the modest town of Winchelsea (not far from Geelong, where Garner was born). He worked as a window cleaner, and had three children with the much more forceful Cindy Gambino, who told the court that Farquharson was 'pretty much a softie. He always gave in to what I wanted.' Though he was a 'good provider', she found it hard to stay in love with her husband. Cindy eventually left him, and soon began a new relationship with a contractor, Stephen Moules, a man more vigorous and successful than Farquharson. She kept the children, and Farquharson had to move out. He was jealous of Moules's access to the children, fearful of being displaced, and angry that the new lover got the better of the Farquharsons' two cars. An old friend testified that he threatened to kill his children and rob Cindy of her dearest gifts; Garner wonders if Farquharson was really trying to commit suicide.

Her narrative is lit by lightning. Hideous, jagged details leap out at us: the old, child-filled car swerving off the road and plunging into dark water; the trapped children (the youngest was strapped into a car seat); Farquharson's casual – or shocked – impotence at the crime scene (his first words to Moules, when he arrived, were 'Where's your smokes?'); the slack, defeated, anguished defendant, weeping throughout the trial; the wedding video of the happy couple, Gambino gliding 'like a princess in full fig, head high', and Farquharson, mullet-haired, 'round-shouldered, unsmiling, a little tame bear'; the first guilty verdict, Farquharson's vanquished defence lawyer standing 'like a beaten warrior ... hands clasped in front of his genitals'.

Garner is a powerful and vivid presence in her nonfiction narratives: she intervenes; she weeps and laughs with the evidence; she is scornful, funny, impassioned, and gives honest expression to biases and prejudices. (She also avails herself of the full, meaty buffet of Anglo-Australian demotic: 'bloke', 'sook', 'sent to Coventry', 'dobbing in', 'spat the dummy', 'bolshie'.) She powerfully sympathises with Farquharson's thwarted opportunities and flattened will, but she cannot hide her distaste for his weakness, which she expresses in tellingly gendered jabs. In court, she compares Stephen Moules physically with Farquharson ('I was not the only woman' to do so), and admits that Moules 'gave off that little buzz of glamour peculiar to the Australian tradie'. She wonders if there was something in Farquharson, by contrast, that brought out 'the maternal in women, our tendency to cosset, to infantilise'. In a striking image near the end of the book, she sees the accused as a big baby, 'with his low brow and puffy eyes, his slumped spine and man-boobs, his silent-movie grimaces and spasms of tears, his big clean ironed handkerchief'. It is hard to resist the conclusion that Garner, in full maternal mode, is arraigning him for not being *more of a man*. Is it unfair to wonder if this tough-minded writer was not also unconsciously demanding of the two University of Melbourne women that they, too, act more like men?

Some of Garner's prejudices are less conscious than others, but I suspect she understands perfectly well that narrative truth – what Elena Ferrante calls 'authenticity' (as distinct from mere verisimilitude) – proceeds from a kind of dangerous honesty that is not always conscious but is, rather, half disclosed, imperfectly controlled. Garner's gradual awakening to her unadmitted anger is what gives her best book, her novel *The Spare Room* (2008), much of its shattering power. Nicola, an old friend who has been diagnosed with stage IV cancer, comes from Sydney to Melbourne to stay for three weeks with the narrator, who is named Helen. (The novel is closely based on Garner's experience in caring for a terminally ill friend; typically, she said that she kept her first name in the text so that she would be forced to admit to all the shameful, 'ugly emotion' she had actually felt.) Nicola is charming, elegant and maddening. She pretends to be much healthier than she is – she gives 'a tremendous performance of being alive', in Garner's savage phrase – and is committed to a kind of social fraudulence that saddens and then gradually enrages her host. Helen longs for Nicola to abandon her bright laugh and fixed smile, a smile that seems to say '*Do not ask me any questions*'. Worse, she has come to Melbourne to seek alternative therapies – vitamin C injections, ozone saunas, coffee enemas – that seem nonsensical to Helen and which only make her friend sicker.

The novel tenderly catalogues that labour of caring which is also the labour of mourning. Helen spends her days and nights washing bedsheets that Nicola has sweated through, bringing morphine pills and hot-water bottles, listening outside the bedroom door to Nicola's snoring, which sounds 'like someone choking', driving her friend to the bogus Institute where she undergoes her hopeless remedies. The simple beauty of the novel's form has to do with its internal symmetry: the two women are locked into a relationship that they can escape only if each admits what she finds most difficult to say. Helen must confess to her exhaustion, her despair at not being a better friend and nurse, her anger at Nicola's terrible, terminal time wasting. And Nicola must admit that time is fading, that she is going to die, that her alternative therapies are an awful distraction, and that she needs proper help, a kind of assistance that Helen is not equipped to give. Nicola says, 'I've never wanted to bore people with the way I feel.'

As in *The Death of Ivan Ilyich* (Garner's book is a contemporary version of Tolstoy's novella), the mortal victim must be brought to comprehend her mortality: Helen tells Nicola, 'You've got to get ready.' There is a deeply moving scene towards the end of the book, when the two friends tearfully embrace in Helen's yard. 'I thought I was on the mountaintop,' Nicola says. 'But I'm only in the foothills.'

> All day long she kept dissolving into quiet weeping. Sometimes I would put my arms around her; sometimes we would just go on with what we were doing. The hard, impervious brightness was gone. Everything was fluid and melting. There was no need for me to speak. She looked up at me and said it herself, as I put a cup into her hand.

> 'Death's at the end of this, isn't it.'

After the anger and the tears, the book ends peacefully. Helen flies with Nicola to Sydney, and transfers her to Nicola's very competent niece. The novel closes: 'It was the end of my watch, and I handed her over.' Helen has done as much as she can do. It is a typical Garner sentence, a writing lesson (all novels should end as completely) and a life lesson: spare, deserved and complexly truthful, both a confession of failure and a small song of success.

Zama: Life at the Limits of Empire

J.M. Coetzee

The year is 1790, the place an unnamed outpost on the Paraguay River ruled from faraway Buenos Aires. Don Diego de Zama has been here for fourteen months, serving in the Spanish administration, separated from his wife and sons. Nostalgically, Zama looks back to the days when he was a *corregidor* with a district of his own to run: 'Doctor Don Diego de Zama! ... The forceful executive, the pacifier of Indians, the warrior who rendered justice without recourse to the sword ..., who put down the native rebellion without wasting a drop of Spanish blood.'

Now, under a new, centralised system of government meant to tighten Spain's control over its colonies, chief administrators have to be Spanish-born. Zama serves as second-in-command to a Spanish *gobernador*: as a Creole, an *americano* born in the New World, he can aspire no higher. He is in his mid-thirties; his career is stagnating. He has applied for a transfer; he dreams of the letter from the viceroy that will whisk him away to Buenos Aires, but it does not come.

Strolling around the docks, he notices a corpse floating in the water, the corpse of a monkey that had dared to quit the jungle and dive into the flux. Yet even in death the monkey is trapped amid the piles of the wharf, unable to escape downriver. Is it an omen?

Besides his dream of being returned to civilisation, Zama dreams of a woman, not his wife, much as he loves her, but someone young and beautiful and of European birth, who will save him not only from his present state of sexual deprivation and social isolation but also from a harder-to-pin-down existential condition of yearning for he knows not what. He tries to project this dream upon various young women glimpsed in the streets, with negligible success.

In his erotic fantasies his mistress will have a delicate way of making love such as he has never tasted before, a uniquely European way. How so? Because in Europe, where it is not so fiendishly hot, women are clean and never sweat. Alas, here he is, womanless, 'in a country whose name a whole infinity of French and Russian ladies – an infinity of people across the world – [have] never heard.' To such people, Europeans, *real* people, America is not real. Even to him America lacks reality. It is a flatland without feature in whose vastness he is lost.

Male colleagues invite him to join them in a visit to a brothel. He declines. He has intercourse with women only if they are white and Spanish, he primly explains.

From the small pool of white and Spanish women at hand he selects as a potential mistress the wife of a prominent landowner. Luciana is no beauty – her face puts him in mind of a horse – but she has an attractive figure (he has spied on her, bathing naked). He calls upon her in a spirit of 'foreboding, pleasure, and tremendous irresolution', unsure how one goes about seducing a married lady. And indeed, Luciana proves to be no pushover. In his campaign to wear her down, she is always a move ahead of him.

As an alternative to Luciana there is Rita, the Spanish-born daughter of his landlord. But before he can get anywhere with her, her current lover, a vicious bully, humiliates her grossly in public. She pleads with Zama to avenge her. Although the role of avenger attracts him, he finds reasons not to confront his formidable rival. (Zama's author, Antonio Di Benedetto, provides him with a neatly Freudian dream to explain his fear of potent males.)

Unsuccessful with Spanish women, Zama has to resort to women of the town. Generally he steers clear of mulattas 'so as not to dream of them and render myself susceptible and bring about my downfall'. The downfall to which he refers is certainly masturbation, but more significantly involves a step down the social ladder, confirming the metropolitan cliché that Creoles and mixed breeds belong together.

A mulatta gives him an inviting look. He follows her into the dingier quarter of the town, where he is attacked by a pack of dogs. He dispatches the dogs with his rapier, then, 'swaggering and dominant' (his language), takes the woman. Once they are finished, she offers in a businesslike way to become his kept mistress. He is offended. 'The episode was an affront to my right to lose myself in love. In any love born of passion, some element of idyllic charm is required.' Later, reflecting on the fact that dogs are as yet the only creatures whose blood his sword has spilled, he dubs himself 'dogslayer'.

Zama is a prickly character. He holds a degree in letters and does not like it when the locals are not properly respectful. He suspects that people mock him behind his back, that plots are being cooked up to humiliate him. His relations with women – which occupy most of the novel – are characterised by crudity on the one hand and timidity on the other. He is vain, maladroit, narcissistic and morbidly suspicious; he is prone to excesses of lust and fits of violence, and endowed with an endless capacity for self-deception.

He is also the author of himself, in a double sense. First, everything we hear about him comes from his own mouth, including such derogatory epithets as 'swaggering' and 'dogslayer', which suggest a certain ironic self-awareness. Second, his day-to-day actions are dictated by the promptings of his unconscious, or at least his inner self, over which he makes no effort to assert conscious control. His narcissistic pleasure in himself includes the pleasure of never knowing what he will get up to next, and thus of being free to invent himself as he goes along. On the other hand – as he intermittently recognises – his indifference to his deeper motives may be generating his many failures: 'Something greater, I knew not what, a kind of potent negation, invisible to the eye, ... superior to any strength I might muster or rebellion I might wage', may be dictating his destiny.

It is his self-cultivated lack of inhibition that leads him to launch an unprovoked knife attack on the only colleague who is well disposed towards him, then to sit back while the young man takes the blame and loses his job.

Zama's incurious and indeed amoral attitude towards his own violent impulses led some of his first readers to compare him with the Meursault of Albert Camus's novel *L'Étranger* (existentialism was in vogue in the Argentina of the 1950s, when *Zama* first appeared). But the comparison is not helpful. Though he carries a rapier, Zama's weapon of choice is the knife. The knife betrays him as an *americano*, as does his lack of polish as a seducer and (Di Benedetto will later imply) his moral immaturity. Zama is a child of the Americas. He is also a child of his times, the heady 1790s, justifying his promiscuity by invoking the rights of man – specifically the right to have sex (or, as he prefers to put it, to 'lose myself in love'). The configuration, cultural and historical, is Latin American, not French (or Algerian).

More important than Camus as an influence was Jorge Luis Borges, Di Benedetto's elder contemporary and the dominant figure in the Argentine intellectual landscape of his day. In 1951 Borges had given an influential speech, 'The Argentine Writer and Tradition', in which, responding to the question of whether Argentina should be developing a literary tradition of its own, he poured scorn on literary nationalism: 'What is our Argentine tradition? ... Our tradition is all of Western culture ... Our patrimony is the universe.'

Friction between Buenos Aires and the provinces has been a constant of Argentine history, dating back to colonial times, with Buenos Aires, gateway to the wider world, standing for cosmopolitanism, while the provinces adhered to older, nativist values. Borges was quintessentially a man of Buenos Aires, whereas Di Benedetto's sympathies lay with the provinces: he chose to live and work in Mendoza, the city of his birth in the far west of the country.

Though his regional sympathies ran deep, Di Benedetto as a young man was impatient with the stuffiness of those in charge of the cultural institutions of the provinces, the so-called generation of 1925. He immersed himself in the modern masters – Freud, Joyce, Faulkner, the French existentialists – and involved himself professionally in cinema, as a critic and writer of screenplays (Mendoza of the postwar years was a considerable centre of film culture). His first two books, *Mundo animal* (1953) and *El pentágono* (1955), are resolutely modernist, with no regional colouring. His debt to Kafka is particularly clear in *Mundo ani-mal*, where he blurs the distinction between human and animal along the lines of Kafka's 'A Report to an Academy' or 'Investigations of a Dog'.

Zama takes up directly the matter of Argentine tradition and the Argentine character: what they are, what they should be. It takes as a theme the cleavage between coast and interior, between European and American values. Naively and somewhat patheti-cally, its hero hankers after an unattainable Europe. Yet Di Benedetto does not use his hero's comical hispanophilism to push the case for regional values and the literary vehicle associ-ated with regionalism, the old-fashioned realist novel. The river port where *Zama* is set is barely described; we have little idea how its people dress or occupy themselves; the language of the book sometimes evokes, to the point of parody, the eighteenth-century novel of sentiment, but it more often calls up the twentieth-cen-tury theatre of the absurd (Di Benedetto was an admirer of Eugène Ionesco and of Luigi Pirandello before him). To the extent that *Zama* satirises cosmopolitan aspirations, it does so in a thoroughly cosmopolitan, modernist way.

But Di Benedetto's engagement with Borges was more far-reaching and complex than mere critique of his universalism and suspicion of his patrician politics (Borges called himself a Spencerian anarchist, meaning that he disdained the state in all its manifestations, while Di Benedetto thought of himself as a socialist). For his part, Borges clearly recognised Di Benedetto's talent and indeed, after the publication of *Zama*, invited him to the capital to give a lecture at the National Library, of which he was Director.

In 1940, along with two writer colleagues associated with the magazine *Sur*, Borges had edited an *Antología de la literatura fan-tástica*, a work that had a far-reaching effect on Latin American literature. In their preface the editors argued that, far from being a debased subgenre, fantasy embodied an ancient, prelit-erate way of seeing the world. Not only was fantasy intellectually respectable, it also had a precursor tradition among Latin American writers that was itself a branch of a greater world tra-dition. Borges's own fiction would appear under the sign of the fantastic; the fantastic, deployed upon the characteristic themes of regional literature, with the narrative innovations of William Faulkner added to it, would give birth to the magic realism of Gabriel García Márquez.

The revaluation of the fantastic advocated by Borges and the writers around *Sur* was indispensable to Di Benedetto's growth. As he testified in an interview shortly before his death, fantasy, coupled with the tools provided by psychoanalysis, opened the way for him as a writer to explore new realities. In the second part of *Zama*, the fantastic comes to the fore.

*

The story resumes in 1794. The colony has a new governor. Zama has acquired a woman, a penniless Spanish widow, to satisfy his physical needs, though he does not live with her. She has borne him a son, a sickly child who spends his days playing in the dirt. Her relations with Zama are entirely without tenderness. She 'allows him in' only when he brings money.

A clerk in the administration named Manuel Fernández is discovered to be writing a book during office hours. The governor takes a dislike to Fernández and demands that Zama find a pretext for dismissing him. Zama reacts with irritation, directed not at the governor but at this hapless young idealist, 'this book-writing homunculus' lost in the outer reaches of Empire.

To Zama, Fernández innocently confides that he writes because it gives him a sense of freedom. Since the censor is unlikely to permit publication, he will bury his manuscript in a box for his grandchildren's grandchildren to dig up. 'Things will be different then.'

Zama has run up debts that he cannot settle. Out of kindness, Fernández offers to support Zama's irregular family – indeed, to marry the unloved widow and give the child his name. Zama responds with characteristic suspiciousness: what if it is all a scheme to make him feel indebted?

Short of money, Zama becomes a boarder in the home of a man named Soledo. Included in Soledo's household is a woman, seen only fleetingly, who is at one point claimed (by the servants) to be Soledo's daughter and at another to be his wife. There is another mystery woman, too, a neighbour who sits at her window staring pointedly at Zama whenever he passes. Most of Part 2 is concerned with Zama's attempts to solve the riddle of the women: are there two women in the household or just one, who performs rapid changes of costume? Who is the woman at the window? Is the whole charade being orchestrated by Soledo to make fun of him? How can he get sexual access to the women?

At first, Zama takes on the riddle as a challenge to his ingenuity. There are pages where, with a nudge from his translator, he sounds like one of Samuel Beckett's heroes of pure intellect, spinning one far-fetched hypothesis after another to explain why the world is as it is. By degrees, however, Zama's quest grows more urgent and indeed fevered. The woman at the window reveals herself: she is physically unattractive and no longer young. Half drunk, Zama feels free to throw her to the ground and '[take] her with vehemence', that is, rape her, then, when he is finished, demand money. He is back on familiar psychic terrain: on the one hand he has a woman whom he can despise but who is sexually available, on the other a woman (or perhaps two women) who, in all her/their 'fearsome charm', can continue to be the unattainable (and perhaps inexistent) object of his desire.

Zama took a long time to gestate but was written in a hurry. The haste of its composition shows most clearly in Part 2, where the dreamlike topography of Soledo's residence will be as confusing to the reader as it is to Zama, drifting from room to darkened room trying to grasp what it is that he is after. Confusing yet fascinating: Di Benedetto lets go of the reins of narrative logic and allows the spirit to take his hero where it will.

There is a rap at the door. It is a ragged, barefoot boy, a mysterious messenger who has appeared in Zama's life before and will appear again. Behind the boy, as if in tableau, a trio of runaway horses are engaged in trampling a small girl to death.

> I returned to my quarters as if harvesting the darkness, and with a new faculty – or so it seemed – of perceiving myself from without. I could see myself gradually transformed into a figure of mourning, the shadows, soft as bat's down, adhering to me as I passed ... I was going to confront something, someone, and I understood that I was to choose it or choose for it to die.

A feminine presence wafts past. Zama raises a candle to the being's face. It is *she*! But who is she? His senses reel. A fog seems to invade the room. He staggers into bed, wakes up to find the woman from the window watching over him, 'compassionate affection, an amorous and self-abnegating pity in her eyes ... [a woman] without mystery.' Bitterly she observes how in thrall he is to the enchantments of 'that other glimpsed figure,' and delivers a homily on the perils of fantasy.

Rising at last from his sickbed, Zama decides that the entire episode of 'harvesting the darkness' is to be explained – and explained away – as the product of a fever. He backtracks from the obscurer regions into which hallucination has been leading him, falters in his hesitant self-exploration, reinstates the dichotomy of fantasy (fever) and reality that he was in the process of breaking down.

To grasp what is at stake at this moment, we need to hark back to Kafka, the writer who did the most to shape Di Benedetto's art, both directly and through the mediation of Borges. As part of his project of rehabilitating the fantastic as a literary genre, Borges had in the mid-1930s published a series of articles on Kafka in which, crucially, he distinguished between dreams, which characteristically lay themselves open to interpretation, and the nightmares of Kafka (the long nightmare of Josef K. in *The Trial* is the best example), which come to us as if in an indecipherable language. The unique horror of the Kafkan nightmare, says Borges, is that we know (in some sense of the word 'know') that what we are undergoing is not real, but, in the grip of the hallucinatory *proceso* (process, trial), we are unable to escape.

At the end of Part 2, Zama, a character in what amounts to a historical fantasy, dismisses as insignificant because unreal the hallucinatory fantasy he has just undergone. His prejudice in favour of the real continues to hold him back from self-knowledge.

*

After a gap of five years, the story resumes. Zama's efforts to secure a transfer have failed; his amours seem to be a thing of the past.

A contingent of soldiers is being sent out to scour the wilds for Vicuña Porto, a bandit of mythical status – no-one is even sure what he looks like – on whom all the colony's woes are blamed.

From the time he spent as *corregidor*, Zama recalls a Vicuña Porto who fomented rebellion among the Indians. Though the troops are to be led by the incompetent, pig-headed Capitán Parrilla, Zama joins them, hoping that a spectacular success will advance his cause.

One dark night on the trail, a nondescript soldier takes Zama aside. It is Vicuña Porto himself, masquerading as one of Parrilla's men and thus in effect hunting himself. He confides that he wishes to quit banditry and rejoin society.

Should Zama betray Porto's confidence? The code of honour says no, but the freedom to obey no code, to follow impulse, to be perverse, says yes. So Zama denounces Porto to Parrilla and at once feels 'clean in every fiber of [his] being'.

Without compunction Parrilla arrests both Zama and Porto. Hands bound, face swollen with fly bites, Zama contemplates being paraded back in the town: 'Vicuña Porto, the bandit, would be no more defeated, repugnant, and wretched than Zama, his accessory.'

But the bandit turns the tables. Murdering Parrilla in cold blood, he invites Zama to join his band. Zama refuses, where-upon Porto hacks off his fingers and abandons him, mutilated, in the wilds.

At this desperate juncture salvation appears in the form of the barefoot boy who has haunted Zama for the past decade. 'He was me, myself from before ... Smiling like a father, I said, "You haven't grown ..." With irreducible sadness he replied, "Neither have you."'

Thus ends the third and last part of *Zama*. In the somewhat too facile lesson that its hero-narrator invites us to draw, search-ing for oneself, as Vicuña Porto has been pretending to do, is much like the search for freedom, 'which is not *out there* but within *each one*.' What we most truly seek lies within: our self as we were before we lost our natural innocence.

Having seen in parts 1 and 2 a bad Zama, a Zama misled by vain dreams and confused by lust, we find in Part 3 that a good Zama is still recoverable. Zama's last act before losing his fingers is to write a letter to his infinitely patient wife, seal it in a bottle, and consign it to the river: 'Marta, I haven't gone under.' 'The message was not destined for Marta or anyone out there,' he confides. 'I had written it for myself.'

The dream of recovering Eden, of making a new start, animated European conquest of the New World from the time of Columbus. Into the independent nation of Argentina, born in 1816, poured wave after wave of immigrants in quest of a utopia that turned out not to exist. It is not surprising that frustrated hope is one of the great subterranean themes of Argentine literature. Like Zama in his river port in the wilds, the immigrant finds himself dumped in an anything but Edenic site from which there is no obvious escape. *Zama* the book is dedicated to 'the victims of expectation'.

Zama's adventures in wild Indian territory are related in the rapid, clipped style Di Benedetto learned by writing for the cinema. Part 3 of the novel has been given great weight by some of his critics. In the light of Part 3, *Zama* is read as the story of how an *americano* comes to cast off the myths of the Old World and commit himself not to an imaginary Eden but to the New World in all its amazing reality. This reading is supported by the rich textual embedding that Di Benedetto supplies: exotic flora and fauna, fabulous mineral deposits, strange foodstuffs, savage tribes and their customs. It is as though for the first time in his life Zama is opening his eyes to the plenitude of the continent. That all this lore came to Di Benedetto not from personal experience – he had not set foot in Paraguay – but from old books, among them a biography of one Miguel Gregorio de Zamalloa, born 1753, *corregidor* during the rebellion of Túpac Amaru, last of the Inca monarchs, is an irony that need not trouble us.

*

Antonio Di Benedetto was born in 1922 into a middle-class family. In 1945 he abandoned his legal studies to join *Los Andes*, the most prestigious newspaper in Mendoza. In due course he would become, in all but name, editor-in-chief. The owners of the newspaper dictated a conservative line, which he felt as a constraint.

Until his arrest in 1976 – for violating that constraint – he thought of himself as a professional journalist who wrote fiction in his spare time.

Zama (1956) was his first full-length novel. It received appropriate critical attention. Not unnaturally in a country that saw itself as a cultural outlier of Europe, attempts were made to supply it with a European parentage. Its author was identified first as a Latin American existentialist, then a Latin American *nouveau romancier*. During the 1960s the novel was translated into a number of European languages, English not included. In Argentina *Zama* has remained a cult classic.

Di Benedetto's own contribution to this debate on paternity was to point out that if his fiction, particularly his short fiction, might sometimes seem blank, lacking in commentary, as if recorded by a camera eye, that might be not because he was imitating the practice of Alain Robbe-Grillet but because both of them were actively involved in cinema.

Zama was followed by two further novels and several collections of short fiction. The most interesting of these works is *El silenciero* (The Silencer), the story of a man (never named) who is trying to write a book but cannot hear himself think in the noise of the city. His obsession with noise consumes him, eventually driving him mad.

First published in 1964, the novel was substantially revised in 1975 so as to give its reflections on noise greater philosophical depth (Schopenhauer comes to figure prominently) and to forestall any simple, sociological reading of it. In the revised edition noise acquires a metaphysical dimension: the protagonist is caught up in a hopeless quest for the primordial silence preceding the divine *logos* that brought the world into being.

El silenciero goes further than *Zama* in its use of the associative logic of dream and fantasy to propel its narrative. As a novel of ideas that includes ideas about how a novel can be put together, as well as in its mystical streak, *El silenciero* very likely pointed the direction Di Benedetto would have followed as a writer, had history not intervened.

*

On 24 March 1976, the military seized power in Argentina, with the collusion of the civilian government and to the relief of a large segment of the population, sick and tired of political violence and social chaos. The generals at once put into effect their master plan, or 'Process for National Reorganisation'. General Ibérico Saint-Jean, installed as governor of Buenos Aires, spelled out what *El Proceso* would entail: 'First we will kill all the subversives, then we will kill their collaborators, then their sympathisers, then those who remained indifferent, and finally we will kill the timid.'

Among the many so-called subversives detained on the first day of the coup was Di Benedetto. Later he would (like Josef K.) claim not to know why he was arrested, but it is plain that it was in retaliation for his activities as editor of *Los Andes*, where he had authorised the publication of reports on the activities of right-wing death squads. (After his arrest, the proprietors of the newspaper wasted no time in washing their hands of him.)

Detention routinely began with a bout of 'tactical interrogation', the euphemism for torture, intended to extract information but also to make it plain to the detainee that he or she had entered a new world with new rules. In many cases, writes Eduardo Duhalde, the trauma of the first torture, reinforced by having to watch or listen to the torture of other prisoners, marked the prisoner for the rest of his or her life. The favoured instrument of torture was the electric prod, which induced acute convulsions. After-effects of the prod ranged from intense muscular pain and paralysis to neurological damage manifested in disrhythmia, chronic headaches and memory loss.

Di Benedetto spent eighteen months in prison, mostly in the notorious Unit 9 of the Penitentiary Services of La Plata. His release came after appeals to the regime by Heinrich Böll, Ernesto Sabato and Jorge Luis Borges, backed by PEN International. Soon afterwards he went into exile.

A friend who saw him after his release was distressed by how he had aged: his hair had turned white, his hands trembled, his voice faltered, he walked with a shuffle. Although Di Benedetto never wrote directly about his prison experience – he preferred to practise what he called the therapy of forgetting – press interviews allude to vicious blows to the head ('Since that day my capacity to think has been affected'); to a session with the cattle prod (the shock was so intense that it felt as if his inner organs were collapsing); and to a mock execution before a firing squad when the one thought in his mind was: what if they shoot me in the face?

Fellow inmates, most of them younger than he, recalled that he seemed bewildered by the brutal prison regime, trying to make sense of the random assaults he suffered from guards when the essence of these assaults was that they should be unpredictable and – like a Kafkan nightmare – make no sense.

Exile took Di Benedetto to France, to Germany, and eventually to Spain, where he joined tens of thousands of other refugees from Latin America. Though he had a contract for a weekly column in a Buenos Aires newspaper and enjoyed a residency at the MacDowell Colony in New Hampshire, he recalled his exile as a time when he lived like a beggar, stricken with shame whenever he saw himself in the mirror.

In 1984, after civilian rule had been reinstalled, Di Benedetto returned to an Argentina ready to see in him an embodiment of the nation's desire to purge itself of its recent past and make a fresh start. But it was a role he was too aged, too beaten down, too bitter to fulfil. The creative energy that prison and exile had taken away from him was irrecoverable. 'He began dying ... on the day of his arrest,' remarked a Spanish friend. 'He continued to die here in Spain ... and when he decided to return to his own country it was only in search of a more or less decent ending.' His last years were marred by recriminations. Having first been welcomed back, he said, he had then been abandoned to even greater poverty than in Spain. He died in 1986 at the age of sixty-three.

During his exile in Spain, Di Benedetto published two collections of short fiction, *Absurdos* (1978) and *Cuentos del exilio* (1983). Some of the pieces in *Absurdos* had been written in prison and smuggled out. The recurring theme of these late stories is guilt and punishment, usually self-punishment, often for a transgression one cannot remember. The best known, a masterpiece in its own right, is 'Aballay', made into a film in 2011, about a *gaucho* who decides to pay for his sins in the manner of the Christian saint Simeon Stylites. Since the pampas have no marble columns,

Aballay is reduced to doing penitence on horseback, never dismounting.

These sad, often heartbreaking late stories, some no more than a page in length – images, broken memories – make it clear that Di Benedetto experienced exile not just as an enforced absence from his homeland but as a profoundly internalised sentence that had somehow been pronounced upon him, an expulsion from the real world into a shadowy afterlife.

Sombras, nada más… (1985), his last work, can most charitably be looked on as the trace of an experiment not carried all the way through. Finding one's way through *Sombras* is no easy task. Narrators and characters merge one into another, as do dream and represented reality; the work as a whole tries doggedly but fails to locate its own raison d'être. A mark of its failure is that Di Benedetto felt compelled to provide a key explaining how the book was put together and offering guidance on how to read it.

Zama ends with its hero mutilated, unable to write, waiting in effect for the coming of the man who a century and a half later will tell his story. Like Manuel Fernández burying his manuscript, Di Benedetto – in a brief testament penned shortly before his death – affirmed that his books were written for future generations. How prophetic this modest boast will be, only time will tell.

Zama remains the most attractive of Di Benedetto's books, if only because of the crazy energy of Zama himself, which is vividly conveyed in Esther Allen's excellent translation. A selection of Di Benedetto's short fiction (his *Cuentos completos* runs to 700 pages), in translations by Adrian West and Martina Broner, has been announced for 2017 by Archipelago Books. It is to be hoped that some enterprising publisher will soon pick up *El silenciero*.

Art Walks a Tightrope

Sebastian Smee

I remember the day that I first fell in love with Bill Henson's work almost thirty years ago. Of course, I have no diary entry to prove it. Such experiences are like the shadows cast by passing clouds – they can't be substantiated or verified. But I know I stood in a small, darkened room at the Art Gallery of New South Wales, surrounded on four sides by blurred black-and-white photographs of pedestrians in crowded city streets. I say 'crowded' and 'city' and 'streets', but the location and nature of these ghostly human congregations were unclear, as was everything else about them. The people, all of different ages, were shown in various aspects of isolation and tender attachment. They were enveloped in shifting accretions of darkness, their hands and faces picked out by pooling, smoky light.

I was suddenly in a new reality, which was also (and this was the breathtaking thing) my own, but made deeper, more enduring. It was as if the skin-tight pocket of time I occupied had suddenly become immensely elastic, and I was intimately connected not just to these anonymous, faraway faces but to something much, much older. I honestly ascribe the beginning of my love of art to this moment, above all others.

Much, of course, has happened since. In 1995, Henson represented Australia at the Venice Biennale, where he exhibited a series of large spliced-up photo-collages showing naked youths in a penumbral landscape littered with abandoned cars. Ten years later, a critically acclaimed retrospective of his work opened in Sydney before travelling to his hometown of Melbourne. It attracted record numbers for an exhibition of contemporary art.

Three years after that, in 2008, a scandal erupted over the image used on an invitation for Henson's upcoming show at Sydney's Roslyn Oxley9 Gallery. It was a photograph of a pubescent girl with budding breasts, simply standing there, her torso and face carved out of darkness.

The whole country knows what happened next. A newspaper columnist went feral. Police removed Henson's photographs from the gallery's walls, and the opening was cancelled. A typhoon of overreaction ensued (on both sides). The offending image was published widely, but with vile black redaction marks covering the model's face and chest. Politicians frothed and fulminated like the bad actors they are.

Many other, more reasonable people had honest, and complex, responses. Some were alarmed by the image, made anxious by what little they could glean of Henson's approach to youth, and baffled by yet more evidence of the peculiar tunnel vision of powerful artists – their strange sense of private immunity to the moral rip-tides sweeping over society at any given time.

Others in the art world and beyond were shocked that art's special dispensation – its right to cherish ambivalence, to speak ancient truths, and to enter the heart in privacy – could be so egregiously violated in a modern, free society.

For many, these apparently contradictory positions proved strangely compatible.

In retrospect, the so-called Henson affair seems eminently foreseeable – though no less lurid and incommensurate for being so. The surprise, perhaps, was only that it hadn't happened before. Nine years later, an acrid odour still lingers in the air, and, although the hysteria has subsided, Henson's name will always, you feel, be associated in some people's minds with creepy weird shit.

That seems a great pity. It makes the decision by the National Gallery of Victoria to mount a show of Henson's recent work appear simultaneously courageous and squarely in line with the fulfilment of its core mission. The exhibition (until 27 August) is hauntingly beautiful. It comprises twenty-three large-scale, deeply shadowed colour photographs with bright white borders and black frames hung against the darkened walls of a single spacious gallery in the NGV's St Kilda Road building. Works by Balthus, Bacon, Degas, Rembrandt, Rubens and Ribera are just around the corner. Henson was given his first show at the NGV when he was only nineteen, and the gallery owns more than 100 of his works. Twenty-one of the images in the exhibition were acquired as a suite by the collector William Bowness and given to the NGV. All were made between 2008 and 2013.

For those who may have seen isolated reproductions of Henson's work but are unfamiliar with his exhibitions, this one reveals, again, what a gift he has not only for creating singular, indelible images but also for combining and arranging them in suggestive, soul-stirring ways. One is struck by the scale of the works, and by the care with which Henson manipulates colour and tone in the printing process, and afterwards. Cumulatively – by force of strange juxtaposition – as much as individually, the photographs break through the carapace of the contemporary, image-saturated mind to admit older, more beautiful and death-haunted recognitions.

Some show ancient sculptures (and in one case portions of a late painting by Rembrandt) in dim museum interiors, where onlookers surround these venerated objects. Blurred and arbitrarily cropped, the living people are captured just as they are. But the camera's alchemy also transmutes them into insubstantial spectres, here one moment, gone the next. The effect is to make the obdurate, centuries-old art objects feel, by contrast, more tremblingly full and alive.

Or is it that they seem more anciently other and dead? The confusion opens up a new susceptibility in the heart.

Other photographs here show solitary nature. A volcanic island asserting its presence against veils of sea and mist. Cascading water arrested – and silenced – in the midst of its roaring vertical plunge. An odd-shaped promontory silhouetted against sea and keening sky. A bosky Italian landscape poised between sensuous invitation and indifference. In the last, Henson choreographs alternating passages of light and dark as the eye moves up the picture plane and the landscape itself recedes. The effect is to reinforce this poetic dynamic of access and obstruction – a dynamic that is in many ways at the very core of his whole sensibility.

Others still show young naked figures, male and female, in states of silent self-absorption – sometimes in what appear to be excruciating agonies of pleasure, often expressionless, always unknowable. Set against pitchy darkness, their bodies float and twist or recline. A young woman's head is propped up by jack-knifed elbows. A hand comes to her mouth in a gesture of feeling and thought in transition. (The same gesture, with similar implications, obsessed Degas for a period in the 1860s.) A boy emerging from the left side of another, remarkable image is suspended in space, foreshortened, one arm dangling.

Seen at close quarters, the knees, hands, necks and thighs of these youths (two of whom appear together several times in poses of great tenderness) have an almost wretched pallor, one that paradoxically evokes great age. One thinks of oxidised metal, weather-damaged marble, or the extraordinary amalgam of coloured oil paint Rembrandt used to describe veins, arteries and ageing skin in his late paintings. One powerful image shows a girl gracefully squatting (the pose suggests a goddess of the hunt on the prowl), with one richly mottled hand pressed to the floor beside her foot.

Perhaps the most beautiful photograph shows the same girl, made slender and insubstantial by encroaching shadow, resting her head on the boy's wrist, which is hinged at the end of a still more slender forearm that mysteriously enters the picture from the right. (Nothing else of him is shown.) Thus unified, the two bodies, each under the spell of what Katherine Mansfield called our 'profound and terrible' desire to make contact, traverse the horizontal picture plane like some giant pictogram from a forgotten language.

Indeed, like a calligrapher brushing white ink on black paper, Henson finds ever new ways to set pale skin and flesh against deep rectangles of black. Some poses echo ancient sculptures – most notably the so-called 'Spinario', a much-copied bronze of a boy pulling a thorn from his foot. Some – the reclining head turning away into darkness – are familiar from countless earlier works by Henson himself.

It would be ideal, at this point, to sign off, as does the Swiss writer Robert Walser in his charming short piece 'A Discussion of a Picture', by saying, 'And with the assumption that things are approximately as I have described them, I shall step away from this picture that I believe I have presented to you with a modicum of grace.'

But such grace eludes me, and so I interrupt our current programming to mutter the smallest of misgivings. The spell of Henson's work is broken for me – shattered, if I'm to be honest – when I become too conscious of his studio lighting. This happens only in three works here: the boy in the pose of the Spinario, the boy seated and embraced from behind, and the younger blond boy turning his forehead into warm, golden light.

It's tremendously hard to speak of how and why a spell is cast, or broken. Can it really be as simple as a shift in the lighting, or a change in surface tension, such that the skimming stone no longer ricochets off the surface but plummets to the deep?

I'm really not sure. When you know what you think of art and how (more or less) to put it in words, it's often because something in the work itself is lacking. The connections between image and feeling or meaning are too obvious. The mind is left with nothing to do but check boxes.

When the reverse occurs, it can be either because you are struggling to make sense of something new or because old, anticipated intensities of feeling elude you. Which can, confusingly, produce its own kind of intense feeling: 'And we,' wrote Rilke, in the last of his Duino Elegies, 'who have always thought of happiness climbing, would feel the emotion that almost startles when happiness falls.' And this feeling, too, is in no way foreign to Henson's visual poetics: one astute writer has detected a quality of self-mourning in the faces of Henson's models, as they emerge from childhood into adulthood, with all its attendant pains.

I have always been aware of the artifice in Henson's work and in most cases succumb instinctively to his invented worlds. As he himself is always saying, art is artifice. And yet when he manipulates his lights to gild shoulders and thighs from behind, setting strands of hair ablaze or picking out patches of perspiration, it sets my teeth on edge. It may simply be that this warmer, golden light clashes (in poetic terms) with the cooler, almost moribund blue and white light in his other works, or that it betokens an aesthetic rhetoric, as of gods descending, or perhaps just high-end fashion photography. In any case, it feels dissonant, and instantly banishes me from Henson's floating world, jamming the signals, as it were, in my heart.

Never mind. All truly affecting art walks a tightrope, and it's never clear what will make either artist or viewer lose balance. Plenty of artists conjure with images from the history of art, but none has been so ambitious in their attempt to marry the immediate, over-brimming present with the haunted past. And the fact remains that no other living Australian artist has produced as many images so full of tenderness, silence and longing.

Towards Joy

Anwen Crawford

I once heard a distinguished American poet quote a Lady Gaga lyric as an example of perfect iambic pentameter. 'I want your psycho, your vertigo schtick' – ten syllables, five feet of metre; he wasn't wrong. I was sitting in a classroom in New York City, and the poet was leading a course on prosody, which is the study of poetic metre but might also concern itself, to quote Ezra Pound, with 'the articulation of the total sound of a poem'. Gaga's line was from her 2009 single 'Bad Romance', one of the songs that launched her on a trajectory towards superstardom. She would become, for a time, the most famous contemporary pop musician in the world.

'I want your psycho, your vertigo schtick.' What is the line doing, apart from keeping the metre? I want: the very bedrock of pop music. Pop music is about many things, but it is mostly about the things that we might want to do with our bodies: playing, dancing, singing, sex of all sorts. Skin and sweat and noises. The repeated *o* of psycho and vertigo is a sound that might be pleasure, might be pain, might be both at once. It's the sadism of Alfred Hitchcock, who took pleasure in making his beautiful blondes – Janet Leigh in *Psycho*, Kim Novak in *Vertigo* – suffer violent deaths. Lady Gaga was a blonde, and she placed herself in this lineage: beauty, danger, tragedy etcetera. The superstar's schtick. As she sang she savoured the phonemes of 'schtick'.

But 'Bad Romance' proved most effective when language broke down – when phonemes, set free from meaning, bloomed across the song like a rash. 'Rah-rah-ah-ah-ah, ro-mah-ro-mah-mah,' sang Gaga, repeatedly. Pop music is about what we feel more than what we say, what goes unsaid, what can't be spoken. *I want.* 'Rah-rah-ah-ah-ah' put Gaga at the edge of language, right where Little Richard was when he shouted, 'A-wop-bom-a-loo-mop-a-lomp-bom-bom.'

Poetry and pop lyrics are forms that share a fascination with language as a material: how can you push it around, or break it apart? And what might that sound like? Through attention to rhythm, and through devices such as rhyme, alliteration, consonance and dissonance (these last two terms also describe harmonic functions within music), the poet produces an array of sensory effects. Language becomes sound, pulse, colour and texture. Pound again: 'Some musicians have the faculty of invention, rhythmic, melodic. Likewise some poets.' Poetry is the literary form that comes closest to music, but literature isn't music, and pop lyrics aren't poetry.

To be fair to my aforementioned teacher, the American poet, I think he knew all this. We shared a fascination with Lady Gaga and a deep dislike of Bob Dylan, or, to be more accurate, a dislike of what Dylan had come to represent: pop music as canon-building, as the reverence of institutions. Once, in that same classroom, we had an argument with another poet, who was determined to convince us that Dylan should be awarded the Nobel Prize in Literature. That was in 2009.

This past October, Bob Dylan was awarded the Nobel Prize in Literature. Plenty of people were made happy by the announcement, but others were disgruntled: why should a pop star be given the Nobel Prize? Underlying such criticism is the assumption that pop music is a lesser form than literature: less serious, less substantial, less deserving of reward or analysis. I was annoyed when Dylan was awarded the Nobel, but my annoyance sprang from an opposite source. I wondered what literature had done to deserve pop music. How is literature, with its hierarchies of genre and judgement, its snobberies and exclusions, worthy of annexing pop to its territory?

I don't hate literature, honestly. (I wouldn't be a writer if that were so.) But I do resent efforts, no matter how well intentioned, to make pop music fit the criteria of an entirely different art form. '[Dylan] can be read and should be read,' commented the Swedish Academy's permanent secretary, Sara Danius, in an interview after she announced the winner of this year's prize. Well, no. Literature should be read. If you want to give Dylan his due, he should be listened to. Listen for the melodies, the vocal timbre and expression, the rhythmic interplay of voice and instruments: all of the things that make lyrics an element of music, not something that can be considered separately from it. I can scarcely think of anything more joyless than reading a lyric sheet as if it were a book.

Judging a lyric by its coherence as a written text – the Nobel Prize website cites a long list of printed Dylan works, beginning with the *Bob Dylan Song Book* (1965), before mentioning any audio recordings – is a poor way of assessing its effect. There is no less useful move in an argument over the worth of any popular musician, Dylan included, than to quote their lyrics out of context, purposely ignoring the musical setting. 'Get sick, get well / Hang around a ink well.' Of course it reads like rubbish on the page.

'Subterranean Homesick Blues', from which the above quote is taken, is as good an example as any in Dylan's catalogue of a song that had an enormous cultural impact not because the words were separate to the music but because the lyrics functioned as part of a larger artefact. Musically, the song borrowed a lot from Chuck Berry's 1956 single 'Too Much Monkey Business' and a bit from Dylan's hero Woody Guthrie. A big part of Dylan's significance in the '60s was his amalgamation of rock and folk styles, and 'Subterranean Homesick Blues' was the sound of this. It was the opening track to his album *Bringing It All Back Home* (1965), which was the first that he recorded using electric guitar.

Some listeners felt that Dylan's switch from acoustic to amplified instruments was a betrayal. Folk was the music of the people, authentic and political, while rock and pop were the sound of vulgar commercialisation, or so the argument went. But folk enthusiasts faced a problem: commercial music forms were the more genuinely popular. Dylan grasped this. The effectiveness of 'Subterranean Homesick Blues' had everything to do with the swaggering, gutsy arrangement and Dylan's mordant vocal; if folk music was defined by its wholeheartedness, then this was something else, and it sounded much cheekier.

Dylan also recognised the visual potency of pop culture. 'Subterranean Homesick Blues' was one of the first songs to be accompanied by a promotional film clip, shot in black-and-white by the documentarian D.A. Pennebaker, who used it as the opening sequence for his tour film about Dylan, *Don't Look Back*, released in 1967. Dylan stands in an alleyway, holding up cue cards to the camera, and on the cue cards are handwritten fragments of the song's lyrics, along with some deliberate misdirections. It's funny because of the gap between what we hear and what we read, with the cue cards – 'Bed, But', 'Man Whole' – making absurd snippets out of what, in song form, is an unbroken diatribe. And then there is Dylan's deadpan expression, his natty waistcoat, his nimbus of bohemian curls: oh yes, he understood the power of an image.

I'm not convinced that awarding Dylan the Nobel Prize in Literature does anything to expand the parameters of literature. Instead, I think that by dragging Dylan into the realm of the literary, by emphasising lyrics as a writing and reading practice rather than a verbal and musical one, we lose what is interesting about him as a performer, and what is compelling about pop music as a whole.

Judgements regarding literary worth and posterity tend to assume that what is valuable about literature are those qualities in it that cannot be wholly measured by the marketplace, and this is good and right. But pop music is an art form that depends upon commodification. There's no getting around that. It relies on mass distribution and advertising (and, decreasingly, on mass manufacture), on the association between buyer and seller, and on the allure of the star system, which is a key part of what is being bought and sold.

Some of the most evocative, transformative and brilliant pop musicians have addressed the tensions between art and commerce in their work. (Dylan certainly has.) But the tension is inherent to the form, uniquely so. Not even cinema, which is expensive and cumbersome to make and to distribute, and has therefore often been tied to the fortunes of commercial studios, is quite so enmeshed with the existence of consumer capitalism.

Indeed, sophisticated systems for cinematic production have existed outside of capitalist economies – Soviet Russian cinema is the paradigmatic example. But pop music? Pop music trades in the effects produced by consumer capitalism: alienation from our labour, estrangement from our desires, isolation from any real sense of community. Literature (or cinema) might make subjects out of these conditions, but can and does function without them. Not so pop music. This is the form's power, and its limitation.

When I lived in New York, I came to love the various ways in which pop music shaped the collective life of the city, attuning its inhabitants to one another. It meant that eight million of us were sharing a cultural location, alongside a physical one. From my tiny bedroom which faced onto a busy Brooklyn street, I could pick out the hit songs and about-to-be-hits by the regularity with which I heard them being played from passing cars. 'Bad Romance' was one of them. The song was unusual, in the context of an American musical landscape that had weathered more than thirty years of hip-hop's loping rhythms, for sounding so stiff. It had no funk at all. The song's rigid beat and grimy, synthesised bassline created a mood that was industrial, almost android. This strange impression was only heightened by the song's video clip, in which Lady Gaga and her dancers emerged from coffin-like pods, like a cluster of aliens.

In October 2009, when 'Bad Romance' was released, the unemployment rate in the US hit 10.1 per cent, the highest in decades. Hopelessness was in the air. 'I want your ugly, I want your disease,' sang Gaga. Like all truly effective pop stars, she both mirrored an existing social mood and modelled a refutation of it. In her songs, malfunction and inadequacy were cherished. Her fans took to calling themselves 'little monsters', which suggested a negation of prevailing systems but also a robust, fighting appetite. *I want.*

How tedious it is, then, when pop stars descend to the level of politicians, costuming themselves in the approbation of institutional power. Political endorsements, knighthoods, Nobel Prizes: just say no. There was Gaga, speechifying for Hillary Clinton on the final night of the US presidential campaign. 'Hillary Clinton is made of steel,' she said, which might make an interesting line in a song, but fell flat as a real-world observation of Clinton's character. Politics is remote and abstract, in so far as the machinations of power feel like something that we have little or no ability to alter. But pop music holds out the promise – an elusive, illusory promise – of transformation, and of transcendence, through means of total delight.

*

In April the world lost Prince, pop's foremost utopian. I miss Prince. I miss his fabulousness, his way of being in the world, which was never only for himself alone, because every song he wrote was also an invitation: *Move with me towards joy*. I miss his sensational beauty, his ski-slope cheekbones and hazel eyes and black hair piled up, his pert waist and perfect arse, the greatest arse in the history of pop music. How ridiculous that anyone should be so beautiful, and how wonderful that he let the world share in it.

I miss the abundance of his musical gift, which he refused to measure against any common schedule. There were songs upon songs and albums upon albums, thousands of concerts, hundreds of afterparties where he played through the night and into the dawn. I miss his playfulness. Nothing was ruled out for being too silly, not zebra-stripe bikini briefs or funk about Batman or the notion of purple rain. The secret of play is to commit to it, and then it isn't silly anymore, it's truthful. I miss his commitment to every performance as if moment by moment it mattered wholly, for that moment. He could make time feel entirely present: not passing, not past, but there. Here. And anything could happen here, including the end of time. I miss his eschatology.

There are so many Prince songs concerning judgement days, including some of his best-loved: '1999', 'Sign 'O' the Times', even 'When Doves Cry', which takes place on the brink of a commingled ecstasy and loss. 'Animals strike curious poses,' Prince sang, summoning a portent in the distinctive, robotic tones that he often reserved for the verses of his songs. Prince is regarded as a consummate funk musician, and he was, but the groove of his dominant '80s recordings is strangely impliable, the Linn drum machines he favoured on albums like *1999* (1982) and

Purple Rain (1984) fixing the arrangements to a grid. Within the shelter of the grid he could go crazy, and did. Lady Gaga learned a lot from Prince.

The stakes are raised in 'When Doves Cry' at around the three-minute mark, when the multi-tracked vocals start to pile in on each other, and robot Prince is pitted against another articulation of himself. 'Why do we scream at each other?' he asks, but on a separate vocal track he *is* screaming, that cry-moan-squeal thing he did that conveyed both perfect pleasure and terrible pain. And so the vagaries of desire surface and resurface in pop music, and desire can't always be put into words, any more than can love, rage or heartbreak. It doesn't mean these things can't be heard.

Prince was a great lyricist, because he understood the points at which words fail. 'I can take you out there and hit this guitar for you,' he told a *Rolling Stone* journalist in 2014, 'and what you'll hear is sex. You will hear something where you'd run out of adjectives, like you do when you meet the finest woman.' Desire was holy in his songs, a form of worship; he sang and played as if sex were a way to steal back time, to exist in the present always, to end estrangement forever. Sex was play, and play the opposite of work: 'Raspberry Beret' is a fantasy of shirking a job in order to have sex. I used to work in a shop, and my workmate and I would wait until it was nearly six p.m. and the shop was closing to put Prince on the stereo. *Sex o'clock*, we'd joke. And then we'd dance around the counter. We went to see Prince play on a work night, once. We were so tired the next day.

Like a poet, Prince had his lexicon. *Baby* and *sky* and *forgive* and *rain*. *Car* and *ride*. *Kiss* and *come*. 'To' was 2 and 'you' was *u*, decades in advance of text messaging. I think he chose the abbreviations because they suggested both interchangeability and intimacy: he was singing to anyone, he was singing 2 u. They also made words into visual symbols, floating through the songs. Stevie Wonder: 'Prince's music was so picturesque that even I could see it.' For a time, Prince changed his name to something that was literally unsayable, a 'Love Symbol' that pointed to all directions on the sexual compass. *Free*. That was another of his favourite words. He was both exuberantly heterosexual and lushly queer: fluid, strange and ungovernable.

The song that follows 'When Doves Cry' on *Purple Rain* is 'I Would Die 4 U'. Prince sings as Prince, and Prince sings as Christ. 'I'm your messiah and you're the reason why.' In his songs, erotic and religious devotion were the twinned sources of his ever-renewing delight. Both were a means of suspending time. The song is potentially infinite; the arrangement has no real end point.

After Prince died, I listened to 'I Would Die 4 U' on a loop. The first four verses are sung on the same note, with no accompanying instruments but the bass and drum machine, hi-hats quivering. During the choruses, the other Prince kicks in, shrieking, begging, being pulled asunder. 'I would die 4 u / Darling if u want me 2.' He always asked permission, and it's hard to overstate just how sexy that could be. He sang of surrender, not of conquest, of mutual and equal pleasure, not of domination, his voice breaking over the words like he was coming, or like he was going. It was the way he sang it.

Publication Details

'Uluru Statement from the Heart' appeared in *A Rightful Place: A Road Map to Recognition*, Black Inc., Melbourne, August 2017.

Michael Adams's 'Salt Blood' appeared in *Australian Book Review*, Number 392, June 2017.

Michael Mohammed Ahmad's 'Bad Writer' appeared in the *Sydney Review of Books*, 4 October 2016.

Lech Blaine's 'The Bystander' appeared in *Griffith Review*, Edition 56, April 2017.

Shannon Burns's 'In Defence of the Bad, White Working Class' appeared in *Meanjin*, Volume 76, Issue 2, Winter 2017.

John Clarke's 'Commonplace' appeared in *Meanjin*, Volume 76, Issue 1, Autumn 2017.

J.M. Coetzee's 'Zama: Life at the Limits of Empire' appeared in the *New York Review of Books*, Volume 64, Number 1, January 2017.

Richard Cooke's 'Bonfire of the Narratives' appeared in the *Monthly*, November 2016.

Anwen Crawford's 'Towards Joy' appeared in the *Monthly*, December 2016.

Nick Feik's 'Killing Our Media' appeared in the *Monthly*, July 2017.

Publication Details

Tim Flannery's 'Extravagant, Aggressive Birds Down Under' appeared in the *New York Review of Books*, Volume 64, Number 4, March 2017.

Helen Garner's 'Why She Broke' appeared in the *Monthly*, June 2017.

Moreno Giovannoni's 'A Short History of the Italian Language' appeared in *Southerly*, 11 May 2017.

Stan Grant's 'A Makarrata Declaration: A Declaration of Our Country' appeared in *A Rightful Place: A Road Map to Recognition*, Black Inc., Melbourne, August 2017.

Sonya Hartnett's 'Hello, Stranger' appeared in *It Happened Off the Leash*, Affirm, Melbourne, November 2016.

Melissa Howard's 'Now No-One Here Is Alone' appeared in *Meanjin*, Volume 75, Issue 3, Spring 2016.

Barry Humphries's 'Up a Wombat's Freckle' appeared in the *Times Literary Supplement*, 21 June 2017.

Micheline Lee's 'The Art of Dependency' appeared in the *Monthly*, August 2017.

Janine Mikosza's 'How Not to Speak Polish' appeared in *Electric Journal*, 18 January 2017.

Amanda C. Niehaus's 'Pluripotent' appeared in *Creative Nonfiction*, Issue 64, Summer 2017.

Harriet Riley's 'Endlings' appeared in *Island*, Issue 146, September 2016.

Jennifer Rutherford's 'House of Flowers' appeared in *Double Dialogues*, Issue 19, December 2017.

Mandy Sayer's 'People Power at the Ponderosa' appeared in *SBS Online*, 16 May 2017.

Keane Shum's 'The Tamarind Is Always Sour' appeared in *Granta*, Issue 138, June 2017.

Robert Skinner's 'Lessons from Camels' appeared in the *Monthly*, August 2017.

Publication Details

Sebastian Smee's 'Art Walks a Tightrope' appeared in the *Monthly*, April 2017.

Sam Vincent's 'Peasant Dreaming' appeared in *Griffith Review: Millennials Strike Back*, Edition 56, April 2017.

James Wood's 'Helen Garner's Savage Self-Scrutiny' appeared in the *New Yorker*, 12 December 2016.

Notes on Contributors

The Editor

Anna Goldsworthy is the author of *Piano Lessons, Welcome to Your New Life* and the Quarterly *Essay Unfinished Business: Sex, Freedom and Misogyny.* Her writing has appeared in the *Monthly*, the *Age*, the *Australian*, the *Adelaide Review* and *The Best Australian Essays.* Described by the *Australian* as a 'musical ambassador,' she is one of Australia's most acclaimed and versatile musicians. As a piano soloist, she has performed extensively throughout Australia and internationally, and as a chamber musician she is a founding member of Seraphim Trio.

Contributors

Michael Adams writes about humans and nature. His work is published in *Meanjin, Australian Book Review*, the *Guardian* and academic journals and books. He teaches in human geography at the University of Wollongong. 'Salt Blood' won the 2017 Calibre Essay Prize.

Michael Mohammed Ahmad is the founder and director of Sweatshop: Western Sydney Literacy Movement. He is the award-winning author of *The Tribe* (Giramondo, 2014). Mohammed's forthcoming novel is *The Lebs* (Hachette, 2018).

Lech Blaine is a writer from Toowoomba. He was an inaugural winner of a Griffith Review Writing Fellowship. In 2017 he received the Queensland Premier's Young Publishers and Writers

Award. Black Inc. will publish his first book, *Car Crash: A Memoir*, in 2019.

Shannon Burns is a writer and critic from Adelaide.

John Clarke (29 July 1948 – 9 April 2017) was a New Zealand–born comedian, writer, and satirist. He was born in Palmerston North, New Zealand, and lived in Australia from the late 1970s. He was a highly regarded actor and writer whose work appeared on the Australian Broadcasting Corporation (ABC) in both radio and television and also in print.

J.M. Coetzee was born in South Africa in 1940. He has published sixteen works of fiction, as well as several volumes of criticism. In 2003 he was awarded the Nobel Prize for Literature. Since 2002 he has lived in Adelaide.

Richard Cooke is a writer, broadcaster and contributing editor to the *Monthly*.

Anwen Crawford is the *Monthly*'s music critic and the author of *Live Through This* (Bloomsbury, 2015).

Nick Feik is the editor of the *Monthly* magazine.

Tim Flannery is an environmentalist. In 2007 he was named Australian of the Year. He delivered the 2002 Australia Day Address to the nation. In 2013 he founded the Australian Climate Council, Australia's largest and most successful crowd-funded organisation. His latest book is *Sunlight and Seaweed* (Text Publishing, 2017).

Helen Garner's most recent book is *Everywhere I Look* (Text Publishing, 2017).

Moreno Giovannoni emigrated from San Ginese at the age of two. A translator and writer who has been published in the *Age, Island, Southerly*, and *The Best Australian Essays 2014* he was the inaugural winner of the Deborah Cass Prize. Black Inc. will publish *Tales of San Ginese* in 2018.

Stan Grant is Indigenous Affairs editor for the ABC and Chair of Indigenous Affairs at Charles Sturt University. He won the 2015 Walkley Award for coverage of Indigenous Affairs and is the author of *The Tears of Strangers* (HarperCollins, 2004) and *Talking to My Country* (HarperCollins, 2016).

Sonya Hartnett writes for children, teenagers and adults. She lives in rural Victoria with her dog, Cole.

Melissa Howard is a freelance writer and copywriter. A PhD candidate at Deakin University, she is working on a collection of personal essays – 'Now No-one Here Is Alone' is the first.

Barry Humphries AO, CBE is an Australian comedian, actor, satirist, artist, and author.

Micheline Lee was born in Malaysia and migrated to Australia when she was eight. She has worked as a human rights lawyer and before taking up writing, as a painter. Her first novel, *The Healing Party*, was shortlisted for the Victorian Premier's Literary Award and is currently longlisted for the Voss prize.

Janine Mikosza is a Melbourne-based writer and artist. Her writing has been published in literary journals, awarded fellowships, and shortlisted for prizes, including the Commonwealth Short Story Prize. She is currently developing a non-fiction manuscript through the Hardcopy program.

Amanda C. Niehaus is a writer and scientist living in Brisbane. Her work has appeared in *Creative Nonfiction*, *AGNI*, *Overland* and *NOON*, among others. Amanda was a 2017 Varuna Fellow and winner of the 2017 Victoria University Short Story Prize and is writing a book based on her prize-winning story.

Harriet Riley is a climate specialist who has consulted to the Gates Foundation, United Nations, and EDF. She studied at Columbia University and the University of Cambridge and is currently developing a TV drama about climate change. 'Endlings' was awarded the 2016 Wildcare Nature Writing Prize.

Jennifer Rutherford is Director of the J.M Coetzee Centre at The University of Adelaide. She has been writing and performing experimental works integrating creative non-fiction and memoir into academic forms for many years. She is currently writing *Méren*, her first full-length novel.

Mandy Sayer is an award-winning novelist and non-fiction writer. Her most recent book, *Australian Gypsies: Their Secret History*, has just been published by New South Press.

Keane Shum leads the Mixed Movements Monitoring Unit at the UNHCR Regional Office for South-East Asia.

Robert Skinner is the editor of the short story magazine *The Canary Press*. He lives without a dog in Melbourne.

Sebastian Smee is the author of *The Art of Rivalry: Four Friendships, Betrayals, and Breakthroughs in Modern Art* (Penguin Random House, 2016). He has worked as an art critic for newspapers and magazines in the US, the UK and Australia. He won the Pulitzer Prize for Criticism in 2011.

Sam Vincent's first book, *Blood and Guts: Dispatches from the Whale Wars* (Black Inc., 2014) was longlisted for the 2015 Walkley Book Award and shortlisted for the 2015 Nib Award for Literature and the 2015 ACT Book of the Year Award. He is writing a book based on the essay 'Peasant Dreaming'.

James Wood has been a staff writer and book critic at the *New Yorker* since 2007. In 2009, he won the National Magazine Award for reviews and criticism. He was the chief literary critic at the *Guardian*, in London, from 1992 to 1995, and a senior editor at the *New Republic* from 1995 to 2007. He is Professor of the Practice of Literary Criticism at Harvard University.